The Four Yogas

The Four Yogas

A Guide to the Spiritual Paths
of Action, Devotion,
Meditation and Knowledge

Swami Adiswarananda

Minister and Spiritual Leader of the
Ramakrishna-Vivekananda Center of New York
and author of *The Spiritual Quest and the Way of Yoga:
The Goal, the Journey and the Milestones*

RAMAKRISHNA-VIVEKANANDA
CENTER OF NEW YORK
"As Many Faiths, So Many Paths"
www.ramakrishna.org

Walking Together, Finding the Way
SKYLIGHT PATHS®
PUBLISHING
Woodstock, Vermont
www.skylightpaths.com

The Four Yogas:
A Guide to the Spiritual Paths of Action, Devotion, Meditation and Knowledge

2006 First Printing
© 2006 by Swami Adiswarananda

Page 289 constitutes a continuation of this copyright page.

Library of Congress Cataloging-in-Publication Data
Adiswarananda, Swami, 1925–
The four yogas : a guide to the spiritual paths of action, devotion, meditation, and knowledge / Swami Adiswarananda.
p. cm.
Includes index.
ISBN 1-59473-143-8
1. Yoga. 2. Yoga, Karma. 3. Yoga, Bhakti. 4. Yoga, Raja. 5. Yoga, Jñana. I. Title: 4 yogas. II. Title.

BL1238.52.A34 2006
294.5'436—dc22

2005029436

10 9 8 7 6 5 4 3 2 1
Manufactured in the United States of America
Jacket Design: Sara Dismukes

SkyLight Paths Publishing is creating a place where people of different spiritual traditions come together for challenge and inspiration, a place where we can help each other understand the mystery that lies at the heart of our existence.

SkyLight Paths sees both believers and seekers as a community that increasingly transcends traditional boundaries of religion and denomination—people wanting to learn from each other, *walking together, finding the way.*

Walking Together, Finding the Way
Published by SkyLight Paths Publishing
A Division of LongHill Partners, Inc.
Sunset Farm Offices, Route 4, P.O. Box 237
Woodstock, VT 05091
Tel: (802) 457-4000
Fax: (802) 457-4004
www.skylightpaths.com

Each soul is potentially divine. The goal is to manifest this divinity within by controlling nature: external and internal. Do this either by work, or worship, or psychic control, or philosophy—by one, or more, or all of these—and be free. This is the whole of religion. Doctrines, or dogmas, or rituals, or books, or temples, or forms are but secondary details.

—SWAMI VIVEKANANDA

Contents

Introduction

The philosophy of yoga tells us that the root cause of all our sorrows and sufferings is loss of contact with our true Self. This Self is called by various names, such as Atman, Purusha, and God. Our loss of contact with the Self is due to our ignorance of the Self as the only reality. Ignorance creates spiritual blindness and subjects us to a world of delusion and desire. This world becomes governed by the seemingly unending rounds of birth and death, pain and pleasure, and happiness and suffering. No material or psychological solution can dispel this ignorance. Our recovery is possible only by reestablishing contact with our true, inmost Self. The message of yoga is that there is no escape from the Self and that knowledge of the Self is our only savior.

Yoga philosophy prescribes four spiritual paths to attain Self-knowledge: karma-yoga, the path of selfless action; bhakti-yoga, the path of devotion; raja-yoga, the path of concentration and meditation; and jnana-yoga, the path of knowledge and discrimination. The purpose of this guidebook is to introduce the reader to each one of these paths and to its corresponding message, philosophy, psychology, and practices, and also to the obstacles that may stand in the way.

Karma-yoga, or the yoga of selfless action, seeks to face the problem of ignorance by eradicating the ego. The ego, born of ignorance, binds us to this world through attachment. The ego creates a dream-land of separative existence that disclaims the rights of others. It wants to achieve the impossible, and it desires the undesirable. Karma-yoga says that our egotistic, selfish actions have created walls around us. These walls not only set us apart from others, but they cut us off from our true Self within. By performing actions in a self-less manner, we can break down the walls that separate us from the Self. The key message of this yoga is to beat the inexorable law of karma by karma-yoga: Release yourself from the chains of attach-ment by practicing nonattachment to the results of action.

Karma-yoga believes that the ego is the sole troublemaker. But when transformed through yoga, the same ego becomes a friend and troubleshooter. Followers of karma-yoga faithfully per-form their actions and renounce the results by making an offer-ing of them into the fire of Self-knowledge. Swami Vivekananda, the great teacher of yoga and Vedanta, teaches us two ways of practicing karma-yoga and nonattachment:

> One way is for those who do not believe in God or in any out-side help. They are left to their own devices; they have sim-ply to work with their own will, with the powers of their mind and discrimination, thinking, "I must be non-attached." For those who believe in God there is another way, which is much less difficult. They give up the fruits of work unto the Lord; they work but never feel attached to the results. Whatever they see, feel, hear, or do is for Him. Whatever good work we may do, let us not claim any praise or benefit for it. It is the Lord's; give up the fruits unto Him.[1]

Bhakti-yoga is the process of inner purification. The message of bhakti-yoga is that love is the most basic human emotion. In its purest form, love is cosmocentric and divinely inspired. But be-cause of the intervention of the ego, love becomes egocentric, obstructing the free flow of love toward the Divine. Lust, anger, jealousy, and greed are the negative emotions created by the impure ego. Bhakti-yoga asks us to purify and transform our egotistic self-love by pouring holy thoughts into our minds and transferring all our love and emotions to God, knowing that God is the only one who truly loves us. Pouring holy thoughts into the mind is accomplished through prayer, ceremonial worship, chanting of holy words, keeping holy company, and studying holy texts. When such holy thoughts are poured into the mind, all unholy and impure thoughts are naturally washed out. The follower of bhakti-yoga establishes a loving relationship with God and eventually realizes God everywhere and in everything. As Swami Vivekananda says:

> We all have to begin as dualists in the religion of love. God is to us a separate Being, and we feel ourselves to be separate beings also. Love then comes between, and man begins to approach God; and God also comes nearer and nearer to man. Man takes up all the various relationships of life—such as father, mother, son, friend, master, lover—and projects them on his ideal of love, on his God. To him God exists as all these. And the last point of his progress is reached when he feels that he has becomes absolutely merged in the object of his worship.[2]

Raja-yoga seeks to attain the Divine by igniting the flame of knowledge of the Self within. Only Self-knowledge can dispel the ignorance that binds the human soul to the world of dreams and desires. To attain Self-knowledge, raja-yoga asks the seeker to develop strong willpower by the relentless practices of concentration and meditation on the Self, with the support of *pranayama,* or control of breath; *asana,* or control of posture; and an uncompromising adherence to austerity and self-control.

Raja-yoga contends that eradication of the ego through karma-yoga is a long process, and most seekers do not have the patience to endure the sacrifice it calls for; bhakti-yoga requires abiding faith in the love of God, which is not always possible for

an average seeker; and the mind is generally too weak and perverted to follow the path of reason, or jnana-yoga (see below).
Impurities of the mind are too deeply embedded and cannot be
uprooted simply by reason. Raja-yoga asks the seeker to confront
the deep-rooted tendencies and restlessness of the mind by cultivating a single thought reminiscent of the Divine. Swami
Vivekananda says:

> When, by analyzing his own mind, a man comes face to face,
> as it were, with something which is never destroyed, some-
> thing which is, by its own nature, eternally pure and perfect
> [the Self], he will no more be miserable, no more be unhappy.
> All misery comes from fear, from unsatisfied desire. When a
> man finds that he never dies, he will then have no more fear
> of death. When he knows he is perfect, he will have no more
> vain desires. And both these causes being absent, there will
> be no more misery; there will be perfect bliss, even in this
> body.[3]

Jnana-yoga is the path of knowledge. Knowledge, according to
jnana-yoga, has two aspects: fire and light. The fire of knowledge
burns all the impurities of our mind, and simultaneously, knowledge enlightens our inner consciousness. But Self-knowledge does
not come by itself. It calls for the practice of discrimination between the real and the unreal, renunciation of all desires—both
earthly and heavenly, mastery over the mind and senses, and an
intense longing for the goal.

The psychology of jnana-yoga tells us that we cannot generate spirituality by artificial means. The mind does not give up its
attachment to worldly pleasures unless it has tasted something
greater and higher. The Self is revealed in the mirror of the mind
that has become purified through self-control and austerity. The
method of jnana-yoga is to persuade the seeker that his or her sole
identity is the Self. By hearing about the Self, reading about the
Self, thinking about the Self, and meditating on the Self, the mind

gradually realizes that the Self is the only reality in this universe and that all else is unreal.

As the seeker in the path of jnana-yoga progresses toward the Self, he or she begins to taste the bliss of the Self and to gain faith in its reality. Self-knowledge, according to jnana-yoga, is true liberation. As Shankaracharya, the foremost proponent of non-dualistic Vedanta, describes in his "Six Stanzas on Nirvana":

> *Death or fear have I none, nor any distinction of caste;*
> *Neither father nor mother, nor even a birth, have I;*
> *Neither friend nor comrade, neither disciple nor guru:*
> *I am Eternal Bliss and Awareness—I am Siva! I am Siva!**
>
> *I have no form or fancy: the All-pervading am I;*
> *Everywhere I exist, and yet am beyond the senses;*
> *Neither salvation am I, nor anything to be known:*
> *I am Eternal Bliss and Awareness—I am Siva! I am Siva!*[4]

Each seeker is called upon to decide which yoga best corresponds to his or her natural disposition. Karma-yoga is advised for the active, bhakti-yoga for the devotional, raja-yoga for the strong-willed, and jnana-yoga for the rational. Traditionally, the seeker may ask for the guidance of an illumined teacher already perfect in yoga; an enlightened teacher will be able to advise which path a seeker is to follow and prescribe specific practices suitable to his or her natural disposition.

Swami Vivekananda emphasized that any seeker may become established in one of the four paths or harmonize them in every-day practice. The goal of all four yogas is freedom from the assumed bondage of the mind and realization of our true identity—the ever-pure, immortal Self, which is non-different from

---

*Siva is the destroyer god, the third person of the Hindu Trinity with Vishnu and Brahmā. Siva is also the symbol of the *sannyasin,* of renunciation, and of Brahman (Ultimate Reality), whose nature is that of Existence-Knowledge-Bliss Absolute.

the universal Self, or the Ultimate Reality. Sri Ramakrishna, the prophet of nineteenth-century India, says, "The mind of the yogi is always fixed on God, always absorbed in the Self."[5]

Yoga must be practiced vigorously and fearlessly. Swami Vivekananda advises:

> [The] various yogas do not conflict with each other; each of them leads us to the same goal and makes us perfect; only each has to be strenuously practiced. The whole secret is in practicing. First you have to hear, then think, and then practice. This is true of every yoga. You have first to hear about it and understand what it is; and many things which you do not understand will be made clear to you by constantly hearing and thinking. It is hard to understand everything at once. The explanation of everything is after all in your self. No one is ever really taught by another; each of us has to teach himself. The external teacher offers only the suggestion, which arouses the internal teacher, who helps us to understand things. Then things will be made clearer to us by our own power of perception and thought, and we shall realize them in our own souls; and that realization will grow into intense power of will.[6]

> Be not afraid of anything. You will do marvelous work. The moment you fear, you are nobody. It is fear that is the great cause of misery in the world. It is fear that is the greatest of all superstitions. It is fear that is the cause of our woes, and it is fearlessness that brings heaven even in a moment. Therefore, "Arise, awake, and stop not till the goal is reached."[7]

This book describes in detail the philosophy, psychology, and methods of practice of the four yogas. It offers a comparative study of the four yogas: their points of agreement and their differences. Special attention has been paid to the pitfalls, roadblocks, and obstacles a seeker is likely to encounter in his or her practice of yoga and also the means to overcome them and realize the goal.

I wish to thank Mr. Jon Sweeney, the cofounder and former editor in chief of SkyLight Paths Publishing, for editing the manuscript. Several other competent editors have also worked on the manuscript, and I am thankful to them as well.

PART ONE

The Way of Karma-Yoga: The Path of Action

1

The Message of Karma-Yoga

To work, alone, you are entitled, never to its fruit.
Neither let your motive be the fruit of action, nor let
your attachment be to non-action.

—BHAGAVAD GITA 2.47

Self-knowledge is the ultimate goal of spiritual quest. The way to Self-knowledge is called yoga. All the maladies of life have their roots in the loss of yoga, which is the loss of contact with the Self, the Ultimate Reality. Karma-yoga shows the way to reach the goal.

Karma-yoga, or the yoga of selfless action, is the central message of the Bhagavad Gita.* Karma-yoga asks us to reconnect ourselves with the Self. Only by this reconnection can we attain freedom of the soul. According to this path, that which stands in the way of our reconnection with the Self is the bondage of egocentric desires, delusions, and false hopes, designated as the

---

Bhagavad Gita literally means "song of the Lord." An important religious text all over the world, the Bhagavad Gita contains the teachings of Sri Krishna and is a manual for the philosophy and practice of yoga.

bondage of karma* accumulated through selfish actions in this life or in previous lives. When we forget or neglect the Self, we are subjected to the world of relative values that is guided by the sixfold change of birth, subsistence, growth, maturity, decline, and death and the pairs of opposites, such as pain and pleasure and ignorance and knowledge.

Each selfish action forges a chain of bondage of the body in the form of addictions, of the mind in the form of delusion and dependence, and of the soul in the form of spiritual blindness. In the words of Swami Vivekananda:

> This feeling of "I and mine" causes the whole misery. With the sense of possession comes selfishness, and selfishness brings on misery. Every act of selfishness or thought of self-ishness makes us attached to something, and immediately we are made slaves. Each wave in the chitta [mind-stuff] that says "I and mine" immediately puts a chain round us and makes us slaves; and the more we say "I and mine," the more the slavery grows, the more the misery increases. Therefore karma-yoga tells us to enjoy the beauty of all the pictures in the world, but not to identify ourselves with any of them. Never say "mine." Whenever we say a thing is ours, misery immediately comes. Do not say "my child" even in your mind. If you do, then will come misery. Do not say "my house," do not say "my body." The whole difficulty is there. The body is neither yours, nor mine, nor anybody's. These bodies are coming and going by the laws of nature, but the Soul is free, standing as the witness. This body is no more free than a picture or a wall. Why should we be attached so much to a body? Suppose somebody paints a picture; why should he be attached to it?

---

*The word *karma* can refer to action in general, duty, or the law of karma (the law of cause and effect). In comparison, *karma-yoga* always refers to selfless action, action performed with nonattachment, or in general, yogic action.

He will have to part with it at death. Do not project that ten-
tacle of selfishness, "I must possess it." As soon as that is
done, misery will begin.[1]

The Bhagavad Gita refers to the ego as a fever and to egocentric
existence as living in a state of delirium.[2]

The deposits of selfish karma in our mind create walls of separation from the totality of existence. These walls cannot be demolished by withdrawal into contemplative silence. Reason, too, is
helpless to break down these walls because strong habits and tendencies of selfish living have affected the very biochemistry of the
mind. The effects of karma created by repeated thoughts, speech,
and action cannot be overcome by mere thought, which is meditation; by speech, which is *japa* and prayer; or by selfish action,
which only adds to the bondage. The separative walls of past
karma can only be demolished by karma-yoga, or selfless action.

If we suffer by becoming lost in the world of the ego, we must
recover ourselves in this very world. If selfish karma has created
devils, karma-yoga will create angels to drive the devils out.
Therefore, the watchwords of karma-yoga are, "Beat the past by
acting in the living present. Brooding and sorrowing over the past
do not and cannot change our lives—neither can dreaming of the
future."

THE EXHORTATION OF KARMA-YOGA

The events of the world do not happen according to our cherished
desires. We often see the virtuous suffer and the vicious prosper.
Nothing is predictable, and yet events seem preordained. Life is
followed by death, pleasure by pain, and good by evil. Naturalists
look upon these sequences of events as chance happenings.
Materialists want to eradicate evil and make everything good.
Transcendentalists try to brush aside the world as an illusion and
so retire into contemplative isolation. Advocates of conventional
religion put their faith in the promise of eternal life hereafter and

regard the world as a passing phase—they somehow endure the pains of this world, hoping against hope to receive their rewards in heaven.

The exhortation of karma-yoga is to face the world. Karma-yoga explains the inequalities and apparent contradictions of the world in terms of the law of karma. Good and evil are subjective explanations and different experiences of the same mind. There is nothing absolutely good or absolutely evil in this world. The world of conflict and contradiction is in the mind, and one's mind is shaped by accumulated karma, or one's past actions. Our present state of life has been shaped by our past actions, and our future will be determined by our present actions. Good actions produce good results and bad ones bad, and the doer of actions must face them both. This is the inescapable and inexorable law of karma, the law of cause and effect. Every person, through each thought, word, and deed, is constantly changing and altering the shape of his or her psychophysical system, which the Bhagavad Gita describes as *svabhava,* or inner disposition.[3] Our actions leave behind results that alter our inner disposition—for better or worse.

Destiny is not fatalism. Destiny, according to karma-yoga, is not the predetermination that makes one lose faith in human endeavor. The Sanskrit word for destiny is *adrista. Adrista* is that which was not previously seen or known. Events appear to be destined for certain persons because they are unable to remember their past. The inner disposition, or *svabhava,* of a person is therefore made up of the accumulated deposits of past thoughts and actions—the total result of all past evolution. The results of actions, or *karmic* deposits, are not destroyed with the death of the body. What has been sown must be reaped. But we can always change our destiny if we follow the path of karma-yoga.

Our bodies and minds are mere vehicles for the working out of the results of our past karma. Karma-yoga asks us to face life by facing the results of our past actions. The tendencies created by one set of actions can be countered only by the performance with equal intensity of an opposite set of actions. The chain of bondage is the chain of karma. That which has been enchained must be unchained. A screw that has been put into a wall with twenty turns can only be taken out with another twenty turns in the opposite direction—to do otherwise would damage the wall. The evolution of a person from sensuality to spirituality cannot be hurried. The effects of egotistic action can be annulled only by the performance of karma-yoga. Karma-yoga is the change of motive inspiring the performance.

One question will naturally occur here: If everything is predetermined by the law of karma, then where is the scope for self-improvement through self-effort? In answer, the Bhagavad Gita points out that the law of karma does not make everything preordained.[4] Like all other natural laws operating in the physical universe, the law of karma operates on the psychophysical level. This law controls the body and mind of a person but has no hold over our indwelling Self, which is infinite, immortal, ever pure, and ever free. The cause of bondage is identification of the Self with the psychophysical system. While the Self of a person is free, its expression becomes conditioned due to the limitations of body and mind.

Karma-yoga is the process of unchaining the Self from the thralldom of body and mind. The deposits of past karma have three parts. The first part is known as *prarabdha* karma or karma that has already borne its fruit in the present life. This part of karma cannot be annulled in any way. No one can deny one's parentage, inner disposition, personality, and so forth, however hard one may try. *Prarabdha* karma can be exhausted only by bearing it with fortitude. Forbearance, according to Shankaracharya, is enduring the effects of *prarabdha* karma without trying to remedy them and without being repentant for not doing so.[5]

The second part of karma is *sanchita* karma, or karma that has not yet started to bear its fruit. The effects of *sanchita* karma remain in the form of desires and thoughts and can be altered. We have control over our *sanchita* karma, but we must act fast. It is possible to uproot those tendencies that are not yet deep rooted and plant good ones in their place. Their effects can be countered through self-effort in the form of right action and austerity.

The third part is called *agami* karma, or karma that is being accumulated in the present life and that will bear its fruit in the future. *Agami* karma can be countered through self-discipline and self-control. Karma-yoga teaches that nothing in this world happens without a cause. No one can enjoy anything unless one has earned it. No suffering is undeserved. We make and unmake our destiny through our own karma. As Swami Vivekananda says:

> Analyse yourselves and you will find that every blow you have received came to you because you prepared yourselves for it. You did half and the external world did the other half; that is how the blow came. That will sober us down. At the same time, from this very analysis will come a note of hope, and the note of hope is this: "I have no control over the external world; but that which is in me and nearer unto me, my own world, is under my control. If the two together are required to make a failure, if the two together are necessary to give me a blow, I will not contribute the one which is in my control—and how then can the blow come? If I get real control of myself, the blow will never come."
>
> From our childhood, all the time we have been trying to lay the blame upon something outside ourselves. We are always standing up to set right other people, and not ourselves. If we are miserable, we say, "Oh, the world is a devil's world." We curse others and say: "What ungrateful fools!" But why should we be in such a world if we really are so good? If this is a devil's world, we must be devils also; why else should we be here? "Oh, the people of the world are so selfish!" True enough; but why should we be found in that company if we are better? Just think of that.

We get only what we deserve. It is a lie to say that the world is bad and we are good. It can never be so. It is a terrible lie we tell ourselves.[6]

Karma-yoga is no idle speculation. It is yoga in action. It is a life of intense activity inspired by knowledge. Genuine spiritual aspiration is bound to have its active expression in everyday life. The pursuit of Self-knowledge, unless it is idle imagination, will make the aspirant act for it. Love of God, if genuine, will make the aspirant express love through every action. The exhortation of the Bhagavad Gita is to act. The cause of a person's downfall is the performance of wrong actions, and a person's rise depends on the performance of right actions. Such a rise is never achieved by escapism, cowardice, or hypocrisy. One is to solve the problems of one's life by living it.

THE WISDOM OF KARMA-YOGA

Activity is not contradictory to Self-realization. Activity, the Bhagavad Gita contends, is the law of life. It is activity that distinguishes the living from the dead. Whether we know it or not, we are always active both inside and outside of ourselves.

All activity pertains to the three *gunas*: *sattva* (tranquility), *rajas* (restlessness), and *tamas* (inertia), which are the three modifications of nature. Since the body and mind of an individual being are material and drawn from nature, they are subject to the influence of the *gunas*. The soul in bondage becomes caught in the ever-revolving wheel of the law of karma because of its identification with the body and mind; the soul follows the body and mind's destiny of birth and death, happiness and misery, and pain and pleasure.

The root cause of bondage is neither the world, the law of karma, nor the *gunas*. The cause of a person's bondage is his or her own attachment. Pain and pleasure or happiness and misery pertain to the body, mind, and sense organs alone. Because of the soul's misidentification with the body and mind, it feels the pleasure and pain of the body, mind, and sense organs to be its own.

There are persons with selfish motives who become attached to the results of their actions. That which is pleasing to the sense organs is regarded by them as good and that which is unpleasant is branded as evil. Bound by attachment, they run after the pleasurable and try to escape the painful. Their attachment does not let them see the universe in its totality and accept its laws. Such attachment dramatically changes the very outlook of their lives. Being attached to life itself, they fear death. Greedy for pleasure, they shun pain. Scarcely do they realize that their likes and dislikes do not change the course of the universe and its laws. Life and its natural laws must be accepted as a whole.

Creation is God's lila, *or play.* The Bhagavad Gita regards the universe as *lila,* or the play of God. In this play, God alone is the actor, action, and audience.[7] The play is at times tragic, at times comic, and at times absurd. To practice karma-yoga is to participate in this *lila,* or the divine sport of the Lord.

Sri Ramakrishna describes God as the Divine Mother who plays a game of hide-and-seek with her created beings. This is a game in which the leader, described as the "granny," bandages the eyes of the players and hides herself. The players are to find her. If the players can touch her, she removes the bandages from their eyes and releases them from the game. But because the granny wants to continue the game, she does not allow all the players to touch her at the beginning. Individual souls are like the players who must go on playing, and the granny will not remove the bandage from their eyes until each one of them finds her and touches her. There are, however, two ways for players to please the granny. They can decide to play well, find her, touch her, and be released, or, if they are tired of playing, they can implore her to remove the bandage and release them altogether. Similarly, an individual soul may perform all activities as ordained by the divine will and exert great effort to attain final liberation.[8] But the second option of genuine self-surrender is only possible for a seeker who has exerted the utmost effort.

Karma-yoga teaches us that life is a play. The play becomes serious when we become competitive and try to fulfill our own desires instead of selflessly carrying out our duties. As a result, we become tense and the game that was played for enjoyment turns into a life-and-death struggle. Being attached to the results of the game, we forget that we were only playing and take our victory or defeat in the game to be real and permanent.

Karma-yoga is the way to freedom. The way out of life's predicaments is not renunciation of activity but renunciation of the results of activity. Since activity is inevitable, we must seek freedom *in* action and not *from* action. The desire to avoid activity is as much prompted by inertia and restlessness as the desire to perform action is prompted by selfishness. The root cause of all bondage is not in the world but in the mind of the bound soul. In truth, no change of place, environment, or duty can free us from our own bondage. Wherever we go, we carry our mind with us, and whatever we want to escape or avoid relentlessly pursues us.

The technique of karma-yoga is neither to avoid activity nor to seek it; it is to act with nonattachment. Nonattachment is the essence of yoga and, therefore, of Self-knowledge. Nonattachment transforms every action into a spiritual practice that is just as important as prayer, meditation, or worship: every action becomes a prayer, every effort a practice of renunciation. Thus, every action, instead of being a source of bondage, becomes a revelation of Self-knowledge. Nonattachment spiritualizes all our thoughts and deeds and bridges the gulf between the sacred and the secular and between knowledge and action.

It is the freedom of karma-yoga that allows us to see the same Self in all beings and things and express that Self-knowledge in our actions. It is worshiping the Divine and meditating on the Divine with eyes open.

Karma-yoga leads the seeker to Self-knowledge. Knowledge of the Self calls for concentration of the whole mind, which is uninterrupted meditation; uninterrupted meditation depends upon unqualified love for the Self; and unqualified love for the Self depends upon the purification of the mind. Sri Krishna in the Bhagavad Gita tells us:

> [T]hose who consecrate all their actions to Me [the Lord, or the Self], regarding Me as the Supreme Goal, and who worship Me, meditating on Me with single-minded concentration—to them, whose minds are thus absorbed in Me, verily I become ere long, O Partha, the Saviour from the death fraught ocean of the world.
>
> Fix your mind on Me alone, rest your thought on Me alone, and in Me alone you will live hereafter. Of this there is no doubt.
>
> If you are unable to fix your mind steadily on Me, O Dhananjaya, then seek to reach Me by the yoga of constant practice.
>
> If you are incapable of constant practice, then devote yourself to My service. For even by rendering service to Me you will attain perfection.
>
> If you are unable to do even this, then be self-controlled, surrender the fruit of all action, and take refuge in Me.[9]

Offering the results of our action into the fire of Self-knowledge through karma-yoga is the first step toward offering our whole mind to the Self.

2

The Philosophy and Psychology of Karma-Yoga

Both renunciation and yoga lead to the Highest Goal;
but of the two, performance of action is superior to
renunciation of action.

—BHAGAVAD GITA 5.2

The philosophy of karma-yoga does not ask us to perform a set of specific spiritual activities. It asks us to act spiritually under all circumstances. The philosophical emphasis of karma-yoga is not on the nature of our duties but on our motive and performance of them. It is not what a person does but why and how he or she does it. True and permanent tranquility of mind is to be attained in the midst of the most intense activity.

The teachings of karma-yoga appear paradoxical to those who identify the attainment of spirituality with the renunciation of all action. Activity, they believe, presupposes desire, and the fulfillment of one desire gives rise to another desire, which then triggers a never-ending chain of karma and desire. Activity, therefore, is the root cause of bondage, forging the chain of cause and effect and keeping the wheel of karma ever revolving. On the one hand, activity requires the assertion of ego, since an individual must have some egotistic incentive in order to act. Even engaging oneself in activity for the good of the world requires some form of desire, the fulfillment or nonfulfillment of which affects the mind of the actor. Liberation, on the other hand, is dependent upon Self-knowledge, and Self-knowledge is not attained until all desires are eradicated, the ego obliterated, and the illusory world of the mind renounced. An ego stuffed with desires can never attain Self-knowledge.

The opponents of karma-yoga say that there is no purpose in striving to make an illusory world perfect—all activity springs from and leads to ignorance. While aspirants of Self-knowledge find no reason to act, the knower of Self does not act, seeing the Self in all and all in the Self. Neither Self-knowledge nor its pursuit necessitates activity.

In the context of these arguments, activity and Self-knowledge appear irreconcilable. But the insight of karma-yoga exposes the very root of the problem of bondage and in a unique way resolves the apparent contradictions between activity and the quest for Self-knowledge. Activity, when performed according to the guidelines of karma-yoga, complements the quest for Self-knowledge. As Swami Vivekananda says:

> If we give up our attachment to this little universe of the senses and of the mind, we shall be free immediately....
>
> But it is a most difficult thing to give up the clinging to this universe; few ever attain to that. There are two ways to do it mentioned in our books. One is called "Neti, neti" ("Not this, not this"); and the other is called "Iti" ("This"); the former is the negative, and the latter is the positive, way. The negative way [of complete renunciation] is more difficult. It is possible for men of the very highest, exceptional minds and gigantic wills, who simply stand up and say, "No, I will not have this," and the mind and body obey their will, and they come out successfully. But such people are very rare. The vast majority of mankind choose the positive way [of karma-yoga], the way

through the world, making use of their bondage in order to break that very bondage. This is also a kind of giving up; only it is done slowly and gradually, by knowing things, enjoying things, and thus obtaining experience and knowing the nature of things until the mind lets them all go at last and becomes unattached. The former way of obtaining nonattachment is by reasoning, and the latter way is through work and experience. The first is the path of jnana-yoga, characterized by the refusal to do any work; the second is that of karma-yoga, in which there is no cessation from work. Almost everyone in the universe must work. Only those who are perfectly satisfied with the Self, whose desires do not go beyond the Self, whose minds never stray out of the Self, to whom the Self is all in all— only those do not work. The rest must work.[1]

THE IMPORTANCE OF NONATTACHMENT

The Bhagavad Gita describes yoga as "same-sightedness"[2] toward every living being and thing and "equanimity of mind"[3] under all circumstances and points out that nonattachment is the very essence of same-sightedness and equanimity. All spiritual aspirants, irrespective of their paths and prescribed spiritual practices, are required to strive for this nonattachment in order to reach the goal.

An aspirant in the path of jnana-yoga discriminates between the real and the unreal and tries to concentrate on the real. The Ultimate Reality of the jnana-yogi is the unity of Pure Consciousness, designated by Vedanta as Brahman, the one without a second. The jnana-yogi rejects all that is unreal, but this rejection is not complete until the jnana-yogi is able to bridge the apparent gulf between the real and the unreal. To see only the diversities of the world is ignorance; to see only the unity of Pure Consciousness is a half-truth. To see the unity of Pure Consciousness in the diversities of the material world is perfect knowledge. Such perfect knowledge, according to karma-yoga, is the result of perfect nonattachment.

The aspirant following the path of raja-yoga is advised to collect and devote the whole mind to the practice of meditation on the inner Self. The raja-yogi meditates on the Self, withdrawing the mind from all objects of the external world. The distracted mind is attached and concentrated on the pursuit of temporary pleasures, and as a result experiences rise and fall, elation and depression, concentration and confusion. These attachments and aversions are at times so subtle and elusive that an individual fails to detect them. But the mind that practices nonattachment finds a more easy equanimity and is able to concentrate only on the Self.

Yet the unruly mind with its deep-seated attachments and aversions is a major obstacle for the aspirant in karma-yoga. The beginner on the path may become intimidated by the immensity of the task. Under such circumstances, the continued practice of nonattachment and dispassion is essential. Weak-minded persons are unable to concentrate because they are incapable of detaching their mind from distracting thoughts. Those who fight with their distractions soon become tired and frustrated, attaching too much importance to the distractions. The more the mind dwells on distractions, the stronger they grow and gain hold over us. Those who mechanically practice severe austerities or who suppress desires only delude themselves. Such practices, if unaccompanied by dispassion, prove to be repressive, and the distracting tendencies continue to lurk in the deeper layers of the mind, waiting for the right opportunity to ambush the aspirant. Those who try to fight with their distractions only torture themselves unnecessarily; those who try to analyze their distractions without having a spiritual goal to realize are prisoners of their own distracting thoughts; and those who give in to their distractions only strengthen them.

Therefore, an aspirant seeking concentration of mind is asked to practice nonattachment toward all distractions. The more we try to ignore a distracting thought, the more we are pursued by it. Aspirants practicing nonattachment separate themselves from the mind and its activities. They remain the witness to whatever comes and goes in the mind. The mind becomes calm when it is watched with nonattachment. Nonattachment, therefore, is the measure of success in the practice of concentration and meditation.

Nonattachment is not indifference. Nonattachment is the natural detachment of the mind from sense objects due to the mind's discovery of something more attractive within, namely, the Self. One naturally loses interest in something when one develops an absorbing interest in something better. As Sri Ramakrishna illustrates, once a person tastes sugar candy, he does not enjoy molasses anymore.[4] Dispassion toward the world and worldly enjoyments is possible only when one has developed a burning passion for God. An aspirant of concentration and meditation, therefore, is required to practice spiritual disciplines with nonattachment to their results.

According to the Yoga scriptures, the mind is made up of various deep-seated tendencies or *samskaras*. Distractions are due to our constantly entertaining and feeding desires that cause distracting tendencies—consciously and unconsciously. Such tendencies cannot be controlled all of a sudden. The more one practices concentration of mind and meditation, the more one adds to one's concentrating tendencies, and the more such concentrating tendencies develop, the more the distracting tendencies lose their potency, become neutralized, and are finally overcome. The stage of overcoming is the stage of perfect nonattachment. But according to the law of karma, bad tendencies cannot be overcome unless good tendencies are overcome too. Bad tendencies continue to exist in the depths of the mind so long as the aspirant clings to good tendencies. It is only when attachment to the good tendencies and aversion for the bad ones are given up that the mind reaches the highest state of *samadhi*, or freedom.

Nonattachment is the essence of self-surrender. Self-surrender is the keynote of the path of bhakti-yoga. Aspirants in the path of bhakti-yoga are called upon to make God the sole object of their love. Their spiritual practices are not for gaining anything here or hereafter but only for the pleasure of their beloved Lord. According to the bhakti-yoga scriptures, the manifestation of love has three stages. The first stage is *sadharani,* or the stage at which aspirants love God for their own pleasure. The second stage is called *samanjasa,* or the stage at which love is for the pleasure of both the aspirant and the Lord. The third stage is called *samartha*, at which stage aspirants love God only for the pleasure of their beloved Lord and become indifferent to their own happiness and unhappiness. The third stage is the stage of pure love, total self-surrender, and perfect nonattachment. Aspirants then see the hand of God everywhere, in everything, and accept pain and pleasure, birth and death, and good and evil as ordained by their beloved Lord. Such aspirants look upon themselves as instruments in the hand of God. They feel joy in being created and in being used in any way by God. They feel happy even when they are broken and discarded after God's mission through them is fulfilled.

All activity, unless performed with nonattachment, is sure to produce some result and make the aspirant's mind cling to that result. Even prayer and meditation are no exceptions to this law. In the light of the teachings of the Bhagavad Gita, the practices of spiritual disciplines such as prayer, contemplation, meditation, repetition of the holy name, study of scriptures, and spiritual austerities, as prescribed by the different paths of yoga, are only various forms of activity. It does not make a difference whether such activity is physical, mental, intellectual, or spiritual. Even spiritual practices cease to be the means to yoga if the results of such practices are not offered to God.

BONDAGE AND LIBERATION

The Bhagavad Gita describes the liberated soul as *sthitaprajna*, "steady in wisdom," and indicates that nonattachment is the measure of such steadiness.[5] Bondage is of the mind, and liberation is of the mind. Bondage is due to the ego and its attachments and aversions, which distort all our values, virtues, and sense perceptions. The ego alienates individuals from the rest of the universe by infusing in them a heightened sense of duality and individuality. Such persons exaggerate their sense of guilt, misery, and unhappiness as well as their virtues, goodness, and happiness.

Liberation in karma-yoga is freedom from the ego. It is nondependence, even-mindedness, and same-sightedness. It is attaining inner maturity. Bondage is selfishness, and liberation is unselfishness. Bondage is self-contraction, and liberation is self-expansion. The keynote of liberation is freedom under all circumstances. The liberated soul of karma-yoga is free from all constraints and conflicts. The liberated soul is free in contemplation of the all-pervading Self as well as free in action. The liberated soul is free because he or she chooses not to choose. The liberated soul desires no desire. Such a soul is greater than the moral person who shuns vice and clings to virtue. The liberated soul is greater than a spiritual person who holds to the unity of spirit as the only reality and looks on the world as a framework of illusion.

There is an incident in the life of the sage Suka that illustrates the idea of perfect nonattachment and liberation. It is said that Suka was born perfect. After receiving spiritual instructions from his father, the sage Vyasa, Suka was sent by him for further instruction to King Janaka, who was not only a great king but also a great sage. King Janaka intuited that Suka would come to his court for Self-knowledge and so made some arrangements in order to test Suka's even-mindedness. In due time, when Suka presented himself at the palace gate of the king, no one greeted him or spoke to him. No one asked him who he was or what he wanted. For three days and three nights, Suka sat outside the royal gate, ignored but with a calm expression on his face. On the fourth day, all the ministers and public dignitaries suddenly appeared to receive him with great pomp and celebration. Still the serene expression on the face of Suka did not change. Then King Janaka, seated in his court in the midst of music and dancing and other amusements, gave Suka a cup of milk full to the brim and asked him to go seven times around the hall without spilling a drop. The young Suka took the cup and in the midst of the music, merriment, and attraction of the beautiful faces around him proceeded to walk seven times around the hall. Established in perfect nonattachment as he was, Suka could not be distracted by anything against his will. He returned the cup of milk to the king without having spilled one drop. King Janaka then told Suka that he had nothing more to teach him. Nonattachment is the highest knowledge, and Suka was already established in it. So King Janaka said to Suka, "What your father has taught you and what you have learned yourself, I can only repeat. You have already known the Truth."

The meaning of liberation is the reconciliation of all dualities to the oneness of the nondual Pure Consciousness. Such reconciliation is possible only when one is established in perfect nonattachment. The symptoms of bondage are feelings of inner division that create, as it were, two souls within one person and thus make the person hypocritical, secretive, and insincere. The liberated soul, on the other hand, is united in thought, word, and deed. The liberated soul is guileless and maintains no secrecy from others.

THE MEANING OF IMMORTALITY

Immortality, the Bhagavad Gita points out, is attained by transcending the realm of maya.[6] Maya is time, space, and causation; it is the realm of relativity governed by the law of karma, the pairs of opposites, and the *gunas*. Anything that is bound by time, space, and causation cannot be permanent and, therefore, immortal. Immortality in terms of time is illogical. Immortality is not within time but beyond time. True immortality cannot be attained in a state of embodiment, whether such embodiment is terrestrial or celestial. What, then, is the way? How can one transcend the bounds of maya?

Maya, the Bhagavad Gita points out, cannot be escaped, avoided, or ignored so long as one is in the state of embodiment.[7] Immortality is not acquired by spiritual discipline, because the practice of spiritual discipline is also within the realm of maya. Maya can be transcended only through nonattachment. Maya does not delude those who know it for what it is. The mirage in the desert, for example, deludes only those who do not know it to be a mirage; but once they know it, they are never again deluded by it. The liberated soul transcends the realm of maya by experiencing it as the dynamic aspect of the Ultimate Reality that pervades all things. Being established in perfect nonattachment, the liberated soul attains immortality, where there is neither birth nor rebirth, nor anything to seek or avoid or gain or lose.

The exhortation of the Bhagavad Gita is for complete liberation through perfect knowledge of the Self.[8] It is this knowledge that makes one realize and experience the Self as one without a second, unborn, immortal, incorporeal, ever pure, ever free, and unaffected by the ideas of time, space, and causation.

3

Karma-Yoga and True Renunciation

The state reached by men of renunciation is reached
by men of action too. He who sees that the way of
renunciation and the way of action are one—he truly
sees. But renunciation of action, O mighty Arjuna,
is hard to attain without the performance of action;
the sage, purified by devotion to action,
quickly reaches Brahman.

—BHAGAVAD GITA 5.5–6

Renunciation is the central theme of the Bhagavad Gita and also its concluding note. But the karma-yogi's renunciation is no world-shunning asceticism. It is a way of life that is dynamic, positive, and creative. The implications of these teachings may be summarized as follows.

First, renunciation is never negative. One can renounce the lower only for the sake of the higher, the lesser for the greater. If a negative conviction were the only basis of renunciation, no one would ever feel inspired to renounce anything. The nothingness of earthly pleasure is realized only in the wake of Self-realization. By attaining knowledge of the ever-blissful Self, one cherishes no more desires.

Second, true renunciation is not for freeing oneself from the cares and worries of life but for attaining a state of spiritual freedom unaffected by honor or dishonor, success or failure, attachments and ambitions. The inspiration for renunciation is longing for Self-knowledge or God-realization. Only by desiring God can one spurn the world and its gross enjoyments. Love of God is the measure of all renunciation. Where there is love of God, renunciation is natural and spontaneous. Renunciation becomes complete when one is able to give one's love to God alone. The way of karma-yoga leads aspirants toward this natural renunciation. Aspirants who develop love of God do not force themselves to renounce the world; the world and its temptations renounce them. Renunciation, when not inspired by yearning for God-realization or Self-knowledge, leads only to self-deception and self-degradation.

Third, no one can renounce unless one has something to renounce. A beggar cannot renounce. A coward cannot be truly nonviolent. In the Bhagavad Gita, the heroic Arjuna refused to fight the war on the plea that nonviolence was the highest ideal; but to Sri Krishna, the plea was nothing but an expression of weakness. To be nonviolent is to renounce violence in thought, word, and deed. A person who does not offer resistance to evil because of weakness and fear cannot derive any benefit from the practice of nonviolence. Such a person does not resist, being incapable of resisting. On the other hand, one who is strong enough to resist evil but chooses not to be violent is truly nonviolent. Nonviolence stems from a position of strength. As Swami Vivekananda aptly points out:

> One man does not resist because he is weak and lazy, and he will not because he cannot; the other man knows that he can strike an irresistible blow if he likes; yet he not only does not strike, but blesses his enemies. The one who from weakness resists not commits a sin and hence cannot receive any benefit from the non-resistance; while the other would commit a

sin by offering resistance. Buddha gave up his throne and renounced his position; that was true renunciation.[1]

Fourth, one who truly renounces feels no attachment to the performance of duties. There are three kinds of renunciation:
tamasika, rajasika, and *sattvika.* In *tamasika* renunciation, a person renounces obligatory duties due to laziness or fear. Such renunciation is degrading and only adds to the dullness of the mind.
In *rajasika* renunciation, one renounces the world from a feeling
of inconvenience or unpleasantness, and such renunciation is essentially escapism and hypocrisy. In *sattvika* renunciation, however, one renounces all claims to the results of one's actions. Only
such renunciation can lead one to knowledge of the Self.

Fifth, true renunciation means the relinquishment of possessiveness. A person of true renunciation is *in* the world but not *of*
the world. It may be easy for us to renounce possessions but quite
difficult to renounce possessiveness. Some who renounce the
world and take up the quest for Self-realization often find it difficult to give up their philosophical views or opinions. Even those
who renounce everything for the sake of God may succumb to the
attachments of honor and fame. The following story illustrates the
meaning of true renunciation.

Once there was a king who developed dispassion, renounced
his kingdom and all his worldly possessions, and repaired to a
deep forest where he built a small hut and began practicing severe spiritual austerities to attain Self-realization. He passed many
days and months in meditation, contemplation, and chanting the
name of God. Then one day, seeing a holy man pass by his forest
dwelling, the king approached the holy man with reverence and
said, "O holy sir, pray enlighten me. Renouncing my kingdom, my
family, and all my possessions, I have repaired to this forest abode
in quest of peace. Living in this small hut and depending upon
the fruits and roots of the forest for my sustenance, I have been
practicing the severest spiritual austerities. Yet, in spite of all my
efforts, I have not achieved inner peace. I beg of you, O holy one,

show me the way." In reply, the holy man only said, "Renounce, O king. Renounce what is yours."

On hearing this, the king began to reflect: "I have renounced my kingdom, my near and dear ones, and all the comforts of life. What else of mine is left to renounce? It may be that the holy man wants me to renounce my hut to make my renunciation complete." So thinking, he demolished his hut and continued his spiritual practices under a tree. Again, days and months passed, but still the mind of the king remained restless. The king then saw the holy man coming his way a second time. On being asked by the king to advise him further, the holy man only repeated what he had said before: "Renounce, O king. Renounce what is yours."

The king became perplexed. He thought, "I have nothing else in my possession except my water vessel, my blanket, my deer-skin, and my rosary. I will also give them up and so complete my renunciation." The king lit a fire and threw his belongings into the flames one by one, watching silently until the fire reduced them all to ashes. He now felt happy, thinking that his renunciation was finally complete and that he would soon be at peace. Yet peace did not come. The king did not know what to do. At that moment, the holy man appeared before him for a third time and, being implored by the king for further instruction, again said, "Renounce, O king. Renounce what is yours," and went on his way.

The holy man's answer further puzzled the king. He thought, "What more is there to renounce except my physical body?" Thinking thus, the king lit a fire, and as he was about to throw himself into it, the holy man appeared for the last time and asked the king, "Do you believe, O king, your body to be your last possession?" The king replied, "Indeed it is so. After my body is burned, nothing will remain of me but my ashes." But the holy man countered, "Renounce, O king. Renounce this 'my-ness' of yours. Prompted by this my-ness, you claim even the ashes of your body to be yours. This my-ness is the root of all bondage, and one who has renounced this truly renounces. You renounced your kingdom and came to live in a hut to practice austerities, but you merely replaced one possession with another. You once called the kingdom yours; then you called the hut yours. You were once attached to a palace, possessions, and comforts; later you became attached to your water vessel, rosary, and the results of your spiritual practice. Possessiveness made you feel that the kingdom, your family, and all other things were for your own selfish enjoyment, but in reality nothing belonged to you. Their existence is not dependent upon your renouncing them or not renouncing them. That which is really yours is this sense of possessiveness. Renounce this possessiveness, O king. Renounce, and be free."

All worldliness is rooted in this my-ness. One who has renounced my-ness has truly renounced the world. Such a person sees God in the depths of contemplation and serves God through every action. To be in the world but not of the world is the most rigorous test of renunciation. Spiritual wisdom is tested when applied in everyday life. Those who renounce all worldly possessions and attachments and devote themselves to the practice of self-control in solitude by repairing to a forest or mountain cave are, no doubt, severe in their austerity. But the austerity of the karma-yogi, who is called upon to remain even-minded in the midst of the pairs of opposites, such as pain and pleasure, praise and blame, is the most rigorous. The karma-yogi's renunciation is relentlessly tested at every step of life.

THE CONNECTION BETWEEN RENUNCIATION AND SERVICE

Renunciation is not mere asceticism, and poverty is not the mark of spirituality. As Swami Vivekananda says, "Live in the midst of the battle of life. Anyone can keep calm in a cave or when asleep. Stand in the whirl and madness of action and reach the Centre.

If you have found the Centre, you cannot be moved."[2] The true renouncer does not merely deny the claims of the ego but actively expresses love of God. The ideal of renunciation is the love of sacrificing oneself for the sake of God. The whole life of a true renouncer is a grand performance of *yajna,* or self-sacrifice. The goal is not just to sit in a cave, meditate, and die. Those who think of winning the race for salvation for themselves neither win nor attain true salvation. One cannot attain true salvation unless one seeks the salvation of others. Renunciation becomes meaningful only when it is balanced and proved through acts of service and self-dedication.

In this regard, the karma-yogi may adopt certain practices from bhakti-yoga or jnana-yoga; for one renounces the world and its enjoyments by loving God alone, and service becomes the active expression of this love. Seeing God in the depths of one's meditation and *samadhi* is incomplete until one is able to see God reflected in all beings and things of the universe and serve them. Service of human beings is veritably the worship of the most visible and living God. God is the sum total of all individual souls.

True service is different from philanthropy. The spirit of philanthropy, which inspires one to do good to others out of compassion, is noble and commendable. But higher than philanthropy is the ideal of service. The knowledge aspect of karma-yoga is to know that we really do good to ourselves when we try to do good to others. Compassion, the basis of philanthropy, may spring from a sense of pity. But there is no scope for pity when we realize that the whole universe is the transfiguration of God. We cannot pity God. We can only serve God by serving all. Such service is the highest form of worship.

Yoga, as outlined by the Bhagavad Gita, embraces one's entire life. Karma-yoga does not make a distinction between meditation and action. Practicing meditation is as important as engaging oneself in acts of service. Self-realization is not a state of inertness but the blossoming forth of spirituality in a dynamic way. It is not passively seeing one's own Self in all beings and things. One who really sees the Self in all and all in the Self feels the joys and sufferings of all beings as his or her own. Seeing God within and serving all beings as God's various transfigurations are two aspects of the same experience.

The ideal of service is to dedicate the results of our actions to God or to offer them into the fire of Self-knowledge kindled within ourselves. Such performance of karma as *yajna* exhausts all *karmic* momentum, on the one hand, and purifies the mind of the aspirant, on the other. Austerity purifies the body and mind, and acts of service constitute the most rigorous austerity. In the words of the Bhagavad Gita: "He who sees inaction in action, and action in inaction, he is wise among men, he is a yogi, and he has performed all action."[3] Swami Vivekananda comments upon this point: "Work, work, day and night, says the Gita. You may ask: 'Then where is peace? If all through life I am to work like a cart-horse and die in harness, what am I here for?' Krishna says: 'Yes, you will find peace. Flying from work is never the way to find peace.'"[4]

It is commonly said, "Throw off your duties if you can and go to the top of a mountain." But even there we cannot escape our minds. Someone once asked a *sannyasin* who had returned from the mountains, "Sir, did you not find a nice place in the Himalayas? How many years did you wander in the mountains?" "For forty years," replied the *sannyasin*. Then the person inquired further, "There are many beautiful spots to select from and to settle down in; why did you not do so?" The *sannyasin* replied, "Because for those forty years, my mind would not give me peace."

Renunciation is the very law of life. By denying the claims of the ego, an individual freely participates in the social aspects of life. All living beings and things form a fellowship of life and keep the universe going. The universal order does not merely meet our physical needs but also provides for our spiritual fulfillment. The *karmic* urge is not merely an urge for the satisfaction of physical wants, but for the realization of a far more profound goal—the spiritual unity and interdependence of all. An individual who disclaims this unity and the law of reciprocity is condemned by the Bhagavad Gita as a thief.[5] We must contribute to the welfare of all beings since we are part of the cosmos. We cannot be truly happy unless we contribute to the happiness of others.

The law of reciprocity has been highlighted by the threefold formula of *yajna* (sacrifice), *dana* (charity), and *tapas* (austerity).

It is imperative that the whole life of a karma-yogi be a *yajna*, or a continual, grateful offering to all. There is an injunction for the observance of five kinds of *yajnas*, or sacrifices, which an individual is to perform daily: duties to one's ancestors, to celestial beings, to plants and animals, to fellow human beings, and to the spiritual preceptors. Duties to ancestors are fulfilled by offering prayers for them, to the spiritual preceptors by following their teachings in one's life, to fellow human beings by unselfishly serving them, to celestial beings by making oblations to them, and to plants and animals by caring for them. The spirit of *yajna* is the sacrifice of egotism in the fire of knowledge. A selfish person who does not pay heed to this injunction to sacrifice violates the universal law of reciprocity and, therefore, stands in opposition to the cosmic order. Such a person, the Bhagavad Gita points out, does not belong to this world: "This world is not for him who makes no sacrifice."[6]

Dana is charity. It is the practice of benevolence without expecting any benefit. One is to give in charity what one loves and values most. *Tapas* is the practice of austerity—of the body, speech, and mind. Austerity of the body is practiced by rendering service to the spiritual preceptor and cultivating reverence for holy men, austerity of speech by unswerving adherence to truthfulness, and austerity of the mind by self-restraint and self-sacrifice. *Tapas* has meaning only in the context of both *yajna* and *dana*. *Tapas* without *yajna* and *dana* is negative; while *yajna* and *dana* without *tapas* are futile. Renunciation and service are, therefore, not two different concepts but two aspects of the same realization. They are not contradictory but complementary.

4

The Practice of
Karma-Yoga

*Being established in yoga, O Dhananjaya, perform
your actions, casting off attachment and remaining
even-minded both in success and in failure. This
evenness is called yoga.*

—BHAGAVAD GITA 2.48

NATURALNESS, EFFICIENCY, AND GRACEFULNESS

The path of karma-yoga has two advantages—it is natural and practical. Karma-yoga never seeks to radically change a person's inner disposition. The personality is formed by one's own inner disposition *(svabhava)* and sense of duty *(svadharma)*. It is neither possible nor desirable to break away from our *svabhava* or deny our *svadharma*. To try to do so is to try to jump out of one's own body and mind. The technique of the Bhagavad Gita leads us to the spiritual goal by following the course of slow, steady steps and not that of sudden, impulsive jumps: "Let no enlightened man unsettle the understanding of the ignorant, who are attached to action. He should engage them in action, himself performing it with devotion."[1] As long as we remain conscious of our social and moral obligations, we must work:

Not by merely abstaining from action does a man reach the state of actionlessness, nor by mere renunciation does he arrive at perfection.[2]

He who restrains his organs of action, but continues to dwell in his mind on the objects of the senses, deludes himself and is called a hypocrite.[3]

Karma-yoga is the practice of even-mindedness at all times and in all places, whether in the workplace or the prayer room. It is the art of spiritual living. Every moment of life can be spiritual. Every call of duty can be a spiritual call. Every challenge can be a spiritual challenge. Every activity, therefore, should be a form of *yajna,* or spontaneous self-sacrifice. Even routine activities can be transformed into the practice of karma-yoga if spiritually motivated. The act of eating, for example, is thought to be different from prayer and meditation, which alone are considered spiritual. But the same act of eating turns into a *yajna* the moment one looks upon God as the enjoyer of the food. The secret of karma-yoga lies not in what we do but the spirit in which we do it. Yoga is in the motive. Examples are given in the Hindu scriptures of a king and a butcher, both of whom attained self-illumination by performing their respective duties in the spirit of karma-yoga.

For instance, King Janaka is described in the Upanishads as an ideal king who combined yoga with enjoyment of the world. He is therefore referred to as *rajarshi,* or a "royal sage." The king ruled over his subjects selflessly, inspiring them to a life of virtue, and often gave shelter to Vedic scholars and knowers of Brahman, while hearing from them about the nature of the Self and Ultimate Reality. Of the great King Janaka, Sri Ramakrishna says:

Why shouldn't one be able to realize God in this world? King Janaka had such realization.... What courage he had, indeed! He fenced with two swords, the one of Knowledge and the other of work. He possessed the perfect Knowledge of

Brahman and also was devoted to the duties of the world....
[King Janaka] worked in the world at the command of God.[4]

Swami Vivekananda also refers to an incident described in the *Mahabharata* about a common butcher who practiced perfect nonattachment to the results of his actions. The butcher came to realize that "no duty is ugly, no duty is impure" since the innermost Self is ever blissful and ever pure. He carried out his commonplace duties with cheerfulness and with a spirit of inner renunciation, knowing they could not affect the unchanging and immortal Self within, and thus attained perfection of the soul.[5]

Dividing life into sacred and secular, work and worship, the active life and the contemplative life is artificial and a waste of time for a yogi of the Self. Aspirants who look upon their prayer time as sacred and all other times as secular only practice self-deception. What they accomplish during prayer and meditation is negated by what they do at other times. The art of karma-yoga is to integrate our whole life by spiritualizing all our duties. The duty of one person, however, need not be the duty of another since the inner disposition of the one is different from that of the other. The soldier who abandons his or her duties and impulsively takes up the contemplative life of an ascetic becomes a misfit and a false ascetic who suppresses the outgoing senses without first conquering internal desires. Such a person is a hypocrite. Thus the repeated exhortation of the Bhagavad Gita is

Better is one's own dharma, though imperfectly performed, than the dharma of another well performed. Better is death in the doing of one's own dharma: the dharma of another is fraught with peril.[6]

The Bhagavad Gita also describes different forms of *yajnas*, or sacrifices, such as those of wealth, food, austerities, self-control, and concentration, which different aspirants perform according to their inner dispositions and moral and intellectual competence.[7] A particular form of *yajna* natural to one may not be natural for another.

When one forces oneself to perform duties that are not natural for one, one invites moral disaster. Forced to be contemplative, most aspirants become tense, isolated, and irritable. The same reactions will follow in the case where a contemplative aspirant is forced to be very active.

An action in accordance with a person's *svabhava* and *svadharma* is always marked by the following three characteristics: naturalness, efficiency, and gracefulness. Naturalness and unostentatiousness go together. The natural is spontaneous. A person does not demand attention for the performance of an action that is natural for her or him. An action that is natural for a person is also enjoyable. Spiritual practices such as contemplation and meditation are looked upon as disciplines so long as they have not become spontaneous.

Similarly, an action that is natural for a person is performed with ease—because the action is in tune with the person's *svabhava* and *svadharma*—and efficiency, because the whole mind participates in the action. The mind's faculties of cognition, volition, and emotion must participate in the performance in a unified way. A skillful performer exerts right effort and spends a proportionate amount of energy. An ordinary person acts either foolishly or feverishly, is either totally passive or overactive, and has either no spiritual goal or an impossible one. But an aspirant in the path of karma-yoga acts spontaneously and freely. The karma-yogi's performance is single-minded, because he or she is wholehearted. An efficient performance brings the joy of spiritual creativity.

And finally, an action that is natural for its performer and spiritually expressive is also graceful. A graceful performance is marked by proportionality, discrimination, rhythm, and harmony. The karma-yogi is like a professional actor for whom the world is a stage and life a drama in which the yogi plays an assigned role and plays it with grace. The illusion and fantasy of the play never overwhelm the yogi. Never for a moment does such a person forget that life is only a play and his or her personality only a costume. Ordinary persons, on the other hand, are amateur actors. They obsessively identify themselves with their roles, and the agonies and exaltations of the drama become their real and personal concerns.

SKILL IN ACTION

The problem of karma is that every action produces a result, forging a chain of bondage for the doer of the action. From a material point of view, the result of an action that is pleasurable may ultimately prove to be painful. For example, one feels unhappy at the loss of acquired pleasurable objects or becomes bored when such pleasure continues too long. From a psychological point of view, an action leaves a subtle deposit of impressions *(samskaras)* in the mind of the doer, and these impressions compel the person, at a future time and under similar conditions, to repeat that same action. Every such *samskara* alters the very texture of the mind of the doer of the action.

The way out of the problem of karma is not abandonment of action through fear, frustration, or disgust but the performance of action without longing for the result. Such performance serves two purposes: it exhausts the propensities of past karma in the mind and, at the same time, keeps us from entanglement in the result. Skill in action and nonattachment are therefore the principal guidelines for right living, because they are the most efficient means of attaining freedom and peace of mind.

No one can say that one's action will produce the desired results. No effort, however efficient and intelligent, can ensure success. Sri Krishna describes five factors that determine the success of any action:

Learn from Me, O mighty Arjuna, the five causes that bring about the accomplishment of a work, as declared in the philosophy of knowledge, which puts an end to all action:

The body, the doer, the different senses, the many and various functions of the vital breaths, and the presiding deity as the fifth.[8]

The first four of these five factors are the field of action, the agent of action, the effort of the performer, and the instruments of action. These four factors indicate that performers of action must have the requisite physical and intellectual fitness for the project. They must be equipped with the necessary instruments and must be efficient in their effort. Yet, even when all these first four factors are fulfilled, the accomplishment of the goal cannot be ensured. No one has control over the fifth factor, which the Bhagavad Gita describes as providential will. One is, therefore, asked to act without being attached or averse to the results of one's actions. The concept of providential will makes it clear that the world process is not governed by mechanical law. The ego has its limitation. The performance of action, however, is necessary in order to realize this fact. A person can never accept this limitation without having exerted the utmost effort. The weak and ignorant believe that everything in life is preordained and therefore give up all efforts; there are others who think that success is solely dependent upon detailed planning and hard work, but very soon they become disillusioned with their philosophy. To be skillful in action is to give equal consideration to all the five factors.

Skill in action is the secret of happiness. For the vast majority of people, happiness depends upon the acquisition of wealth, talent, fame, power, health, and beauty. They multiply their desires, and struggle hard to gratify them, but they very soon realize that happiness is not something that can be bought or borrowed. Happiness is the result of a peaceful mind, and the mind becomes peaceful when it is free from all attachment. Without peace of mind, the world seems hollow and distasteful. No artificially manufactured happiness can substitute for peace of mind. Peace of mind, again, is not for a person who tries to escape the duties of life. Peace of mind results from the practice of nonattachment.

The ideal of karma-yoga is particularly significant for modern times, when so many people seek life's fulfillment in terms of greater pleasure or lesser pain, and yet suffer from chronic tension, anxiety, and insecurity. Modern societies spend vast amounts of money searching for techniques that can help achieve peace of mind. Many people undertake spiritual practices not for God-realization but for concentration, balance, and inner peace. Yet hollowness only piles upon hollowness, tension upon tension, and fear upon fear.

THE WAY OF MATURE LIVING

Karma-yoga is a call for enlightened and mature living, which is free, responsible, expressive, and creative. It is living that combines fullness of vision with maturity of action. The characteristic marks of mature living, according to the teachings of karma-yoga, are the following:

Mature living is realistic living. Mature persons cannot afford to be carried away by personal whims and attachments. They are realistic in their views and balanced in their judgments. To always be optimistic is to be a visionary; to always be pessimistic is to be fearful of life itself. Mature living follows the path of moderation. It asks us to neither seek nor avoid anything but carry out those duties and obligations of life that fall upon us in a natural way.

Mature living accepts life as a whole. We often forget that the sufferings and miseries of life make vital contributions to the growth of our inner being. One who has not suffered in life can never attain wisdom. The moments of suffering, in fact, impart more enduring lessons of wisdom to us than the moments of pleasure. The reversals of life guard us from lapsing into the state of psychological rigor mortis. They force us to correct our past mistakes and enable us to reassess our values and priorities. The moments of suffering and misery are not only moments of crisis but moments of possibility and revelation. Only at such moments do we seriously discriminate between the real and unreal. Those who have not suffered for the sake of truth do not care to understand it nor can they truly appreciate it. The moments of suffering reveal the authenticity latent in us. Our spiritual wisdom and love of God are tested when we suffer for their sake.

Mature living exhorts us to get hold of ourselves. An immature person always blames the external world and finds fault with it. Mature living asks us to reverse the process and correct ourselves. As Swami Vivekananda says:

> This is the great lesson to learn: be determined not to curse anything outside, not to lay the blame upon anyone outside, but be a man, stand up, lay the blame on yourself. You will find that that is always right. Get hold of yourself.
>
> Is it not a shame that at one moment we talk of our manhood, of our being gods, of our being able to know everything, do everything, of our being blameless, spotless, the most unselfish people in the world—and the next moment a little stone hurts us, a little anger from a little Jack wounds us, any fool in the street makes us—these "gods"—miserable! Could this happen if we were really such gods? Is it true that the world is to blame? Could God, who is the purest and noblest of souls, be made miserable by any of our tricks? If you are really so unselfish, you are like God. How can the world hurt you? You will go through the seventh hell unscathed, untouched. But the very fact that you complain and want to lay the blame upon the external world shows that you feel the external world; the very fact that you feel, shows that you are not what you claim to be. You only make your offense greater by heaping misery upon misery, by imagining that the external world is hurting you, and crying out: "Oh, this devil's world! This man hurts me; that man hurts me!" and so forth. It is adding lies to misery.

We have to take care of ourselves—that much we can do—and give up minding others for a time. Let us perfect the means; the end will take care of itself. For the world can be good and pure only if our lives are good and pure. It is an effect, and we are the means. Therefore let us purify ourselves. Let us make ourselves perfect.[9]

Mature living is integrated. All the priorities of life should be subordinated to one single goal. To immature persons, the different priorities of their professional life, family life, social life, and spiritual life appear as conflicting pursuits with no connection to one another. As a result, immature persons feel divided within, as if they were living two lives. They often feel like hypocrites. Mature living asks us to follow a mature goal of life and subordinate all goals to that goal.

According to karma-yoga, the most worthy and mature goal of life is Self-knowledge. By knowing one's own Self, one knows the whole world. This Self, the common Self of all, is our true identity. All values and virtues of life are meaningful only in the context of the Self. It is said that a person should sacrifice the interest of the family for the sake of the country and the interest of the country for the sake of the world; but for the sake of the Self, one should sacrifice everything.

In this regard, Hinduism outlines the four basic values of life: *dharma,* or moral perfection; *artha,* or acquisition of wealth; *kama,* or fulfillment of legitimate desires; and *moksha,* or Self-realization. The first three values are meaningful only in the context of the fourth and should be subordinated to it. Life becomes a problem when any one of these four values is overemphasized. Material success and the fulfillment of desires, unless conducive to moral perfection and directed toward Self-realization, only lead to the disintegration of a just society and the deprivation of one's inner being.

Mature living asks us to practice even-mindedness in pain and pleasure. Pleasure and pain are different feelings experienced by the same mind. We often find that the more we increase our pleasure, the more we increase our pain. The more new remedies are invented for old diseases, the more new diseases multiply in number. As we expand the frontier of our knowledge, we are confronted with new frontiers of ignorance. The more we try to control nature, the more it eludes our grasp. New additions to the comforts and amenities of life made available by science and technology may be offset by the resulting pollution of the environment, erosion of human individuality, and mechanization of life.

The philosophy of karma-yoga compares the world to a dog's curly tail and contends that just as it is useless to try to straighten a dog's curly tail, so it is futile to try to eradicate all evil from the world. There will never be a time when there is only good and no evil. Imperfection, insufficiency, and change are the very conditions of life. Therefore, the watchword of karma-yoga is *service* and not charity or philanthropy. The world does not need our charity; no one depends on our good will. The world will not stop if we do not give in charity—although being charitable is better than doing nothing and having apathy toward the suffering of our fellow human beings. Still, the mature attitude is that of service, which teaches us to feel blessed and privileged for being allowed to help another person. The world process, according to karma-yoga, is eternal, and the universe is the transfiguration of God alone. God does not need our help or charity. It is a blessed privilege to serve God and God's children. If karma-yoga teaches us to do good to others, it is because we come nearer to God by doing good than by doing evil.

Mature living is neither defensive nor aggressive. Mature living is sincere, honest, and frank. The more immature one is, the more walls of defense one raises around oneself. Such immature persons are exclusive, secretive, and private. The more they seek exclusiveness, the more isolated they feel, until finally they explode into fanaticism, skepticism, cynicism, or other aggressive forms of desperate living. The same desperation impels them to dominate others. Pretension and ostentation are attempts to appear different from what one really is. A person who does not have any holy qualities, but who wants to appear holy, often poses as pious. But no hypocrite can be a yogi.

Mature persons are spontaneous and authentic. They have nothing to hide from others and nothing to display. They are humble because they are strong, and open because they see the reflection of the Self in all.

Mature living is conscious and creative. Karma-yoga is a life of action punctuated by contemplation. If action represents becoming, contemplation indicates being. Being indicates Self-consciousness and becoming indicates responsiveness to the external world. But becoming is impossible without being. A life of action not supported by contemplation loses its direction and purpose.

A mature person is always anxious to learn. Sri Ramakrishna says, "As long as I live, so long do I learn."[10] The mark of true knowledge is humility. An enlightened person knows the limitations and insufficiency of the ego. Such a person draws lessons when criticized—if such criticism is fair and not malicious.

Mature living is free from all dependence. The secret of a happy life is freedom from dependence. As long as we need something or someone to make us happy, we are at the mercy of that thing or person and, therefore, miserable.

Mature living is marked by forbearance and adaptability. Mature persons are never the cause of anxiety for others. They possess an inner stability and have the capacity to adjust to the needs of the particular time, place, circumstance, culture, and custom. A karma-yogi must have an inner steadiness to withstand the frustrations of life—frustrations from within and without. Immature persons easily collapse under such pressures and experience rise or fall with the rise or fall of their emotions. Mature persons, on the other hand, are firmly grounded in themselves. They are forbearing because their minds are strong. Intolerance and impatience indicate an overcharged mind that releases its tensions through violent outbursts of anger and lust.

Mature living is sattvika *living. Sattvika* living is marked by balance, efficiency, and joy. Our inner disposition consists of our moods, temperament, instincts, and desires, which unconsciously impel us to act in certain ways. This inner disposition, although inherited to a certain extent, is constantly altered by our actions and choices. Any action that is consciously done today becomes an unconscious impulse tomorrow; any mood or desire that is allowed to be repeated becomes part of our character. Our inner disposition influences our actions, and our actions influence our inner disposition.

In this regard, the Bhagavad Gita describes, in general, three types of inner dispositions: *rajasika* (adolescent), *tamasika* (infantile), and *sattvika* (mature).

Rajasika persons are generally restless and adolescent. They are full of ambitions, concerned with their gain or loss, beset with innumerable anxieties, and bound by a hundred ties of hopes and expectations. Such persons are often under the control of their fluctuating emotions and moods. They tend to make a decision before deliberating, later regret it, but never bother to change their habit. In their spiritual quest, *rajasika* persons seek the fulfillment of desires instead of spiritual joy. Of the four basic values of life discussed above, the *rajasika* person is most interested in *artha* and *kama,* or the acquisition of wealth and fulfillment of legitimate desires.

Tamasika living is generally delusional and infantile. A *tamasika* disposition is dull, brooding, and inactive. Such individuals generally drift aimlessly in life and procrastinate endlessly. Their spiritual practices are sometimes based on occultism or dogmatism, and even their practices of austerity and worship neglect basic moral values.

But *sattvika* individuals are free from egotism and utilitarian motives, even-minded under all circumstances, and endowed with efficiency, enthusiasm, and discrimination. Such persons are guided by an illumined *buddhi,* or intellect, which sees things and persons in the light of unity. Self-knowledge is the prime consideration for such persons, and all other life goals are subordinated to this one goal.

Each of these inner dispositions relates to the *gunas,* the three constituent elements of all material things and of the psychophysical system of every individual. While there is one common Self abiding in all individuals—free, immortal, ever pure, and unchanging—the psychophysical system of each individual is different from all others because of its particular *guna* structure. The three *gunas* are interdependent and abide together in every individual in varying proportions, influencing all moral judgment and spiritual motivation. Again, while the light of the Self shines within every individual in the same way, its shining through the body and mind depends on the proportion of the three *gunas. Sattva* may be compared to pure glass through which the light shines clearly, *rajas* is like tinted glass that distorts the light, and *tamas* is like black glass that altogether blocks the light. The goal of spiritual discipline is to make the body and mind pure by the cultivation of the quality of *sattva,* so that the pure light of the Self can shine forth.

As a guideline for mature living, the Bhagavad Gita extols the cultivation of a *sattvika* attitude toward action.[11] The *guna* structure of each of us is partly inborn and partly formed by our actions. Since a peculiar *guna* constitution impels a person to adopt a certain attitude toward life, a conscious change in conduct can very well change his or her *guna* structure. Thus all individuals, by consciously cultivating *sattva* in thought, word, and deed—that is, in meditation, *japa* (repetition of a holy name), and action—can methodically change the character of the mind.

Also, the Bhagavad Gita points out that action is nothing but *gunas* acting on *gunas*.[12] An individual must know that the rise and fall of the mind, the feelings of elation and depression, are due to the particular nature of the mind itself, and the individual should, therefore, remain detached from such changes by contemplating the immutable, ever-pure Self. And finally, it is important to realize that *tamas* can be controlled by *rajas* and *rajas* by *sattva*. Inertia is to be overcome by activity, and activity is to be oriented toward a spiritual goal, which ultimately brings peace of mind in the midst of action.

MORALITY AND SPIRITUALITY

Moral practices endow a spiritual seeker with a steel frame foundation upon which the spiritual structure can be raised. In order to practice karma-yoga, the seeker's moral foundation is to be developed by observing the following six virtues:

First, the seeker must give up longing for and brooding over the results of action. Such longing or brooding creates attachment to or aversion for the results of action, which is an obstacle along the path of Self-realization. The seeker must perform action selflessly, rising above all praise and blame, gain and loss. The practice of karma-yoga is always difficult for a person who is insensitive, oversensitive, or calculating.

Second, the seeker must pay as much attention to the details and means of work as to its goal. Mere thinking about the goal does not help attain the goal. The karma-yogi must work for it with all sincerity, attention, and dedication. To practice karma-yoga means to move toward the goal with measured and steady steps.

Third, the seeker must know that there is no such thing as perfect action. As fire produces smoke, every action reveals an element of imperfection. The yogi must know that the path to the goal is fraught with difficulties. He or she must be able to practice nonattachment and anticipate these difficulties, so as not to be ambushed by such obstacles.

Fourth, the seeker must be endowed with zeal and discrimination. It is necessary to remain composed in the midst of both success and failure. Zeal is the spirit that makes the seeker practice karma-yoga with enthusiasm, without becoming depressed or disillusioned when faced with difficulties. Discrimination gives the seeker right understanding of the difference between the desirable and the undesirable, between the real and the unreal. Karma has the tendency to create turbulence, and a discriminating seeker must remain unperturbed in the practice of yoga.

Fifth, a karma-yogi must be humble. Karma-yoga is the practice of the presence of God at every step, and this is not possible unless the seeker is humble. The more one feels the presence of God, the more one discovers the smallness of the selfish ego. Only a humble person can consecrate the results of all action to God. Humility is the very basis of nonattachment. Success, failure, praise, and blame are the inevitable results of karma. An egotistic person can easily become distracted by blame or praise. Failure and blame bring a sense of guilt, while success and admiration inflate the ego. The seeker who is humble is neither elated by success nor depressed by failure, but modestly offers all results to God.

Sixth, the motto of an aspiring karma-yogi must be "Seek not. Avoid not." On the one hand, if one seeks responsibility beyond one's spiritual capacity, one may lose the very sight of yoga. On the other hand, if one avoids work that naturally presents itself—work that is sometimes unpleasant—one is giving in to escapism, and no escapist can practice karma-yoga.

5

Karma-Yoga for Self-Knowledge

*He who does the work he ought to do and does not
seek its fruit—he is a sannyasi and he is a yogi; not he
who does no work and maintains no sacred fire.*

—BHAGAVAD GITA 6.1

Knowledge of one all-pervading Self or total absorption in God-consciousness is the culmination of all yoga. It is the state of *nirvikalpa samadhi,* in which all ideas of plurality and diversity dissolve into one undivided Pure Consciousness, indicated by Vedanta scriptures as the one all-pervading Self, immortal and immutable. The Self has been compared to an infinite circle whose circumference is nowhere but whose center is everywhere. Knowledge of the Self is a supreme revelation and is possible only when *samadhi* reaches the stage of *nirvikalpa samadhi,* where knowledge, knower, and known become one through uninterrupted meditation on the Self.

The state of uninterrupted meditation is a wholehearted response of the mind to the object of meditation. Such response demands a full commitment of all the faculties of the mind to the goal. Meditation is more than mere thinking about and imagining the object of meditation. It is an intense and uninterrupted feeling for the Chosen Ideal based on knowledge. As long as one is unable to feel, one thinks and reasons; but as one begins to feel, all reasoning gradually comes to a stop, and one's feeling gradually leads to the state of meditation.

The state of meditation cannot be reached unless the aspirant feels pure love and attachment for the object of meditation. Pure love merges into meditation, and meditation culminates in *samadhi,* in which state love, lover, and beloved lose their separate identities. Self-knowledge or God-realization is the most concentrated form of love. The commitment of the heart is thus the most vital prerequisite for meditation for the psychological reason that the mind dwells on the object a person loves most.

Love for the object of meditation is an intensified attachment to and identification with the object. Such loving attachment is not possible unless the mind is detached from its countless preoccupations. The mind of an average person is a slave to worldly attachments, desires, and instincts and thus is incapable of selflessly loving anyone or anything. The average person is unable to meditate on a fixed ideal, having no mind left to devote. He or she is at the mercy of endless desires and impulses and is unable to concentrate—not to speak of practicing meditation. Remaining constantly preoccupied with the objects of the senses and harassed by attachments, the average mind finds no time to devote to the spiritual quest.

Gathering the scattered mind is, therefore, the first step toward the practice of meditation. The scattered mind has been likened to a packet of tiny mustard seeds that have been scattered all over the harvest field. The process of gathering the mind is as painstakingly difficult as gathering the scattered mustard seeds one by one. The Bhagavad Gita points out:

> For a sage who wants to attain yoga, action is said to be the
> means; but when he has attained yoga, serenity is said to be

the means. [Through serenity, the sage is gradually established in Truth.]

When a man has no attachment to the objects of the senses or to works, and when he has wholly renounced his will, he is said to have attained yoga.[1]

Karma-yoga is nonattachment in practice and the most effective means for the spiritual training of the mind. Our character is tested only in the field of activity. One who is really great is always great, and such greatness is manifested even in the most commonplace duties of everyday life. As Swami Vivekananda says:

If you really want to judge the character of a man, do not look at his great performances. Every fool can act as a hero at one time or another. Watch a man do his most common action; those are indeed the things which will tell you the real character of a great man. Great occasions rouse even the lowest of human beings to some kind of greatness; but he alone is the really great man whose character is great always, the same wherever he may be.[2]

THREE STAGES OF PRACTICE

The first stage of karma-yoga is purification of the mind through selfless activity, which exhausts the excess of *rajas* and *tamas*. Aspirants at this stage practice detachment from all thoughts other than those concerning the object of their spiritual interest. For beginners, work and worship are distinct practices, leading the mind in different, and sometimes opposite, directions. The beginners' spiritual life is guided more by law than by love, and their inspiration for the practice of karma-yoga is not yet spontaneous.

The beginner is an afflicted soul, eager to end all the sufferings of life. The practice of detachment can create a vacuum in the beginner's mind. While there is a feeling of distaste for worldly pleasures and a dispassion toward worldly things, there is as yet no natural love and longing for the spiritual ideal. But it is not enough for an aspirant to have distaste for worldly enjoyment. Such distaste never becomes permanent until one develops a taste for spiritual practices and through them feels spiritual joy. What is important is what an aspirant enjoys, not what he or she does not enjoy.

In the transition from the first stage of karma-yoga to the second, the aspirant glimpses a new spiritual horizon. It is the transition from the stage of an "unripe ego" to that of a "ripe ego." The ego is unripe when it is *rajasika*, that is, inflated and arrogant, or *tamasika*, indulging in self-pity and self-punishment. A *rajasika* ego tries to solve the problems of life all by itself. Such an ego looks on spiritual practices as decisive techniques and relies solely on its own strength to achieve the desired end. The *sattvika* ego, on the other hand, combines self-effort with the bhakti-yoga practice of self-surrender. In the Bhagavad Gita, Sri Krishna advises Arjuna to "remember Me and fight."[3] To fight is to make self-effort, and to remember one's spiritual ideal is to surrender oneself to the Lord. The keynote of the spiritual quest is nonattachment, and nonattachment is possible only when self-effort is guided by self-surrender. A karma-yogi is advised to perform spiritual practices and then surrender the results to God. Genuine and sincere self-surrender never indulges in self-pity and idleness. One who has genuinely and sincerely surrendered to God actively strives for knowledge of the Self.

In the second stage of karma-yoga, the aspirant is no longer guided by a life of law but lives a life of love. Work becomes worship. The Supreme Brahman is felt as the indwelling Atman, or Self. The practice of spiritual disciplines becomes the practice of the love of God. The worker is now a devotee. The devotee no longer struggles to control the mind, subdue passions, or overcome emotions. The disciplines previously practiced for purification of mind now become natural and spontaneous acts of worship performed for the pleasure of the spiritual ideal.

The most important contribution of the second stage of karma-yoga is the establishment of an emotional link between the spiritual ideal and the aspirant. Here, karma-yoga draws on the philosophy of bhakti-yoga. So long as the aspirant is guided by a need for discipline, the spiritual quest is never creative or enjoyable. Control of the mind remains a battle unless one is able to turn the mind to a spiritual ideal. Liberated from its involvement in worldly matters, the mind must have some absorbing ideal to which it can devote itself. Directing the mind in the second stage is possible because the aspirant's loving attachment for the spiritual goal makes it easy to control the mind.

The quest for Self-knowledge now becomes the absorbing preoccupation of the aspirant's mind. The more one becomes absorbed in contemplation of the spiritual ideal, the more worldly pleasures drop away. The Bhagavad Gita asks an aspirant of meditation to be "completely serene," "fearless," "disciplined in mind" and "steadfast in the vow of a *brahmachari*."[4] Achieving complete mastery over these virtues is comparable to forcing a turbulent river back to its source. But the Bhagavad Gita indicates that the secret of mastery consists of no more than "regarding Me [the Lord, the Self] as the Supreme Goal."[5] No aspirant can expect to attain steadfastness in the vow of self-control without an uncompromising love for God. Self-knowledge is never the result of austerities or spiritual disciplines. The yogi loses interest in the world and worldly pleasures, preoccupied with the indwelling and infinite Self alone.

Like bhakti-yoga, karma-yoga emphasizes the positive aspect of Self-realization. It contends that it is psychologically irresponsible and unnecessary to make the mind a vacuum in order to fill it with the thought of God. It is harmful to teach a person austerity, meditation, and other spiritual practices before a positive spiritual inspiration has been aroused. Loving attachment for the spiritual ideal acquired during the first stage leads the aspirant to the state of meditation in the second stage. But the state of steady meditation is far from that of Self-knowledge and *samadhi*. One reaches the state of *samadhi* only after perfecting the practice of meditation.

According to Patanjali, the aspirant's mind in the state of meditation is charged with *samskaras* of *sattva* quality.[6] The impressions of *rajas* and *tamas* do not become destroyed at this stage but remain submerged. As long as the aspirant depends on *sattvika samskaras,* he or she continues to remain vulnerable to the possible upsurge of *rajasika* and *tamasika samskaras.* The state of meditation is still within the bounds of the three *gunas.* Self-knowledge, on the other hand, is transcending the *gunas.* It is above action and non-action, neither active nor passive. Self-knowledge is a revelation in the depths of *samadhi,* which is attained when meditation becomes uninterrupted and natural for the aspirant, and naturalness in meditation comes in the course of time as the result of repeated practice.

In this regard, karma-yoga is a twofold practice of negative and positive practices. Negatively, it exhausts the attachments of egotistic karma. Positively, it helps in the cultivation of deep attachment to the Self. Attachments to various sense objects are replaced by one deliberately cultivated attachment to the Self in meditation.

The third stage of karma-yoga is the natural culmination of the second stage. It is the stage of total transcendence of all duality. The free souls who reach this transcendence see the presence of one all-encompassing Self everywhere, both with eyes open and eyes closed, both in good and in evil. Self-knowledge alone can destroy all bondage and ignorance. The practices of penance, austerity, and even meditation cannot destroy the cause of error and ignorance. Hence, they cannot liberate the soul. Knowledge of the Self alone can make this liberation possible. According to Shankaracharya, Self-knowledge is like a lamp of shining wisdom within:

Characterized by discrimination [the lamp of wisdom is] fed with the oil of contentment due to divine love; fanned by the wind of earnest meditation on the Lord; furnished with the wick of right intention; purified by the cultivation of piety, chastity, and the other virtues; held in the chamber of the heart devoid of worldliness; placed in the sheltered recess of the mind withdrawn from sense-objects and untainted by attachment and aversion; shining with the light of right knowledge generated by incessant practice of concentration and meditation.[7]

According to Shankaracharya's interpretation of the Bhagavad Gita, meaningful liberation is possible only through knowledge of the Self or Brahman—not through action or a combination of action and knowledge. As darkness cannot dispel darkness, action cannot remove ignorance. Ignorance is the very result of action. Only knowledge of the Self destroys the very root of ignorance and all illusory perceptions. Such knowledge reveals itself as the grace of God. God alone is the path as well as the goal. Through the practice of karma-yoga, one prepares for responding to the call of grace by renouncing all egotism and self-love.

THREE METHODS OF PRACTICE

The aspirant of karma-yoga may be a dualist having faith in some form of personal God, a nondualist whose goal is Self-realization through discrimination and renunciation, or the aspirant may not adhere to either of these two conventional spiritual attitudes, following the agnostic practice of simply being good and doing good. It may be noted, however, that the practice of karma-yoga and nonattachment becomes less difficult if inspired by faith in a spiritual ideal.

A karma-yogi having faith in some form of personal God looks upon God as the real doer of all actions; such a karma-yogi is but an instrument in God's hands. For the dualist, work is worship of the Lord. Service is offered to God through the service of God's children. Karma-yoga is essentially one of the practices of bhakti-yoga for a devotee of God. The root cause of all bondage and suffering is the ego. The ego dies hard and refuses to be altogether obliterated. The devotee of the personal God, instead of seeking obliteration of the ego, cultivates the harmless ego of a servant and looks upon God as Master.

The practice of karma-yoga for a nondualist is offering the results of actions in the fire of Self-knowledge. The nature of this offering has been thus described in the Bhagavad Gita:

> To him Brahman is the offering and Brahman is the oblation, and it is Brahman who offers the oblation in the fire of Brahman. Brahman alone is attained by him who thus sees Brahman in action.[8]

The Ultimate Reality for the nondualist is the inmost Self, one without a second—immutable, incorporeal, and absolute. Here, karma-yoga adopts the philosophy of jnana-yoga. All diversities and dualities comprise not-Self and are creations of the mind. Karma-yoga is the offering of all that is not-Self in the fiery knowledge of the Self. For the nondualist, all actions are the preoccupation of the senses with their objects, of *gunas* with *gunas*. The Self is the unconcerned witness to the workings of the mind and the senses. The knower of the Self sees action in inaction and happily dwells in the body, neither working nor causing work to be done. The goal of the nondualist is to separate the Self from not-Self and be established in knowledge of the Self. For the nondualist, practices of charity, austerity, service, contemplation, repetition of a holy name, and meditation are all practices of knowledge.

The spirit of karma-yoga is the practice of unselfishness. It makes no difference whether the karma-yogi is Hindu, Christian, Jewish, Muslim, Buddhist, a priest, a laborer, a CEO, a soldier fighting a just war for the sake of truth, and so forth. Even the practice of spiritual disciplines, such as prayer and worship, are forms of activity. The mind remains active at all times, and it is positively harmful for it to lapse into inaction or inertia. The spiritual quest, according to karma-yoga, is not the renunciation of action but the renunciation of longing for the results of action. Unselfishness is an attitude of the mind, which is expressed in the motive behind the action and not in the action itself. An action is never truly unselfish unless it is inspired by a spiritual motive. Therefore, karma-yoga is a dual practice: work and worship, action and meditation. The practice of meditation helps the aspirant withdraw the scattered mind from its selfish preoccupations. It enables us to be truly selfless in activity, and such activity helps us to meditate with a pure mind.

The true karma-yogi can enjoy solitude in the midst of intense activity. It is not true that activity brings weariness. Longing for the results of action—and not action itself—causes weariness. Such longing makes one anxious and, therefore, weak. An active life is the counterpart of the contemplative life. The two go hand in hand. Even the actions of a karma-yogi without contemplation lose their spiritual direction; contemplation without action lapses into laziness. Meditation is not relaxation, as is often thought nowadays. One is to practice meditation with great energy. The aspirant must practice meditation regularly in order to easily invoke the meditative mood at will. Meaningful meditation can only be tested in the midst of intense activity—not by its length of time or by what one "feels" during meditation.

The true karma-yogi carries an atmosphere of tranquility within that emanates like the fragrance of a flower. When such a meditative tranquility emanates from a seeker, it will not remain unperceived by others. If activity is the practice of being good and doing good, meditation is the means to help one *be* good in order to *do* good. Doing good is never possible unless one is good, but no one can become good unless one does good. Karma-yoga is the only yoga where this paradox is reconciled.

By action, the karma-yogi does good, and by meditation, becomes good—both at the same time.

Karma-yoga purifies the heart that loves God, and this culminates in knowledge of God as the inner Self. The practice of karma-yoga leads either to God-realization or Self-realization and becomes manifested as spiritual activity for the welfare of all beings.

THE IDEAL EXEMPLAR OF KARMA-YOGA

It is one thing to attain realization of the Self but quite another to become steady in that realization. When Self-realization has become spontaneous and intuitive, it enables the seeker to see the abiding presence of one common universal Self unfolding and infolding itself in the midst of all pluralities and diversities. The *sthitaprajna*, or one steady in realization, integrates both *jnana* (knowledge of the one in the midst of the many) and *vijnana* (knowledge of the many as the one). Sri Ramakrishna describes these two types of knowledge:

> Brahman alone has become everything. Therefore to the vijnani this world is a "mansion of mirth." But to the jnani it is a "framework of illusion." Ramprasad* described the world as a "framework of illusion." Another man said to him by way of retort:
>
> *This very world is a mansion of mirth;*
> *Here I can eat, here drink and make merry.*
> *O physician [addressing Ramprasad], you are a fool!*
> *You see only the surface of things.*
> *Janaka's [an illumined king] might was unsurpassed;*
> *What did he lack of the world or the Spirit?*
> *Holding to one as well as the other,*
> *He drank his milk from a brimming cup!*

---

*Ramprasad was a Bengali mystic and composer of songs about the Divine Mother.

The vijnani enjoys the Bliss of God in a richer way. Some have heard of milk, some have seen it, and some have drunk it. The vijnani has drunk milk, enjoyed it, and been nourished by it.[9]

The *sthitaprajna* is like the *vijnani*. The *sthitaprajna*'s experience of *samadhi* is *sahaja,* or spontaneous and effortless. The *sthitaprajna* is a free soul, ever steady in knowledge of the Self. The *sthitaprajna* sees the presence of God not merely in the good and noble but also in the wicked and ignoble. The state of steady wisdom is a state of transcendence that does not overlook, rationalize, or destroy the lower values of life but fulfills them all, just as adulthood does not deny childhood but completes it.

A *sthitaprajna* is also known as a *jivanmukta,* or one who is truly free while still living. Although the realization of truth is private and cannot be communicated to others, the *sthitaprajna* can be identified by his or her actions, habits, and character as a tree is known by its leaves, flowers, or fruit. The Bhagavad Gita describes the character of the *sthitaprajna* as the following:[10]

- The *sthitaprajna* is *dvandatita,* or free from the conflicts of the pairs of opposites, such as pain and pleasure, virtue and vice, honor and dishonor, and good and evil. In short, the *sthitaprajna* is free from all attachments and aversions.

- The *sthitaprajna* demonstrates the reality of the Self, the divinity of all beings, and the unity of all existence through his or her conduct.

- Steady in wisdom, the *sthitaprajna* enjoys the constant bliss of the Self, irrespective of the changing phenomena of the universe. The rise and fall of mind and pain and pleasure of body never make the *sthitaprajna* waver in steadiness of wisdom.

- Though behaving like an ordinary person, the *sthitaprajna* is ever conscious of the reality of oneness.

- Though engaged in actions, being free from ego and free from motive, the *sthitaprajna* is not a doer of actions. Though having a physical body, the *sthitaprajna* is merely a dweller within the body and is unidentified with it.

- Firmly grounded in the wisdom of the one Self, the *sthitaprajna* is at peace and ease with everything in all situations.

- The wisdom of the *sthitaprajna* is wisdom of a cosmic oneness with all beings that cannot be contained in any temple or exhaustively described by any scripture.

- The *sthitaprajna* is not bound by the injunctions of the scriptures, the traditions of society, or the laws of ethics. Yet the *sthitaprajna*'s freedom does not impose itself on anyone, nor does it violate the rules of morality and ethics.

- The *sthitaprajna* does not belong to a particular culture, sect, nation, or society; the *sthitaprajna* is for all beings of all times.

- Whatever the *sthitaprajna* does is conducive to the welfare of all beings. When the *sthitaprajna* does good, he or she has no expectations or desires. The *sthitaprajna*'s very nature is to do good.

- The *sthitaprajna* is a *seer* of truth, no longer its *seeker*. The *sthitaprajna* is not just pure but purity itself. A person conscious of his or her purity is also conscious of impurity. The *sthitaprajna* is not just holy but holiness itself, not just a knower of truth but the very embodiment of truth. The Bhagavad Gita declares: "The yogi who is happy within, who rejoices within, and who is illumined within attains freedom in Brahman, himself becoming one with Brahman."[11]

- While steady wisdom indicates seeing action in inaction and inaction in action, it does not stand for a philosophy of inaction. The *sthitaprajna* continues to act, lest by following his or her example, the vast majority of people should be led to practice inertia in the name of spirituality.

- The *sthitaprajna* lives on the borderline between absolute and relative consciousness.

- The *sthitaprajna* is a *jnani,* a *bhakta,* and a yogi.

- Ever established in the state of yoga, the *sthitaprajna* remains in constant union with God and, at the same time, is the ideal exemplar of karma-yoga, demonstrating steady wisdom through every action.

- The *sthitaprajna*'s knowledge of Ultimate Reality is universal and dynamic.

- The *sthitaprajna*'s spiritual vision is integral and all-embracing.

- For the *sthitaprajna,* God is both immanent and transcendent at the same time. Dedicated service is as important as offerings of worship, and meditation is no less an action than everyday activity.

6

Obstacles in Karma-Yoga

Know that what they call renunciation is the same as
yoga, O Pandava; for no one who has not renounced
his desire can ever become a yogi.
—BHAGAVAD GITA 6.2

There are a number of obstacles that make the practice of karma-yoga extremely difficult. Many aspirants, in spite of vigilance and discrimination, lose spiritual direction and fail to reach the goal. Aspirants in this path are easily misled because these obstacles are often unperceived and change their forms frequently. Unlike other paths of yoga, which are distinctly defined, the day-to-day practice of karma-yoga cannot be charted beforehand. Depending upon the aspirant's inner disposition, the practice of karma-yoga can follow the mode of jnana-yoga or that of bhakti-yoga. Jnana-yoga and raja-yoga necessitate withdrawal from the world. Bhakti-yoga, although it does not ask for complete withdrawal, advocates performance of some specific activities, such as charity, austerity, and pilgrimage, which are essential for the growth of love of God. Karma-yoga, in contrast to the other paths, asks an aspirant to be in the world under all circumstances. The karma-yogi's place of *sadhana,* or spiritual practice, is neither the sanctum of a temple nor a solitary retreat but the very center of activity, the arena of the world. The yoga of action demands involvement and participation, instead of withdrawal and seclusion.

The practice of any path to yoga has both internal and external aspects: *antaranga* and *vahiranga.* In the paths of bhakti-yoga, raja-yoga, and jnana-yoga the external practices are meant for promoting and heightening the internal practices, which are considered more vital. For the karma-yogi, however, the two aspects of the practice—meditation and action—are of equal significance. While selfless action helps to purify the mind, meditation enables the aspirant to maintain the spirit of yoga in the midst of activity. Attachment and detachment are the two practices the karma-yogi is required to follow. Selfless action is attaching the entire mind to one's duties, while meditation is detaching the same mind from the results of duty. Truly speaking, only an adept in meditation can practice karma-yoga.

COMMON OBSTACLES

The most common obstacles in the path of karma-yoga are attachment, false success, loss of right perspective, egotism, and loss of meditative balance.

Attachment

Most aspirants in the path of karma-yoga lose sight of their goal: nonattachment. It is not easy to eradicate all the ego's attachments. Sometimes attachment takes the form of lust and at other times the forms of greed, anger, and possessiveness. Sometimes it takes possession of the senses, sometimes the will, sometimes the mind, and sometimes the intellect. Attachment can wear the mask of affection and compassion for one's family or friends, and even concern for the welfare of a spiritual institution. It comes in different disguises and on different pretexts.

The Bhagavad Gita indicates attachment as the greatest enemy of the karma-yogi.[1] It obscures the faculty of discrimination and deludes the yogi against his or her own will. Even the most adept aspirants fall due to their attachments. Moreover, those who have freed themselves from gross attachments may give in to subtle ones. They may not be attached to worldly possessions but still have the desire for honor and fame. Ascetics and monks who have renounced everything for the sake of God-realization are not exempt from this danger. They often hanker after recognition and veneration and cannot renounce attachment to their dogmatic philosophical or theological views.

Attachment often justifies itself as duty and takes hold of the mind. Deluded by worldly attachments, many aspirants busy themselves day and night, obsessed with the idea of fulfilling their self-appointed duties. This obsession is really slavish attachment. Attachment impels many aspirants to compromise their principles and gradually carries them away from the path of yoga.

False Success

Success in the field of action is not necessarily success in karma-yoga. That which makes karma, or activity, karma-yoga is the motive. Where the spiritual motivation behind action is sacrificed for the sake of worldly success, there is no yoga. Such worldly successes are spiritual failures and only degrade the aspirant.

Loss of Right Perspective

Karma-yoga is not philanthropy. It is not even doing good to others. The keynote of karma-yoga, as formulated by Swami Vivekananda, is "for one's own liberation and the welfare of the world." Doing good to others is the path to this goal. The ideal of the karma-yogi is selfless service and not mere philanthropy, social service, or altruism. To serve fellow human beings in distress or in need by seeing the presence of God in them is a form of worship, and it is therefore a privilege to serve them. Karma-yoga ceases to be spiritually effective when this aspect of selfless service is lost.

The practice of karma-yoga for an aspiring karma-yogi is a spiritual austerity that is the severest of all austerities. Aspirants in other paths of yoga practice austerities in solitude. But the karma-yogi practices austerity by serving everyone equally—even if cheated a million times—and this is not an easy practice. It requires the vision of a sage to see God in all and to serve them even when they are ungrateful and hostile. It is especially difficult to maintain a spirit of service when cheated, criticized, and ignored. It calls for divine power to accept defeat in the battles of life in the same spirit as one accepts victory. The spirit of karma-yoga, therefore, cannot be sustained unless the aspirant remains anchored to the spiritual ideal.

Egotism

An exceedingly difficult obstacle for the karma-yogi is the stubborn ego that constantly seeks its own gain and satisfaction. The goal of a karma-yogi is to keep the Self in sight and throw the ego overboard, but the ego again sneaks in, unnoticed, and begins to claim the results of action for itself. Satisfaction of the ego gradually becomes the unconscious motive behind all activity and the practice of karma-yoga. Giving in to the demands of their ego, aspirants quickly ruin all their past efforts in karma-yoga.

Loss of Meditative Balance

Action (karma) often creates a sense of competition and jealous intoxication, which in many cases disturbs the aspirant's meditative state of mind and discriminative anchor. The more the aspirant feels restless, the more he or she seeks activity to escape inner restlessness. In the end, activity begun in the spirit of yoga becomes blind activity that only intensifies inner anxiety and ultimately brings a fall in the path of yoga. Meditation and action represent one's subjective attitude and objective performance. While subjective attitude without objective performance is escapism and serves no purpose of karma-yoga, no amount of objective success can compensate for the loss of one's subjective attitude.

WAYS TO OVERCOME OBSTACLES

Of the five obstacles in the path of karma-yoga, attachment is the root obstacle; false success, loss of right perspective, egotism, and loss of meditative balance are its offshoots. Here are some guidelines for overcoming these obstacles:

Steadfastness in Meditation

The practice of meditation is vitally important for a karma-yogi. Steadfastness in meditation alone can lead an aspirant in the right direction. Regular and daily practice of meditation helps the aspirant overcome attachments that invariably develop for anyone engaged in activity. The compass needle quickly regains its position whenever deflected and points toward the true north. The mind of the karma-yogi must return to its ideal as soon as the assigned activity is completed.

The karma-yogi is required to keep three-fourths of the mind in meditation and one-fourth on work. It is natural for a beginner to find it difficult to maintain such a balance between meditation and action. Activity often means dealing with a certain amount of tension, frustration, difference of opinion, and misunderstanding. Such experiences can overwhelm an aspirant not firmly rooted in meditation. The beginner is advised, therefore, to balance work with regular, effortful periods of meditation and remembrance of the spiritual ideal. The beginner must carry the mood of meditation into the field of activity. As Sri Ramakrishna says, a turtle may reside in the river, but its mind is fixed on its eggs lying on the bank; a nurse takes care of her master's children as though they were her own, but her mind continually longs for her own home and her own children.[2] An aspirant practicing karma-yoga must cultivate and develop this spiritual balance so that the mind naturally gravitates toward the spiritual goal.

Self-Analysis

The practice of karma-yoga requires involvement in the world while remaining unaffected by it. Such involvement becomes mechanical unless one regularly practices self-examination and honest introspection. An aspirant is advised to periodically withdraw from the field of action and devote some time for self-analysis to make sure he or she is on track.

Discrimination

No practice of karma-yoga is possible without the practice of discrimination. An aspirant on this path must know which kind of work is desirable and which is not. It is said that there are three types of offerings: material assistance, intellectual training, and spiritual wisdom. One can give to others only what one has in abundance. An aspirant must therefore assess his or her talents and fitness before accepting responsibility for any work. The yogi must serve according to his or her strength and the opportunities available. It is vital for an aspirant to maintain the right attitude in the midst of activity. One should even reduce one's activities if they begin to disturb one's spiritual balance. Unless one is discriminative, one's own mind will be an obstacle at every step along the path.

Many aspirants believe they are free from attachment; but as soon as they encounter an object of enjoyment, their old habits of reckless living ambush them. An aspirant is truly free from attachment when he or she feels no temptation or curiosity for objects of enjoyment when near them. Discrimination plays a vital role in self-control. It is restraining the mind with a spiritually inspired intellect. One method of renouncing attachments is to repeatedly tell the mind that attachments will take a toll on the character and eventually bring complete downfall in the path of yoga. It is the nature of the mind to obey autosuggestions, and it will gradually accept them if repeated regularly and genuinely.

Forbearance

The karma-yogi must be forbearing under all conditions. One endowed with forbearance can overcome all difficulties, and only a humble person can be truly forbearing. As Swami Vivekananda says, "duty is seldom sweet."[3] An aspirant who grumbles about the nature of duty finds all duties distasteful. An aspirant in the path of karma-yoga is required to put up with the pressures and tensions common to all activities. The yogi must know that there is no such thing as an ideal environment for the practice of karma-yoga. The karma-yogi's only role is to selflessly give without expectation of return. The results of action may bring success, failure, praise, blame, honor, or dishonor. The yogi's supreme duty is to offer all results to God.

An aspirant of karma-yoga must know that there are people ready to do harm even when served with all graciousness. It is said that when Iswar Chandra Vidyasagar, a great personality of nineteenth-century India, legendary for his charity and philanthropy, was told that someone had spoken derogatively of him, he remarked, "I don't remember having done any good to him. Why should he speak ill of me?" An aspirant of karma-yoga is required to persist in yoga under all circumstances—favorable and unfavorable. It is the nature of a good person to be unselfish and self-sacrificing. The practice of forbearance is necessary for aspirants to allow them to adjust to various situations that will confront them along the way. One must be flexible, gracious, but also uncompromising in one's principles.

Renunciation

Above all, the karma-yogi is a person of renunciation. Karma-yoga calls for unselfish activity, but mere unselfish activity is not karma-yoga. No aspirant, however lofty his or her philosophy of life, can remain steadfast in yoga without the spirit of renunciation. Karma-yoga is not just duty for duty's sake. The karma-yogi's spirit of renunciation must burn like a steady flame in his or her heart. Whenever this flame of renunciation grows dim, the darkness of ignorance becomes deeper and denser. Where there is no renunciation, there is no discrimination, no meditation, no self-examination, and no yoga.

PART TWO

The Way of Bhakti-Yoga:
The Path of Devotion

7
The Message of Bhakti-Yoga

*Bhakti, love of God, is the essence of all spiritual
discipline. Through love one acquires renunciation
and discrimination naturally.*

—SRI RAMAKRISHNA

Bhakti-yoga is the yoga of love. There are two aspects of the
spiritual quest: the commitment of the head and the commitment of the heart. The commitment of the head—that is to
say, reason—highlights the necessity of the spiritual quest, in-
forms us about the path, and provides an intellectual understanding of spiritual truth. The commitment of the heart, which
is bhakti-yoga, makes spiritual quest positive, absorbing, and spiritually nourishing. Realization of God comes through one's own
personal experience and is the very soul of spiritual quest. One
may pore over books, reason relentlessly, practice prayer, meditation, and austerities diligently, yet may find the journey mechanical, tasteless, dry, and uninspiring. Devotion makes
renunciation easy, self-mastery possible, and concentration and
meditation natural.

The renunciation of the karma-yogi is always difficult; human attachments have many gross and subtle forms. The human ego refuses to die. The renunciation of the raja-yogi has to be maintained by willpower and force, which often provoke the mind to react violently. The jnana-yogi's renunciation is the harshest of all renunciations. It is uncompromising and merciless from the very beginning. To look upon the visible world around us as an illusion is no easy task. The jnana-yogi has to cut the Self off from everything by the "sheer force of rational conviction."[1] But in the renunciation of a bhakti-yogi, a devotee of God, Swami Vivekananda says:

> There is no violence, nothing to give up, nothing to tear off, as it were, from ourselves, nothing from which we have to separate ourselves violently.... In this renunciation auxiliary to devotion there is no harshness, no dryness, no struggle, no repression or suppression. The bhakta has not to suppress any single one of his emotions; he only strives to intensify them and direct them to God.[2]

A sensual person may intensely crave the pleasures of the senses, but as the same person becomes educated and exposed to higher forms of enjoyment, he or she begins to desire intellectual pleasures, and the cravings for sense enjoyment gradually diminish. Swami Vivekananda describes this evolution of love and says:

> No man can enjoy a meal with the same gusto or pleasure as does a dog or a wolf; but those pleasures which a man gets from intellectual experiences and achievements, the dog can never enjoy.
>
> At first, pleasure is associated with the lower sense-organs; but as soon as an animal reaches a higher plane of existence, the lower pleasure becomes less intense. In human society, the nearer a man is to the animal, the stronger is his pleasure in the senses; and the higher and the more cultured a man is, the greater is his pleasure in intellectual and other

such finer pursuits. So, when a man goes even higher than the plane of the intellect, higher than that of mere thought, when he reaches the plane of spirituality and of divine inspiration, he finds there a state of bliss compared with which all the pleasures of the senses, or even of the intellect, are as nothing.[3]

In this regard, devotion holds the key to the door of the inner recess of the heart, where God dwells as the inmost Self of all, and where the devotee can taste the highest and most pure bliss of God.

Karma-yoga helps us collect our scattered mind that was entangled in many things through attachment; bhakti-yoga focuses our mind on the spiritual goal; raja-yoga brings concentration and absorption into the ideal; and jnana-yoga reveals the face of God. The collected mind without devotion to God is dangerous. There is no revelation without concentration, and there is no concentration without devotion.

God is our very own and loves us unconditionally. It is out of love that God incarnates from age to age, listens to our prayers, and redeems us by divine grace. "We love him, because he first loved us" (1 John 4:19). The bhakti-yogi's love of God is not sentimental. It is inspired by knowledge—the knowledge that nobody in this world really loves us. Whatever love we receive is really God's love flowing through human channels.

Bhakti-yoga tells us that love is the most natural and basic instinct of life. In its purest form, it is cosmocentric. But when polluted and perverted by self-love, it becomes egocentric. The ego blocks the free flow of love toward all beings and things equally. Seen through the eyes of devotion, the bhakti-yoga practices of worship, prayer, and meditation are loving service to the Lord.

THE EXHORTATIONS OF BHAKTI-YOGA

Grasp the essentials of the spiritual path. A spiritual seeker must understand that communion with the Divine is the most essential part of the spiritual quest. All else is secondary.

Taste the bliss of the Divine. The Divine has been described as Existence-Knowledge-Bliss Absolute. The blissful aspect of the Divine is the most important. Only by tasting this bliss can the seeker overcome all obstacles and temptations and be freed from bondage.

Seek divine intervention. Know for certain that all human efforts are futile without divine intervention. The water of the ocean cannot rise to the sky by itself. Only the sun can lift the water up.

Seek judgment from above. Bhakti-yoga asks us to leave everything in the hands of God.

Be God's temple. The Lord is ever seated in every human heart as the inmost Self. Be assured that God listens to our prayers and gives us the best when we surrender our will to God's will. No sincere prayer ever goes unanswered.

Be a playmate in the cosmic drama. Play the role that has been assigned to you by God. Know God to be your real father, real mother, real well-wisher, and true redeemer.

In brief, the yoga of devotion is natural because it is heart-directed and heart-centered; it is human; it is less exacting; it is not just for the selected or elected but is available to all; it is guided by feeling, not by reason; and its approach to the Divine is positive and joyful. God, according to this path, is a person, not an abstract principle. The individual soul is created by God to be God's playmate. Earthly life is for proclaiming the message that God is the provider of everything and our sole protector. Suffering is forgetting God, who alone loves us. Bondage is the inability to love all as our brothers and sisters. Liberation is homecoming, by which the soul reaches its destiny that is God.

Bhakti-yoga emphasizes purification of the mind through love of God—not forcible control or suppression of the mind. It seeks not ego-eradication but ego-transformation. Its watchword is "I am His" as distinguished from "I am He." Its way is to seek divine support by giving our "power of attorney" to God. True love of God gives the seeker the taste of divine bliss that alone makes the spiritual quest meaningful. Finally, bhakti-yoga maintains that our self-effort is futile without divine grace—divine grace that is the gift of God. Those who sincerely and intensely pray for this grace surely receive it. God is ever bound by a devotee's love, and God never fails the true devotee. This is the promise of the Lord in the Bhagavad Gita: "My devotee never perishes."[4]

8

The Philosophy and Psychology of Bhakti-Yoga

One is able to realize God just through love. Ecstasy of feeling, devotion, love, and faith—these are the means.

—SRI RAMAKRISHNA

THE NATURE OF ULTIMATE REALITY

Ultimate Reality, according to bhakti-yoga, is a supremely lovable personal God who is both immanent and transcendent, all good, the object of highest love, and the abode of all fulfillment. God is our inner controller, the one goal of all spiritual aspiration, and the ultimate refuge of all beings. The Upanishads describe Brahman, Ultimate Reality, as Sat-Chit-Ananda, or Existence-Knowledge-Bliss Absolute, and the bhakti-yogi tries to get a taste of that absolute bliss in communion with the Ultimate. All joys of the phenomenal universe are but sparks of that absolute joy. The universe of multiplicity and plurality emanates from God and is therefore real—not illusory. God, the world of souls, and the world of matter form an organic unity, just as the individual soul and its physical body form an organic whole. Just as a part is inseparable from the whole, so the *jiva*, or individual, is inseparable from God. It is realistic, bhakti-yoga says, to think of the Divine with a name and form so long as we believe in name and form.

THE MEANING OF CREATION

According to bhakti-yoga, the world of matter is fundamentally real and undergoes real evolution, but such evolution is neither an unconscious process nor an elusive projection of maya. The world, though evolving constantly as a cosmic process, is subordinated to and dependent upon God and serves God's purpose. God of the bhakti-yogi is not only the efficient cause of the universe but also its formal, material, and final cause—that is to say, God is all in all. Creation is not an absolute act beginning in time or a process of mechanical evolution. Creation is *lila,* or the play of God. Bhakti-yoga contends that the Upanishads support such a view of creation:

> All this is Brahman. From It the universe comes forth, in It the universe merges, and in It the universe breathes.[1]

> As the spider sends forth and draws in its thread, as plants grow on the earth, as hair grows on the head and the body of a living man—so does everything in the universe arise from the Imperishable.[2]

That which has been indicated by the Upanishads as Brahman is described by bhakti-yoga as personal God, the source and support of the universe, controller of the cosmic process, and giver of salvation to all beings. The *jiva,* or individual soul, is therefore an essential attribute of God and inscrutably bound to God just as the attribute of a substance is related to the substance itself. Inseparably joined to God, the individual soul is eternal and yet has a personality as well as free will. Free will is the gift of God and finds its fulfillment only when exercised in accordance with the universal will of God.

BONDAGE AND LIBERATION

The soul in bondage is like the prodigal son who has forsaken his all-loving father. Such bondage is due to the individual's feeling of separation, which alienates the *jiva* not only from God but also from the inmost Self. Created as an eternal playmate of God, the *jiva*, deluded by ignorance, refuses to play the assigned role. But those unwilling to submit to God's will face the universal will as the inexorable law of karma and experience untold suffering.

Liberation, according to bhakti-yoga, is the return of the prodigal son to his all-loving father. It is the loving surrender of the individual to the Lord by having faith in the Lord's love and forgiveness. The spirit of this liberation is the saying "Thy will be done."

THE WAY TO LIBERATION

Bhakti-yoga emphasizes the positive aspect of liberation. Different schools of thought look upon liberation variously as release, as withdrawal, and as enjoyment. To the Nyaya system of Hindu philosophy,* liberation is a release from pain with no positive enjoyment of bliss—an abstract existence without knowledge and happiness. To the Samkhya and Yoga systems,† liberation is the eternal isolation of the soul from the bonds of nature. Buddhism looks upon liberation as nirvana, which is complete annihilation of the self. And to the different schools of Vedanta, liberation is twofold: realizing the bliss of the Self and regaining freedom from the law of karma and the pairs of opposites, such as pain and pleasure, virtue and vice, and birth and death.

---

*The Nyaya system of philosophy founded by Gautama is Indian Logic, one of the six systems of orthodox Hindu philosophy.

†The Samkhya and Yoga philosophies (raja-yoga) are also two systems of orthodox Hindu philosophy, founded by Kapila and Patanjali, respectively.

Bhakti-yoga, however, does not speak of this twofold aspect of liberation. Liberation is the experience of the unalloyed bliss of God both within and without. Freedom from the miseries of life naturally follows from the experience of this divine bliss. Bhakti-yoga describes liberation as a state of absolute joy and blessedness. All worldly and heavenly pleasures appear insignificant in comparison with this bliss. The Upanishads designate this bliss as Ananda: "from bliss, verily, are these beings born; by bliss, when born, do they live; into bliss [at the time of dissolution] do they enter, do they merge."[3]

Liberation is a gift of God. It cannot be acquired through austerity, penance, or meditation. Liberation is the redeeming grace of God who responds to our sincere prayers and who is sensitive to our needs, ever desirous of our love. God's grace is a heralding light that dispels the darkness of ignorance in our hearts and sets us free. Such grace is unconditional, spontaneous, and ever redeeming. The darkness of ignorance that had accumulated for thousands of years becomes dispelled as soon as the light of God's grace shines upon it. As Sri Ramakrishna says:

> You may try thousands of times, but nothing can be achieved without God's grace. One cannot see God without His grace. Is it an easy thing to receive grace? One must altogether renounce egotism; one cannot see God as long as one feels, "I am the doer."
>
> God doesn't easily appear in the heart of a man who feels himself to be his own master. But God can be seen the moment His grace descends. He is the Sun of Knowledge. One single ray of His has illumined the world with the light of knowledge. That is how we are able to see one another and acquire varied knowledge. One can see God only if He turns His light toward His own face.[4]

Bondage, according to bhakti-yoga, springs from a feeling of "I and mine." Liberation is the state where the feeling of "I and mine" transforms into that of "thou and thine." Such liberation is not a complete absorption of the individual into God. It is the companionship of the Lord by being the Lord's messenger on earth. Liberation is *videhamukti,* or liberation after death, and not *jivanmukti,* or liberation while living. The highest liberating experience of bhakti-yoga has been described as *chetana samadhi.* In the words of Sri Ramakrishna:

> What is samadhi? It is the complete merging of the mind in God-Consciousness. The jnani experiences jada samadhi, in which no trace of "I" is left. The samadhi attained through the path of bhakti is called "chetana samadhi". In this samadhi there remains the consciousness of "I"—the "I" of the servant-and-Master relationship, of the lover-and-Beloved relationship, of the enjoyer-and-Food relationship. God is the Master; the devotee is the servant. God is the Beloved; the devotee is the lover. God is the Food, and the devotee is the enjoyer. "I don't want to be sugar. I want to eat it."[5]

Sri Ramakrishna compares the God-consciousness of the jnana-yogi with that of the bhakti-yogi and says:

> The jnani experiences God-Consciousness within himself; it is like the upper Ganges, flowing in only one direction. To him the whole universe is illusory, like a dream; he is always established in the Reality of Self. But with the lover of God the case is different. His feeling does not flow in only one direction. He feels both the ebb-tide and the flood-tide of divine emotion. He laughs and weeps and dances and sings in the ecstasy of God. The lover of God likes to sport with Him. In the Ocean of God-Consciousness he sometimes swims, sometimes goes down, and sometimes rises to the surface—like pieces of ice in the water.[6]

Liberation, according to bhakti-yoga, is the unalloyed bliss of God-consciousness either in the state of *samadhi* or while perceiving the manifold diversities of the universe. To experience

God only as one's inner Self is not complete liberation but a halfway house for the bhakti-yogi. Such an experience does not take into account the manifold universe in which God is equally revealed. The state of complete absorption of the individual Self into Brahman, the Supreme Reality, is not the desired goal of the bhakti-yogi, because in such a state there remains no trace of the experiencer of liberation and, therefore, no account of the experience. The state of liberation is not being one with absolute bliss but consciously experiencing that bliss. Without such experience, liberation would be reduced to the state of nothingness, a void, for which, the bhakti-yogi argues, no one would feel any longing. It is the taste of the bliss of God that makes liberation a meaningful and tangible goal, attracting souls in bondage to the attainment of liberation.

According to bhakti-yoga, the only means to attain liberation is to attain pure love of God. Sri Krishna in his last message to Uddhava reveals this secret and says:

> O Uddhava, neither Yoga, nor knowledge, nor piety, nor study, nor austerity, nor renunciation captivates Me so much as a heightened devotion to Me. I, the dear Self of the pious, am attainable by devotion alone, which is the outcome of faith.... Piety joined to truthfulness and compassion or learning coupled with austerity, never wholly purifies a mind which is devoid of devotion to Me.[7]

The path of bhakti-yoga is God loving, not God fearing. God is often thought of as the inner controller or supreme power, and the seeker feels a sense of awe in the presence of God rather than an attraction. Bhakti-yoga's conception of God is personal, intimate, and loving. For the beginner in the path of bhakti-yoga, the worshiper and the worshiped are two distinct entities separate from each other. But as love grows in the heart of the worshiper, he or she begins to approach God, and God begins to approach the devotee. In the end only the object of worship remains. Love, the lover, and the beloved become one. This is the great power and attraction of divine love, which is greater and more essential to a seeker than knowledge, study, or work. The sacred texts of bhakti-yoga point out:

> A man cannot please a king by merely knowing about him and seeing his palace, nor can a man satisfy his hunger by mere knowledge and sight of food; similarly a man cannot be satisfied by knowledge or perception of God until love comes.[8]

The instinct of love is universal. Psychologically speaking, love is the most basic human emotion. However, when love's natural flow is obstructed, it expresses itself in the forms of negative emotions, such as lust, greed, jealousy, and anger. The sole object of all love is God. It is for the sake of God dwelling as the Self in every heart that one person loves another. Love, when not directed toward God, is mere human attachment and cheap sentiment, which only forge the chains of bondage. Yet the same human attachment, when directed toward God in all sincerity and longing, becomes the cause of liberation.

Bondage is the inability to love and express oneself freely and fully, which ends in repression, suppression, and perversion of emotions. Liberation comes when one is able to love all equally by seeing God in them. It is the result of an intense longing to commune with the world, with one's innermost Self, and with God. Sri Ramakrishna describes this intensity of love:

> God reveals Himself to a devotee who feels drawn to Him by the combined force of these three attractions: the attraction of worldly possessions for the worldly man, the child's attraction for its mother, and the husband's attraction for the chaste wife. If one feels drawn to Him by the combined force of these three attractions, then through it one can attain Him.
>
> The point is, to love God even as the mother loves her child, the chaste wife her husband, and the worldly man his

wealth. Add together these three forces of love, these three powers of attraction, and give it all to God. Then you will certainly see Him.[9]

All the bhakti-yogi needs to do is fill the mind with the thought of God. The more the mind is filled with thoughts of God, the more undesirable thoughts and tendencies are automatically washed out. The farther a person travels toward the East, the more the West is left behind. Swami Vivekananda recounts the following story that beautifully describes the attitude of the bhakti-yogi:

> Ramakrishna used to tell a story about some men who went into a mango orchard and busied themselves in counting the leaves, the twigs, and the branches, examining their colour, comparing their size, and noting down everything most carefully, and who then got up a learned discussion on each of these topics, which were undoubtedly highly interesting to them. But another man, more sensible than they, did not care for all these things and instead began to eat the mangoes. And was he not wise? So leave this counting of leaves and twigs and this note-taking to others. This kind of work has its proper place, but not here in the spiritual domain. You never see a strong spiritual man among these "leaf-counters." Religion, the highest aim, the highest glory of man, does not require so much labour. If you want to be a bhakta, it is not at all necessary for you to know whether Krishna was born in Mathura or in Vraja, what He did, or the exact date on which He imparted the teachings of the Gita. You only need to feel the craving for the beautiful lessons about duty and love in the Gita. All the other particulars about it and its author are for the enjoyment of the learned. Let them have what they desire. Say "Shantih, shantih!" [Peace, Peace] to their learned controversies, and you yourself "eat the mangoes."[10]

The teachings of bhakti-yoga do not deny human emotions and human aspirations, but they do ask that these be given to God. Even hatred and anger, when directed toward God, become the cause of liberation: "On whatever object a corporeal being may concentrate his whole mind with his intellect, either through love or through hate or through fear, he attains the form of that very object."[11] The psychology behind this idea is that the mind becomes concentrated on God and purified as easily through intense hatred and anger as through love and attachment.

Renunciation of the pleasure of the senses, bhakti-yoga says, is impossible until the seeker has tasted the bliss of God. All efforts to control the lower self are meaningless and futile unless such efforts are inspired by an intense love of God. Mere intellectual knowledge or indirect perception of God does not fill the heart. It is only through pure love that one can realize God directly and fully. One who has attained this realization does not reason any more. As Sri Ramakrishna says, "If a man but once tastes the joy of God, his desire to argue takes wing. The bee, realizing the joy of sipping honey, doesn't buzz about any more."[12] All the spiritual practices prescribed by the teachings of bhakti-yoga are practices of the love of God. Such love, as it becomes intensified, unknowingly takes the form of meditation.

Questions that often come to the mind of a seeker are, Does God really listen to my prayers for devotion? Will my longing for God really result in my realizing God? In answer, Sri Ramakrishna tells us:

> I can assure you of that a hundred times. But the prayer must be genuine and earnest. Do worldly minded people weep for God as they do for wife and children? At Kamarpukur the wife of a certain man fell ill. The man thought she would not recover; he began to tremble and was about to faint. Who feels that way for God?[13]

One should pray to God with sincere longing. God cannot but listen to prayer if it is sincere.[14]

There are certain signs of God-realization. A man who longs for God is not far from attaining Him. What are the outer indications of such longing? They are discrimination, dispassion, compassion for living beings, serving holy men, loving their company, chanting God's name and glories, telling the truth, and the like. When you see those signs in an aspirant, you can rightly say that for him the vision of God is not far to seek.

The state of a servant's house will tell you unmistakably if his master has decided to visit it. First, the rubbish and jungle around the house are cleared up. Second, the soot and dirt are removed from the rooms. Third, the courtyard, floors, and other places are swept clean. Finally the master himself sends various things to the house, such as a carpet, a hubble-bubble for smoking, and the like. When you see these things coming, you conclude that the master will very soon arrive.[15]

9
Preparatory Practices in Bhakti-Yoga

Living in solitude now and then, repeating God's name and singing His glories, and discriminating between the Real and the unreal—these are the means to see Him.

—SRI RAMAKRISHNA

To practice bhakti-yoga is to be drunk with the bliss of God. A song Sri Ramakrishna loved to sing describes the state of divine intoxication:

> I drink no ordinary wine, but Wine of Everlasting Bliss,
> As I repeat my Mother Kali's name;*
> It so intoxicates my mind that people take me to be drunk!
> First my guru gives molasses for the making of the Wine;
> My longing is the ferment to transform it.

---

*The Divine Mother Kali is a symbol of the Cosmic Power of Brahman, or the Absolute. She is the totality of the universe, a glorious harmony of the pairs of opposites. She deals out death as she creates and preserves human life. Kali has three eyes, the third being the symbol of Divine Wisdom of the Self and of Ultimate Reality; they strike dismay into the wicked, yet pour out affection for her devotees.

Knowledge, the maker of the Wine, prepares it for me
then;
And when it is done, my mind imbibes it from the bottle of the
mantra,
Taking the Mother's name to make it pure.
Drink of this Wine, says Ramprasad [the poet], and the four
fruits of life are yours.[1]

In modern times, Sri Ramakrishna's life is an example of uninterrupted divine ecstasy. He would become deeply intoxicated by uttering the name of God but once. In divine inebriation, he would stumble in his steps; his disciples would have to hold him so he would not fall. At times ordinary people, not understanding this divine inebriation or God-intoxication, took him to be a common drunk. Sri Chaitanya* also used to experience these states of divine ecstasy, and never did his mind forget the bliss of God. Sri Ramakrishna described Sri Chaitanya's experience: "In the inmost state he would remain in *samadhi*, unconscious of the outer world. In the semi-conscious state he would only dance. In the conscious state he chanted the name of God."[2]

This state of complete absorption cannot be attained all at once. The bhakti-yogi must proceed gradually and surely. The beginner should not practice meditation before having mastered concentration; and concentration on a subtle object should be practiced after having mastered concentration on a physical object. Concentration, most importantly, is not possible unless one feels a loving attachment for the object of concentration.

PREPARATORY LOVE

Preparatory love is developing a loving attachment toward God. Pure love is giving one's whole mind to God. According to bhakti-

---

*Sri Chaitanya was a prophet born in Bengal, India, in 1485, who emphasized the path of divine love for the realization of God.

yoga, preparatory love may with effort and longing grow into pure love. God holds the hand of an aspirant who has attained pure love; until then, the aspirant at the stage of preparatory love must hold onto God's hand. As Sri Ramakrishna describes:

> Only those who have developed raga-bhakti [supreme love] for God may be called His sincere devotees. God becomes responsible for them. If you enter your name in a hospital register, the doctor will not discharge you until you are cured. Those who are held by God have nothing to fear. The son who holds to his father, while walking along the narrow ridge of a paddy-field, may slip if he absent-mindedly lets go his father's hand; but if the father holds the son by the hand, there is no such danger.[3]

Preparatory love has been designated as formal love. At this stage, aspirants follow spiritual practices as rigid disciplines, adhering to the strict injunctions of the scriptures. They consciously count how many times they chant the name of God, meticulously repeat the rounds of meditation, and elaborately procure all the ingredients for ceremonial worship. But as their love for God deepens, all external ceremonials gradually become transformed into internal meditation. As Sri Ramakrishna says, "The *sandhya* merges in the Gayatri, the Gayatri in Om, and Om in *samadhi.*"*[4]

In the first stage, the aspirant develops faith in the words of the scriptures and seeks holy company. Bhakti-yoga greatly extols holy company as a means to attain *bhakti,* or love of God. Nothing is more purifying and inspiring than holy company. Mere study of scriptures and practice of austerities can never inspire us. We feel truly inspired only when we see spiritual truths translated in the lives of holy persons. Our minds are such that they naturally acquire the nature of a thing on which we allow them to dwell.

---

*The *sandhya* is ceremonial worship, the Gayatri is the highest Vedic prayer, Om is considered the most sacred word, and *samadhi,* absorption into the Divine, is the final goal of yoga.

The aspirant who keeps holy company naturally develops the spiritual virtues of discrimination, humility, self-control, and purity that lead to the love of God. The company of holy souls who demonstrate Reality is a rare blessing.

Ramanuja* speaks of the following seven practices of preparatory love:

Viveka, *or discrimination regarding food.* According to the Upanishads, purity of food helps cultivate a pure mind. Food becomes impure for three reasons:

1. *Jati,* or the nature of the food itself. Bitter, malodorous, or stale food should be avoided.

2. *Ashraya,* or the person from whom one receives food. Swami Vivekananda says, "The idea is that each man has a certain aura around him, and whatever thing he touches, a part of his character, as it were, his influence, is left on it. It is supposed that a man's character emanates from him, as it were, like a physical force, and whatever he touches is affected by it."[5]

3. *Nimitta,* or defects of food arising from the presence of external impurities. While Ramanuja emphasizes the purity of the food we eat, Shankaracharya points out that anything we draw in through our sense organs is also to be considered food. A spiritual seeker must engage only in pure actions, speak pure words, and meditate on pure thoughts to nourish a pure mind.

Vimoka, *or freedom from desires.* An aspirant of bhakti-yoga must get rid of all worldly desires and desire nothing but God.

Abhyasa, *or physical and mental practice.* Thoughts, words, and deeds must be in unison. Performance of rituals with the hands,

---

*Ramanuja was a great teacher of bhakti-yoga and the foremost interpreter of the school of qualified nondualistic Vedanta.

chanting of holy names with the mouth, and meditation on the Lord with thoughts—these allow for concentrating the mind and keeping the mind focused on the bliss of God.

Kriya, *or doing good to others.* As discussed in the context of karma-yoga, the Bhagavad Gita speaks of the fivefold daily sacrifice: the aspirant must study something holy and good every day; must engage in the worship of God in some form and revere the saints and holy persons; must fulfill the sacred duty to his or her ancestors; must look to the welfare of family members, neighbors, and society; and must fulfill duties for the protection of plants and animals.

Kalyana, *or adherence to truthfulness, straightforwardness, compassion, nonviolence, and charity.* Charity can take the form of offering food and money, secular education, or spiritual knowledge. Most importantly, charity should be thought of as an offering to God, and one must give God what one loves most.

Anavasada, *or not yielding to despondency.* "Despondency," Swami Vivekananda says, "is not religion, whatever else it may be."[6] One should know that if one's prayers are sincere and heartfelt, they will surely be answered by God.

Uddharsha, *or avoidance of excessive merriment.* The mind of an aspirant who indulges in excessive merriment easily becomes excited by impulsive surges of emotions—emotions that may be spiritual but may also be the passions of the baser urges, especially lust and anger. The aspirant should, therefore, control the emotions, because excessive merriment may be followed by a violent downward reaction of the mind.

According to the *Bhakti Ratnavali or A Necklace of Devotional Gems,* the steps of preparatory love may be summarized into nine principal spiritual practices: hearing the sacred texts; singing and chanting the glories of God; loving remembrance of one's Chosen Ideal; worship of God; loving service to God; saluting God;

assuming the attitude of a servant of God; companionship with God; and self-surrender to God.

The practice of hearing the sacred texts comprises listening to scriptural injunctions, songs, and hymns of the Divine, and reading devotional scriptures and the sacred texts describing the glory of the Chosen Ideal. Singing and chanting the glories of God includes singing hymns congregationally or individually. One should then remember God throughout the day and in all activities. Worshiping God includes worshiping the Chosen Ideal both externally with ceremonials and internally by contemplation and meditation. Service to God includes dedicating all actions to the Chosen Ideal. Salutations before God signify one's sense of submission to the Chosen Ideal and surrender to the will of God. Cultivating the attitude of a servant of God is offering one's whole life to God. Companionship with God is establishing a human and intimate relationship with one's Chosen Ideal. This attitude is not one of fear and awe but friendship. "There is no fear in love; but perfect love casteth out fear" (1 John 4:18). The devotee then surrenders or abandons all he or she possesses, all confidence, honor, and pride, and takes refuge in God.

SELECTION OF THE CHOSEN IDEAL

The second stage of practice is the selection of one's Ishtadevata, or Chosen Ideal. The Ishtadevata is the aspirant's most favorite form of God on which the aspirant meditates. Each aspirant has a unique and different inner disposition and temperament; therefore, each should be able to worship God according to his or her own nature by establishing a human relationship with God.

Bhakti-yoga gives an aspirant the freedom to choose a personal Ideal and the way of experiencing God. The omnipresent, all-pervading Ultimate Reality, conditioned by an aspirant's inner disposition and temperament, assumes the form of the aspirant's

Chosen Ideal out of love and kindness. An aspirant in the path of bhakti-yoga is, therefore, advised to hold the Chosen Ideal sacred and the relationship with the Ideal strictly private. There are two reasons for this injunction: first, one person's Chosen Ideal need not be the Ideal of another; second, the faith of the beginner in spiritual quest is not yet strong and may easily be disturbed by the negative suggestions of dogmatists or atheists. By keeping the Ideal private, the aspirant protects him- or herself from all such adverse influences. In the beginning, an aspirant whose faith is not yet natural and spontaneous is required to be unquestioningly loyal to the Chosen Ideal in order to develop undeviating love for the Ideal. An Ideal, once chosen, must be chosen forever. The aspirant may love and appreciate other Ideals, but for the Chosen Ideal the aspirant has a special love and devotion. Swami Vivekananda warns the beginner about being too liberal in the early stages of spiritual quest:

> We find, as a rule, that liberal and sympathetic sects lose the intensity of religious feeling, and in their hands religion is likely to degenerate into a kind of politico-social club life. On the other hand, intensely narrow sectarians, while displaying a very commendable love for their own ideals, are seen to have acquired every particle of that love by hating everyone who is not of exactly the same opinion as themselves. Would to God that this world were full of men who were as intense in their love as they were world-wide in their sympathies! But such are few and far between. Yet we know that it is practicable to educate large numbers of human beings into the ideal of a wonderful blending of both the breadth and the intensity of love; and the way to do that is by this path of Ishta-nishtha [or steadfast devotion to the Chosen Ideal].
>
> Every sect of every religion presents only one ideal of its own to mankind; but the eternal Vedantic religion opens to mankind an infinite number of doors for ingress into the inner

shrine of Divinity, and places before humanity an almost in-
exhaustible array of ideals, there being in each of them a manifestation of the Eternal One.[7]

Absolute loyalty and devotion for one's Chosen Ideal is the one
and only injunction for the beginner on the path of bhakti-yoga.
Later on, when one's love for the Chosen Ideal becomes deep and
firm, one will naturally see the reflection of the Ideal in all the
other manifestations of God, irrespective of their names and
forms.

The Chosen Ideal of an aspirant may be any form of God. The
Chosen Ideal may also be a prophet or an incarnation of God.
According to bhakti-yoga, the most natural object of love is a
human form of God. We can best love God in a human way by
establishing a human relationship with God. Bhakti-yoga advocates worship of the Chosen Ideal through concrete images and
symbols that are reminiscent of the Chosen Ideal.

10

Characteristics of the Teacher and the Aspirant

He who is the Lord of the Universe will teach everyone.... He is our Inner Guide.

God cannot be realized without love and longing. Unless one has learnt to love God, one cannot realize Him.

—Sri Ramakrishna

CHARACTERISTICS OF THE TEACHER

The bhakti-yoga aspirant may select the Chosen Ideal (see the previous chapter) or may approach a teacher for this purpose. According to the traditions of bhakti-yoga, one who introduces an aspirant to the Chosen Ideal and initiates him or her into the worship of that Ideal is known as a guru, or spiritual teacher. The role of the teacher in the path of bhakti-yoga is vitally important. The teacher is a specialist who explores the layers of the aspirant's mind and selects the path most beneficial to the aspirant. Needless to say, a teacher must be qualified to teach. Through an analogy, Sri Ramakrishna describes the dilemma we face in the hands of an incompetent teacher:

One day as I was passing the Panchavati on my way to the pine-grove, I heard a bullfrog croaking. I thought it must have been seized by a snake. After some time, as I was coming back, I could still hear its terrified croaking. I looked to see what was the matter, and found that a water-snake had seized it. The snake could neither swallow it nor give it up. So there was no end to the frog's suffering. I thought that had it been seized by a cobra it would have been silenced after three croaks at the most. As it was only a water-snake, both of them had to go through this agony. A man's ego is destroyed after three croaks, as it were, if he gets into the clutches of a real teacher. But if the teacher is an "unripe" one, then both the teacher and the disciple undergo endless suffering. The disciple cannot get rid either of his ego or of the shackles of the world. If a disciple falls into the clutches of an incompetent teacher, he doesn't attain liberation.[1]

Swami Vivekananda also describes:

There are many who, though immersed in ignorance, yet, in the pride of their hearts, fancy they know everything and not only do not stop there, but offer to take others on their shoulders; and thus, the blind leading the blind, both fall into the ditch. "Fools dwelling in darkness, wise in their own conceit and puffed up with vain knowledge, go round and round, staggering to and fro, like blind men led by the blind." ... The world is full of these. Everyone wants to be a teacher; every beggar wants to make a gift of a million dollars! Just as such beggars are ridiculous, so are such teachers.[2]

According to the texts of Yoga, a spiritual teacher must have the following qualifications: The teacher must be a *shrotriya,* or a knower of the true spirit of the scriptures. The scriptures are sometimes contradictory and must be recognized for what they are: mere attempts to describe that which is indescribable. A teacher, therefore, must know the essence of the scriptures and instruct the aspirant accordingly. The teacher must be *Brahmanishtha,* or one who has experienced God directly. Spirituality can be taught only by transmitting it. Such transmission alone can spiritually awaken the aspirant. The teacher must be an awakened soul who has enough spiritual potency to transmit spiritual power to the seeker without being drained of his or her own spirituality. The teacher must also be sinless. The strength of a teaching depends upon the purity of the teacher. Imparting spiritual instruction is not just stimulating the intellect of the aspirant or temporarily stirring up the emotions. It is the transmission of purity that is never possible unless the teacher is pure. Finally, the teacher must be utterly unselfish, caring only for the welfare of the student. Spiritual instruction loses its potency when imparted with a motive, no matter what the motive may be. The teacher conveys the instruction to the aspirant through the medium of motiveless love; therefore, any motive on the teacher's part distorts the medium of instruction and ultimately renders the spiritual teaching ineffective.

One in whom all these conditions are fulfilled is known to be a perfect teacher. But how does an aspirant find such a teacher? According to bhakti-yoga, it is not by chance that one meets such a perfect teacher. One finds a true teacher only if one's longing for God is intense, pure, and sincere. At this stage, God provides the aspirant with a true teacher. As Christ told us of God's grace, "Ask, and it shall be given to you; seek, and you shall find; knock, and it shall be opened unto you; For every one that asketh receiveth; and he that seeketh findeth; and to him that knocketh it shall be opened" (Matt. 7:7–8). In spiritual life, what we are given depends upon what and how we seek. The laws of the spiritual realm leave nothing to chance. Swami Vivekananda says:

> Religion, which is the highest knowledge and the highest wisdom, cannot be bought, nor can it be acquired from books. You may thrust your head into all the corners of the world, you

may explore the Himalayas, the Alps, and the Caucasus, you may sound the bottom of the sea and pry into every nook of Tibet and the desert of Gobi, but you will not find it anywhere until your heart is ready to receive it and your teacher has come. And when that divinely appointed teacher comes, serve him with childlike confidence and simplicity, freely open your heart to his influence, and see in him God manifested. Those who come to seek the truth with such a spirit of love and veneration—to them the Lord of Truth reveals the most wonderful things regarding truth, goodness, and beauty.[3]

CHARACTERISTICS OF THE ASPIRANT

Receiving the grace of a perfect teacher depends upon the fitness of the aspirant. An aspirant must be ready to receive the teaching. The necessary qualifications for an aspirant in the path of bhakti-yoga are as follows:

The aspirant must have faith in God and in God's divine dispensation.

The aspirant must have devotion and loyalty to one, and only one, Chosen Ideal, one method of worship, and one teacher.

The aspirant must feel some relish in repeating the name of God and meditating on God. Spiritual quest for the aspirant must be more than an intellectual endeavor or spiritual discipline. The aspirant must not only become disinterested in the world but should equally become interested in developing love of God.

The aspirant must be humble and forbearing: humble like a blade of grass and forbearing like a tree. The aspirant must give honor to all, faithfully repeat the name of God, and sing God's glories. The bondage of ignorance has often been described in the scriptures as maya's net, and there are only two methods to escape from this net. One can completely identify with God and become too big for the net; or, one can make oneself smaller than the smallest, the humble servant of God, and slip right through the net of maya. Bhakti-yoga advises an aspirant to choose the second alternative.

The aspirant must surrender body, mind, ego, and will to the Lord under all circumstances. His or her spiritual practices are solely for the pleasure of the Lord and not for attaining any spiritual merit here or hereafter. The aspirant accepts everything as the will of the Lord and remains unmoved in the midst of the greatest joy or sorrow. The following parable, narrated by Sri Ramakrishna, describes the ideal self-surrender of a bhakti-yogi:

In a certain village there lived a weaver. He was a very pious soul. Everyone trusted him and loved him. He used to sell his goods in the market-place. When a customer asked him the price of a piece of cloth, the weaver would say: "By the will of Rama the price of the yarn is one rupee and the labour four annas; by the will of Rama the profit is two annas. The price of the cloth, by the will of Rama, is one rupee and six annas." Such was the people's faith in the weaver that the customer would at once pay the price and take the cloth. The weaver was a real devotee of God. After finishing his supper in the evening, he would spend long hours in the worship hall meditating on God and chanting His name and glories. Now, late one night the weaver couldn't get to sleep. He was sitting in the worship hall, smoking now and then, when a band of robbers happened to pass that way. They wanted a man to carry their goods and said to the weaver, "Come with us." So saying, they led him off by the hand. After committing a robbery in a house, they put a load of things on the weaver's head, commanding him to carry them. Suddenly the police arrived and the robbers ran away. But the weaver, with his load, was arrested. He was kept in the lock-up for the night. Next day he was brought before the magistrate for trial. The villagers learnt what had happened and came to court. They said to the magistrate, "Your Honor, this man could never commit a robbery." Thereupon the magistrate asked the weaver to make his statement.

The weaver said: "Your honor, by the will of Rama I finished my meal at night. Then by the will of Rama I was sitting in the worship hall. It was quite late at night by the will of Rama. By the will of Rama I had been thinking of God and chanting His name and glories, when by the will of Rama a band of robbers passed that way. By the will of Rama they dragged me with them; by the will of Rama they committed a robbery in a house; and by the will of Rama they put a load on my head. Just then, by the will of Rama the police arrived, and by the will of Rama I was arrested. Then by the will of Rama the police kept me in the lock-up for the night, and this morning by the will of Rama I have been brought before Your Honor." The magistrate realized that the weaver was a pious man and ordered his release. On his way home the weaver said to his friends, "By the will of Rama I have been released."[4]

According to the *Srimad Bhagavatam,* there are three types of aspirants: inferior, average, and superior. The inferior aspirant worships God in the form of an idol but does not care for God's devotees or anyone else. The average aspirant develops love for God and friendliness toward God's devotees. But the superior aspirant does not distinguish between his or her own Self and the Self of others, having equal regard for all living beings and full control over gross sense desires. The *Srimad Bhagavatam* testifies that the Lord "destroys all the accumulated sins of those who take His name even once in a distressed state. No wonder then that a devotee who ties himself to His lotus feet with the cords of love never misses Him from his heart. Such a devotee is the greatest among the [devotees] we have been speaking about."[5]

Sri Krishna describes the perfect aspirant in the Bhagavad Gita:

He who never hates any being and is friendly and compassionate to all, who is free from the feelings of "I" and "mine" and even-minded in pain and pleasure, who is forbearing, ever content, and steady in contemplation, who is self-controlled and possessed of firm conviction, and who has consecrated his mind and understanding to Me—dear to Me is the one who is thus devoted to Me.

He by whom the world is not afflicted and whom the world cannot afflict, he who is free from joy and anger, fear and anxiety—he is dear to Me.

He who is free from dependence, who is pure and prompt, unconcerned and untroubled, and who has renounced all undertakings—dear to Me is the man who is thus devoted to Me.

He who rejoices not and hates not, who grieves not and desires not, who has renounced both good and evil and is full of devotion—he is dear to Me.

He who is alike to foe and friend, unaltered in honour and dishonour; who is the same in cold and heat, in pleasure and pain; who is free from attachment, who is unchanged by praise and blame; who is silent, content with whatever he has; homeless, firm of mind, and full of devotion—that man is dear to Me.[6]

Aspirants need not worry about beginning their spiritual quest without having all of these virtues. The important point is that they should be firmly committed to the goal of the quest and faithful to their God. If these qualities are present, all other virtues will be bestowed upon the sincere aspirant. Bhakti-yoga can be practiced by anyone, under any conditions, and it is never too late to cultivate *bhakti*. The Bhagavad Gita points out:

Even the most sinful man, if he worships me with unswerving devotion, must be regarded as righteous; for he has formed the right resolution.

He soon becomes righteous and attains eternal peace. Proclaim it boldly, O son of Kunti, that My devotee never perishes.[7]

This assurance of Sri Krishna has again been repeated in *The Last Message of Sri Krishna:* "Even a devotee of Mine who not being a master of his senses is troubled by sense-objects, is generally not overcome by them, owing to his powerful devotion."[8]

According to the traditions of bhakti-yoga, the guru not only fixes the Chosen Ideal for the aspirant, but also initiates the aspirant into the specific spiritual practices of the path. Generally, initiation is imparted by the teacher, who utters a mantra reminiscent of the aspirant's Chosen Ideal and who asks the aspirant to regularly repeat the mantra. The mantra is like a seed that remains planted in the mind of the aspirant, ready to sprout in the course of time. The potency of any initiation depends upon the spiritual strength and realization of the particular teacher and his or her spiritual heritage. The mantra, method of meditation, and mode of worship vary according to the nature of the initiation and the aspirant. Each aspirant's mantra, method of worship, and meditation are his or her own private and individual concern. The aspirant is therefore advised to keep silent about the initiation rites and not reveal them to others. Each seeker, bhakti-yoga contends, must follow his or her own conviction because each is different from others with regard to inner tendencies. Each has to struggle in his or her own way to reach the goal, and each assimilates the spiritual instruction and makes progress individually. The aspirant, therefore, must be loyal to the teacher and follow the instruction to the letter.

Bhakti-yoga asks for developing a spiritual root, and love of God is the fruit of bhakti-yoga. Those who expect the fruit must first develop a root. The practice of bhakti-yoga has often been compared to the process of farming. In farming, the farmer must obtain a plot of land; the seeds are to be procured and properly planted; they must be fertilized and watered; the surrounding area must be weeded; the farmer must wait for the seeds to sprout into a plant and then the plant to grow into a tree; and the tree will bring forth flowers and then produce fruits. In the spiritual farming of bhakti-yoga, the plot of land is the individual's mind. The soil of the mind is plowed and tilled by the awakening of spiritual consciousness. The spiritual seed is provided by the teacher in the form of guiding a seeker to a Chosen Ideal. Choosing the Ideal is a commitment of the seeker to a specific aspect of the Divine that is a manifestation of the infinite, all-pervading Ultimate Reality. The seed must be fertilized by the sincere prayer of the heart and watered by tears of longing. In the early stages, the plant needs to be fenced around by orthodox observances to protect it from empty intellectualism and dry erudition. The seeker needs to weed around the plant through discrimination, dispassion, and self-control. He or she should be loyal to the plant and not abandon or ignore it. Then the plant grows into a tree and brings forth the flowers of purity, contentment, faith, spiritual emotions, taste of bliss, and the total transformation of the seeker's personality. And finally comes the spiritual fruits of supreme devotion and constant communion with the Divine. The seeker becomes blessed, and the Lord is pleased with the seeker's patience and loyalty and grants the seeker the fruit of pure devotion.

11

Spiritual Disciplines in Bhakti-Yoga

The aim of human birth is to love God. Realize that love and be at peace.

—SRI RAMAKRISHNA

METHODICAL SPIRITUAL PRACTICES

Having committed to one Chosen Ideal, one teacher, and one teaching, the seeker now enters the stage of practicing the spiritual disciplines of bhakti-yoga in a methodical way. These spiritual practices can be divided into four categories, as follows.

Ceremonial Worship

Ceremonial worship of the Chosen Ideal as described in the sacred texts is one of the important practices of bhakti-yoga. Sri Ramakrishna says:

> [Bhakti] is to adore God with body, mind, and words. "With body" means to serve and worship God with one's hands, go to holy places with one's feet, hear the chanting of the name and glories of God with one's ears, and behold the divine

image with one's eyes. "With mind" means to contemplate and meditate on God constantly and to remember and think of His lila. "With words" means to sing hymns to Him and chant His name and glories.[1]

Ceremonial worship is seeking the Chosen Ideal using all the sense organs. Such worship has a deep spiritual significance. The cause of bondage is the attachment of the mind to the world and worldly objects, and the mind perceives worldly objects through its outward-seeking sense organs. One must purify one's whole body and mind. The *Bhakti-Ratnavali or A Necklace of Devotional Gems* says:

> The human ears that have not listened to recitals of Divine glory are mere caves, and the voices of men who have not sung of it are mere croakings of frogs. A man's head, though decorated with silken turban, is a mere burden to bear, if it is not accustomed to bowing down to the Lord; his arms, though wearing shining golden ornaments, are purposeless like those of a corpse, if they are not used in the service of the Lord. The eyes that are not accustomed to seeing Divine images are equal to the eyes of a peacock feather, and the legs of people who do not walk to, and go round, holy places are comparable to trees. A man who has never touched the holy dust, sanctified by the feet of the devotees of the Lord is indeed a living corpse....

> That alone is real faculty of speech which is used for reciting the Lord's attributes and His glories; those alone are real hands which are used for the service of the Lord; that alone is the real mind which contemplates on the Lord as dwelling in everything; and that alone is the real power of hearing which is utilized for listening to the description of the Supreme Being. Again, that alone is the real head which bows down before the two symbols of the Lord, His image and His devotees; they alone are the real eyes which see them both (the images and

the devotees); they alone are the real limbs which become purified by the waters with which the feet of holy images and holy men are washed.[2]

Through ceremonial worship, the seeker touches the feet of the Chosen Ideal's image. The seeker tastes the food that was offered to the Chosen Ideal to purify the organ of taste. The seeker visualizes the beauty of the Chosen Ideal to purify the eyes. The seeker smells the fragrance of the flowers offered to the Lord. The seeker hears only the holy name and glories of God. By engaging all sense organs in this worship, the seeker very soon replaces worldly attachments with an attachment to the Chosen Ideal and is ready to practice mystic or inner worship, such as concentration and meditation.

The practice of worship and other disciplines is necessary for a seeker as long as he or she has not attained *samadhi*. Sri Ramakrishna beautifully describes the purpose of ceremonial worship and says:

After a man has attained samadhi all actions drop away. All devotional activities, such as worship, japa, and the like, as well as all worldly duties, cease to exist for such a person. At the beginning there is much ado about work. As a man makes progress toward God the outer display of his work diminishes, so much so that he cannot even sing God's name and glories.[3]

A beginner in the path of bhakti-yoga performs ceremonial worship of the Chosen Ideal through a symbol or an image, which is the concrete representation of the Ideal. But according to the Hindu scriptures, worship done through an image or a symbol is inferior to mystic or inner worship. Better than image worship is *japa*, or the repetition of a holy name. Still better is mental worship, and the highest form of worship is to see the Chosen Ideal within oneself and in all. The symbols a seeker uses are at first visible, concrete, and tangible. Then at the second stage, the seeker uses symbols such as thoughts, words, or sounds. Finally, he or she goes beyond all symbols. In the beginning, however, these symbols, images, and rituals are indispensable aids in the practice of concentration of mind and cultivation of love of God. We think and act symbolically; our thoughts and ideas are nothing but symbols.

A beginner may find it very difficult to uninterruptedly focus the mind on some abstract thought. The deity for the beginner remains manifested in the image, and he or she worships the deity with such physical ingredients as flowers, incense, and candles. Before the beginner begins the worship, he or she invokes the Lord in the image, decorates the Lord with garlands of flowers, and feels the living presence manifested in the image. The beginner regards the Chosen Ideal as most beloved and every act of worship as a service to God.

But the seeker eventually comes to look upon the image of the deity as the reflection of the altar within the heart where the deity remains manifested permanently. The advanced seeker looks upon the body as a veritable temple and the heart as the inmost shrine. The seeker thinks of the form of the deity as luminous and loving. In this worship, the items of offering, such as flowers, are actually offerings of good deeds and thoughts. According to Tantra,* a worshiper is asked to look upon the heart as the altar of the Chosen Ideal, the life breath as incense, the inner fire as light, the ocean of divine bliss as food, all perceptions of sound as well as those of air as a fan, and the action of the sense organs and the vagaries of the mind as a dance.[4] The seeker is asked to symbolically offer the flowers of guilelessness, humility, desirelessness, calmness, integrity, simplicity, discrimination, compassion, freedom from greed and jealousy, nonviolence, and control of the senses.

---

*Tantra is a system of religious philosophy in which the Divine Mother, or Power (Shakti), is the Ultimate Reality.

A seeker in the path of bhakti-yoga may worship the Chosen Ideal with all the paraphernalia of external rituals but knows in his or her own heart of hearts that the one to whom all worship is directed is all-pervading and beyond all comprehension of the human mind. How can the all-pervading Lord be worshiped? How can a seat be given to the omnipresent? What light can illumine the light of all lights? The worshiper, therefore, is asked to conclude all worship with the following prayer:

> O Lord, in my worship I have attributed forms to Thee, who art formless. O Thou teacher of the world, by my hymns I have, as it were, contradicted Thy indescribable nature. By going on pilgrimage I have, as it were, denied thy Omnipresence. O Lord of the universe, pray, forgive me these three transgressions.[5]

The bhakti-yogi must also practice *bhajana,* or the performance of such spiritual actions as chanting of hymns and rendering personal service to one's spiritual teacher, holy persons, and the devotees of the Lord. In his last message, Sri Krishna assures Uddhava, his friend and disciple, that any sincere action of the devotee pleases the Lord: "Those who knowing or not knowing how much, what, and of what sort I am, worship Me with their whole soul given up to Me are in My opinion the best of My devotees."[6]

Just as proper conduct is conducive to the cultivation of the love of God, so the *bhakti* scriptures describe certain behavior that is destructive of *bhakti.* A seeker is therefore instructed to avoid the following behavior:

- While visiting a temple, expecting special attention because of one's wealth, position, or power

- In a place of worship, before a holy personality, or before a guru, sitting with outstretched legs or in a disrespectful posture, lying down, indulging in gossip or argument, or speaking in a loud voice

- Telling lies

- Showing favor or disfavor

- Speaking ill of a saint or holy person

- Judging the character of the teacher

- Neglecting to show proper regard for the teacher

- Disregarding the scriptures

- Taking the name of God in vain

- Repeating the name of the Lord mechanically, without making effort to taste the joy of repeating the name

The purpose of the above negative injunctions is to help the seeker avoid distractions and focus the mind on the Chosen Ideal. Positive practices to focus the mind include chanting hymns; studying sacred texts; listening to discourses; singing praises of the Lord, individually or congregationally; repeating the name of the Lord, silently or loudly; and meditating on God. The seeker is advised to undertake such practices to increase his or her *bhakti* and longing for God.

Japa, or Repetition of a Holy Name

The second category of methodical spiritual practice in bhakti-yoga is *japa*, where a seeker repeats the mantra, or holy name, taking the name itself as the embodiment of the Chosen Ideal. Meditation is often preceded by the practice of *japa*. *Japa*, when practiced consciously, leads the mind to concentration. Sri Ramakrishna explains the efficacy of the practice and says:

> One attains God through japa. By repeating the name of God secretly and in solitude one receives divine grace. Then comes His vision. Suppose there is a big piece of timber lying under water and fastened to the land with a chain; by proceeding along the chain, link by link, you will at last touch the timber.[7]

Japa may be performed aloud, semi-audibly, or mentally. Mental *japa* is the most efficacious of all. In the beginning, seekers may take the help of a rosary in repeating the holy name. The more adept repeat the holy name while keeping count on their fingers. Superior seekers repeat the holy name mentally. It is said that if the efficacy of repeating the holy name aloud is considered one unit, repeating the name semi-audibly is ten units, uttering to oneself with the movement of the lips is one hundred units, and mentally repeating the holy name is a thousand units. Mental *japa* can be practiced even when one is engaged in other activities. Through prolonged practice of *japa*, the seeker develops the habit of repeating the holy name without conscious effort. Sometimes such a seeker practices *japa* with every breath.

Among the various postures prescribed for the practice of *japa* and meditation, the seated posture is generally preferred. If *japa* is practiced while standing or walking, the seeker is likely to become distracted, and if practiced while lying down, the seeker may fall asleep. In order to achieve perfection in *japa*, it should be accompanied by meditation on the meaning of the mantra. Yaska in his *Nirukta* says, "He who repeats a Vedic mantra without understanding its meaning is like an ass carrying a load of sandal wood; it knows only the weight of the load but does not enjoy the fragrance."[8] The Upanishads advise the spiritual seeker to contemplate the true meaning of the mantra while repeating the mantra faithfully and vigilantly.[9]

Although any time is good for the practice of *japa*, the conjunctions of the day and night are considered most auspicious. Midnight and midday are also regarded as auspicious for such practice. *Japa* is the surest stepping-stone to meditation. Only those who practice *japa* for long periods of time are able to concentrate their minds in meditation. In this sense, *japa* is considered indirect meditation. Continuous and rhythmic repetition of the holy name or mantra fills the mind with holiness and the mind unconsciously reaches the state of meditation. *Japa* is the surest way of controlling the mind. Even the most turbulent and distracted mind becomes calm and tranquil with steady and regular practice.

True meditation is spontaneous. In order to meditate one must have a mood, and a beginner cannot predict when this mood will come. Under such circumstances, it is easier for a seeker to concentrate the mind on a holy name. One such repetition with a concentrated mind is equivalent to a million mechanical repetitions not accompanied by devotion. It is the same with regard to meditation. A brief period of meditation with intense devotion is equal to many hours of meditation unaccompanied by the right mood.

In the beginning, *japa* is always mechanical. The average person is dominated by fleeting moods, feelings, and emotions. Such a mind can never consciously concentrate on one thought alone. The average mind easily gets tired in the practice of *japa*. But, in the course of time, the same mind, by dwelling on a certain idea for a length of time, develops an affinity for that idea. As a result of effortful repetition of the holy name, the mind develops the habit of repeating it unconsciously and regularly. With regard to the practice, Swami Vivekananda answers a number of vital questions:

Q. Sometimes one gets tired of Japa (repetition of the Mantra). Should one continue it or read some good book instead?

A. One gets tired of Japa for two reasons. Sometimes one's brain is fatigued, sometimes it is the result of idleness. If the former, then one should give up Japa for the time being, for persistence in it at the time results in seeing hallucinations, or in lunacy, etc. But if the latter, the mind should be forced to continue Japa.

Q. Sometimes sitting at Japa one gets joy at first, but then one seems to be disinclined to continue the Japa owing to that joy. Should it be continued then?

A. Yes, that joy is a hindrance to spiritual practice, its name being Rasasvadana (tasting of the sweetness). One must rise above that.

Q. Is it good to practice Japa for a long time, though the mind may be wandering?

A. Yes. As a person breaks a wild horse by always keeping his seat on its back.

Q. You have written in your *Bhakti-Yoga* that if a weak-bodied man tries to practise Yoga, a tremendous reaction comes. Then what to do?

A. What fear if you die in the attempt to realise the Self! Man is not afraid of dying for the sake of learning and many other things, and why should you fear to die for religion?[10]

If *japa* is practiced regularly and with great yearning, the seeker develops relish in repeating the mantra or the holy name. The teachers of bhakti-yoga say that a seeker must repeat the name of God with every breath, for no one knows which breath will be his last.

The system of Tantra extols the practice of *purascharana*—that is, performing japa along with a spiritual vow. The seeker should resolve to perform a specific number of *japa* and must fulfill that resolve. According to one view, *purascharana* is the vow of daily repeating the mantra one thousand times from one dark fortnight to the next or continuously repeating the mantra from sunrise to sunset. According to another view, *purascharana* is the vow of continuously repeating the mantra 1.2 million times. The essential aspect of *purascharana* and other such vows is for seekers to reassure themselves that they are faithful to the mantra and the Chosen Ideal.

Contemplation

The third category of spiritual practice in bhakti-yoga is contemplation, or loving remembrance of one's Chosen Ideal. In the state of contemplation, the mind remains delightfully absorbed in various thoughts of God. This is an absorption on the brink of meditation. Aspirants in such a state think of divine grace and the qualities of the Lord. If the Chosen Ideal of the aspirant is a divine incarnation, he or she thinks of the incarnation's life and teachings and remains absorbed in them. Such devotees while reading a text describing the life and sports of the beloved Lord may mentally transport themselves to the place and time where the incidents occurred. Devotees reading the Bible hear Christ delivering the Sermon on the Mount as if they were there on that day. Devotees reading the Bhagavad Gita transport themselves to the battlefield and visualize the dialogue between Krishna and Arjuna. It is said that Sri Chaitanya once made a pilgrimage to southern India and saw a pundit who was reading the Bhagavad Gita while another man, seated nearby, was listening and weeping. Sri Chaitanya asked this man, "Do you understand all this?" The man answered, "No, revered sir, I don't understand a word of the text." "Then why are you crying?" Sri Chaitanya asked. The man then said, "I see Arjuna's chariot before me. I see Lord Krishna and Arjuna seated in front of the chariot. I see Lord Krishna expounding the wisdom of Bhagavad Gita. I see this and I weep."[11] Such absorption is an ideal example of contemplation.

Contemplation in bhakti-yoga involves the faculty of imagination heightened by emotion. Imagination, when not properly guided, becomes the cause of distraction; after all, many of the distractions that bother a person during spiritual practice are due to unconscious imagination. The mind perhaps recalls various images and past actions that frighten the beginner. Contemplation utilizes the faculty of imagination and focuses it on one's spiritual goal. Lack of imagination is the reason persons often feel dry in spiritual practice or lose interest in meditation. The same power of imagination that was associated with one's past worldly actions and unholy thoughts, bhakti-yoga argues, can be used to remember and contemplate one's Chosen Ideal.

Meditation

The fourth and culminating practice in bhakti-yoga is meditation, an expression of supreme love toward the object of devotion. The more intense the aspirant's love, the greater the depth of meditation. Teachers of bhakti-yoga have defined *bhakti* meditation in different ways:

> One's own natural affections for one's Chosen Ideal will mature into extreme love: the absorbed state of mind then noticeable is called Bhakti, and its essence is love.[12]

> What is called bhakti is a state of mind in which, being melted by the force of spiritual discipline, the mind constantly flows toward the Lord.[13]

> Firm love for God more than for anything else, with full consciousness of His glory and magnitude, is Bhakti—and from this Bhakti alone results Release [liberation]. Supreme love following in the wake of previous knowledge and lasting for ever is designated as Bhakti.[14]

Meditation is common in many traditions, but according to bhakti-yoga, it is marked by two distinct characteristics. First, unlike meditation in other yogas, which emphasize the subject of meditation—that is, the meditator—bhakti-yoga emphasizes the object of meditation, or the Chosen Ideal. Second, while meditation in the other yogas is a result of conscious effort, meditation in bhakti-yoga is unconsciously attained through the aspirant's intense love for the Ideal. Loving meditation is one of the stages of divine enjoyment and inebriation. Such loving meditation is the means as well as the end. It is eternal companionship of the Lord. The intensity of this divine inebriation makes the aspirant speechless and absorbed in meditation.

Meditation, according to bhakti-yoga, is *dhruva smriti,* or a willing and continuous remembrance of one's favorite form of the Lord. Ramanuja comments, "Meditation [in bhakti-yoga], again, is a constant remembrance [of the thing meditated upon], flowing like an unbroken stream of oil poured from one vessel to another. When this kind of remembering has been attained [in relation to God], all bondages break. Thus it is said in the scriptures regarding constant remembering as a means to liberation."[15]

Meditation in bhakti-yoga begins with an intense love of God and gradually develops into complete absorption into the form of God on which the aspirant meditates. It begins with *bhava*, or partial absorption. This is like the state of an angler who has been sitting by a lake. The fish comes and swallows the bait and the float begins to tremble. The angler is on the alert, gripping the rod, watching the float steadily and eagerly, without looking around or speaking to anyone. Next is *mahabhava*, or divine intoxication. As Sri Ramakrishna says, "If a drunkard takes too much liquor he cannot retain consciousness. If he takes only two or three glasses, he can go on with his work."[16] Then comes *prema*, or divine madness. Sri Ramakrishna says, "When prema is awakened, a devotee completely forgets the world; he also forgets his body, which is so dear to a man."[17] Finally, the devotee reaches the stage of complete absorption. In this state of intense love, the aspirant unthinkingly attains *kumbhaka*, or suspension of breath, and is overtaken by *samadhi*, just as a weary person is taken over by deep sleep. According to the *bhakti* aphorisms of the sage Narada: "The devotee may first become intoxicated with bliss. Then, having realized That, he becomes inert and silent and takes his delight in the Atman."[18]

But perfect meditation—toward complete absorption—is to be achieved by stages. The aspirant first meditates on the luminous Lord as adorned with ornaments; next, on the Lord without ornaments; then, on oneness with the Lord; and finally, on the indwelling Self. Proceeding through these stages is the natural path of bhakti-yoga, since it is easier for the vast majority of aspirants to concentrate on a personal God, with name, form, and attributes.

In the preparatory stages of love, the aspirant practices meditation and *japa* as a matter of discipline. The seeker is an afflicted soul. The seeker's love for the Chosen Ideal is not yet completely unselfish and spontaneous, but with the achievement of pure love, the bhakti-yogi attains the final goal. Sri Ramakrishna beautifully describes the meaning of spiritual disciplines in bhakti-yoga and says, "How long must a man continue the sandhya [formal worship]? As long as he has not developed love for the Lotus Feet of God, as long as he does not shed tears and his hair does not stand on end when he repeats God's name."[19]

The secret of meditation in bhakti-yoga is absolute self-surrender—not out of fear but out of pure and spontaneous love for one's Chosen Ideal. Self-surrender is not possible until the aspirant feels the living presence of God. Sri Ramakrishna describes two kinds of self-surrender:

The nature of one kind [of aspirant] is like that of the young monkey, and the nature of the other kind is like that of the kitten. The young monkey, with great exertion, somehow clings to its mother. Likewise, there are some aspirants who think that in order to realize God they must repeat His name a certain number of times, meditate on Him for a certain period, and practice a certain amount of austerity. An aspirant of this kind makes his own efforts to catch hold of God. But the kitten, of itself, cannot cling to its mother. It lies on the ground and cries, "Mew, mew!" It leaves everything to its mother. The mother cat sometimes puts it on a bed, sometimes on the roof behind a pile of wood. She carries the kitten in her mouth hither and thither. The kitten doesn't know how to cling to the mother. Likewise, there are some aspirants who cannot practice spiritual discipline by calculating about japa or the period of meditation. All that they do is cry to God with yearning hearts. God hears their cry and cannot keep Himself away. He reveals Himself to them.[20]

Self-surrender is the keynote of bhakti-yoga. Sri Ramakrishna designates self-surrender as giving one's "power of attorney" to God.

An incident in the life of Sri Ramakrishna illustrates the true spirit of self-surrender. Sri Ramakrishna's beloved disciple Girish Chandra Ghosh* was by nature averse to practicing disciplines or even following any routine. After meeting Sri Ramakrishna only a few times, Girish wholeheartedly surrendered to Sri Ramakrishna and asked, "What shall I do from now on?" Sri Ramakrishna answered, "Remember God every morning and evening." But this was too much for Girish to comply with. He was a playwright and actor and, before meeting Sri Ramakrishna, had led a hectic lifestyle. His mind was restless and his tendencies outgoing. Girish knew that if he were to follow a routine, he would feel no peace until that routine was intentionally broken. But there was no hypocrisy in Girish; he could never be insincere. He therefore kept silent at the words of Sri Ramakrishna. Seeing Girish hesitate, Sri Ramakrishna said, "Well, if you cannot do that, remember God once before taking food and before going to bed." Girish still remained silent because he knew he could not even do that. He had no schedule for eating or sleeping, nor did he know if he would eat or sleep at all. Seeing Girish's helpless condition, Sri Ramakrishna finally said in a state of divine consciousness, "Very well, if you cannot even do this, then give me your 'power of attorney.'" Girish, then, heaved a sigh of relief and assented. He was overwhelmed by the abundance of grace showered upon him by Sri Ramakrishna.

Girish thought that since he had given his "power of attorney" to Sri Ramakrishna, he would no longer have to bother about spiritual practices. Little did he realize that he had voluntarily bound himself out of love and faith—a bond far greater than any

---

*Girish Chandra Ghosh was one of the greatest Bengali dramatists and an ardent disciple of Sri Ramakrishna.

bond of daily prayers or vows. Girish recalled this incident later in life and said, "Did I know then that so much lay hidden in the simple giving of the 'power of attorney'? I now find that at some time there is an end to spiritual practices like *japa*, austerities, and devotional exercises but there is no end to the work of a person who has given the 'power of attorney,' for he has to watch every step and every breath to know whether he acts and moves depending on Him and His power or on this wretched 'I.'"[21]

Self-surrender means absolutely surrendering one's ego to God and abiding only by God's will. True surrender is practiced without complaining and questioning. Self-surrender to God depends upon the faith of the aspirant. It is through faith that the aspirant realizes the living presence and protection of God. Where there is no faith, the deity on the altar is a mere picture, an image, or a lifeless symbol; the holy name a verbal formula; and worship an empty show. Bhakti-yoga requires aspirants to have true faith in their spiritual practices. It is not the duration of meditation or the number of repetitions of the holy name but the extent of faith with which these are practiced that makes the difference in the path of bhakti-yoga.

Faith and self-surrender are not possible unless one has attained pure love—love without desire, selfishness, and fear. As long as love is selective, it is not pure; as long as it is not love for all, it is incomplete. No liberation is possible without this pure love that embraces all beings and things, seeing in them the presence of God.

Bondage, bhakti-yoga contends, cannot be broken by discrimination, self-analysis, or reasoning but only by choosing the most loving object to love. The essence of yoga is to withdraw the mind from sense objects and fix it on God alone. But the mind has to keep occupied with something. It constantly has to imagine, think, and meditate on some object. The path of bhakti-yoga points out that since the mind mostly indulges in jealousy, anger, hatred, desire, and attachment, let it make God the target of all its outbursts—let the seeker make a beginning with what he or she has been naturally endowed. Let a seeker adopt whatever means possible to think of God. As the seeker's mind becomes filled with the thoughts of God, contrary thoughts formed by careless habits of the past drop off of themselves.

EXPERIENCE OF ABSORPTION: THE STAGE OF PURE LOVE

The practice of spiritual disciplines leads the seeker to the next stage of bhakti-yoga, known as *raganuga-bhakti* (supreme love). At this stage, the seeker develops an intense desire to establish various human relationships with God. Devotion to one's Chosen Ideal becomes spontaneous and takes the form of a particular *bhava,* or human attitude toward the Divine: *santa* (peace), *dasya* (servant-master), *sakhya* (friendship), *vatsalya* (mother-child), and *madhur* (lover-beloved). As Sri Ramakrishna describes:

> Santa, the serene attitude. The rishis of olden times had this attitude toward God. They did not desire any worldly enjoyment. It is like the single-minded devotion of a wife to her husband. She knows that her husband is the embodiment of beauty and love, a veritable Madan.
>
> Dasya, the attitude of a servant toward his master. Hanuman had this attitude toward Rama. He felt the strength of a lion when he worked for Rama....
>
> Sakhya, the attitude of friendship. Friends say to one another, "Come here and sit near me." Sridama and other friends sometimes fed Krishna with fruit, part of which they had already eaten, and sometimes climbed on His shoulders.
>
> Vatsalya, the attitude of a mother toward her child. This was Yasoda's [Krishna's mother's] attitude toward Krishna.... Yasoda would roam about with the butter in her hand, in order to feed Krishna.

> Madhur, the attitude of a woman toward her paramour.
> Radha had this attitude toward Krishna.... This attitude in-
> cludes all the other four.[22]

Bhava is the mature form of *bhakti* for the Chosen Ideal. It is the
state of being absorbed in meditation as the result of loving attachment. The *bhavas* are marked by eight manifestations of
deep spiritual emotions that lead the seeker to complete absorption in the Chosen Ideal: suspension of breath, perspira-
tion, horripilation, a choked voice, trembling of the body, change
in complexion, shedding of tears, and loss of consciousness.
The manifestations of these spiritual emotions have been cate-
gorized into four stages identifying the varying degrees of intensity of love the seeker experiences on the way to the goal:
smoldering, glowing, flaming, and blazing. Each stage of intensity is marked by how much a seeker is able to control these
spiritual emotions.

In the smoldering stage, the seeker experiences one or two of
the manifestations of spiritual emotions but is able to suppress
them. Sri Rupa Goswami, one of the renowned teachers of bhakti-
yoga, gives the following example of devotion in this stage:

> As he went on hearing the praise of Hari,* the Enemy of sin,
> the hairs of the priest's eye-lids became suddenly moistened
> with tears, his cheeks grew ruddy, and his nose perspired.[23]

At the stage of glowing, the seeker experiences two or three of the
manifestations of emotions and holds them in check, but with
much difficulty. An incident in the life of a devotee of Sri Krishna
exemplifies this stage:

> Oh dear! when the sound of his reed-pipe came from within
> the distant caves, with great difficulty did I succeed in con-
> cealing the lump in my throat, and the huskiness of my voice,

---

*Hari is a name of God.

> but, alas, failed altogether in suppressing the tremor of my
> body. And from this, my intelligent relatives suspected that I
> was in love with Sri Krishna.[24]

At the stage of flaming, a seeker simultaneously experiences four or five of the manifestations of emotions with great intensity and can no longer control them. As an example of flaming devotion, it is said that the sage Narada would become so overjoyed on simply beholding Sri Krishna that he could not even utter the name of Sri Krishna, could not play on his lyre due to the trembling of his body, and could hardly even see Sri Krishna due to tears filling his eyes.[25]

Above all other stages is the stage of blazing devotion, in which a seeker experiences five or more manifestations of spiritual emotions simultaneously and at their maximum intensity. In this fourth stage, the seeker loses all body consciousness and becomes absorbed in the thought of God. As the following incident describes, when Sri Chaitanya danced before the image of the Lord, he experienced such an intensity of devotion:

> What a wonderful change in his body takes place [as he sees
> the Lord]!... With difficulty he utters the first or second letter
> of the name of [the Lord] and his voice is choked in the at-
> tempt. Tears flow from his eyes with the rapidity of a current
> of water flowing from a waterspout. They wet all his neigh-
> bours' clothes. His fair complexion sometimes turns golden
> like the rising sun, and is sometimes as tender and beautiful
> as the *Mallika* flower. Now he stands immovable and now he
> rolls on the earth and now again stands inert like a log of dry
> wood.[26]

When one becomes perfect in devotion, one reaches the state of *bhava samadhi, savikalpa samadhi,* or *chetana samadhi.* The highest state of *bhava* is *mahabhava,* and higher than *mahabhava* is the state of *prema.* The seeker who attains *prema* lives and moves in constant communion with the Lord. It is the highest intensity of divine love, where one's love is uncontrollable like a blazing fire that even one's tears of devotion cannot extinguish. Sri Ramakrishna says:

> The sum and substance of the whole matter is that a man must love God, must be restless for Him. It doesn't matter whether you believe in God with form or in God without form. You may or may not believe that God incarnates Himself as man. But you will realize Him if you have that yearning. Then He Himself will let you know what He is like. If you must be mad, why should you be mad for the things of the world? If you must be mad, be mad for God alone.[27]

In this state of *prema,* the slightest sensation kindles great spiritual feeling in the seeker. By repeating the name of the Chosen Ideal only once, the seeker becomes completely inebriated with God-consciousness:

> When, hearing the name of Hari or Rama once, you shed tears and your hair stands on end, then you know for certain that you do not have to perform such devotions as the sandhya any more. Then only will you have a right to renounce rituals; or rather, rituals will drop away of themselves.[28]

Absorption in *samadhi* and communion with the Divine is the one goal of bhakti-yoga. A seeker practicing bhakti-yoga with sincerity, faith, and loyalty is sure to reach the goal in due time. Fulfilling the instruction of the teacher, being faithful to the teaching, and being devoted to the Ideal are, again, the three most important aspects of bhakti-yoga practice. One who attempts to progress on this path fulfills the highest purpose in life—to love God.

12

Obstacles in Bhakti-Yoga

*You may speak of the scripture, of philosophy, of
Vedanta; but you will not find God in any of these.
You will never succeed in realizing God unless your
soul becomes restless for Him.*

—Sri Ramakrishna

Obstacles will arise for a seeker on the path of bhakti-yoga,
and the seeker must know how to overcome them. The
major obstacles in the path are bad company, idle gossip, dogmatism, emotionalism, disloyalty, indolence, gullibility, fastidiousness, and ostentation.

BAD COMPANY

The great bhakti-yoga sage Narada advises seekers to shun bad
company by all means. Many seekers of bhakti-yoga become
stalled on the path due to this obstacle. By coming into contact
with unspiritual people, dormant passions of one's mind, such as
lust and greed, become aroused. Company with such people
slowly and imperceptibly leads the seeker to indulge in conversations relating to sense enjoyment, which causes the seeker to
stray from the path of yoga. As the Bhagavad Gita describes:

> When a man dwells on objects, he feels an attachment for them. Attachment gives rise to desire and desire breeds anger.
>
> From anger comes delusion; from delusion, the failure of memory; from the failure of memory, the ruin of discrimination; and from the ruin of discrimination the man perishes.[1]

Association with those who are averse to spiritual practice fills the mind of the seeker with doubts and desires. Therefore, a seeker should avoid the company of those who are addicted to sense pleasures, averse to prayer and meditation, and even those who keep the company of such worldly people. A beginner must avoid hearing or seeing anything that inflames the mind with sense desires. It is said in the *Mahabharata*:

> You have no desire for a thing till you know what it is like. It is only after you have seen it, or heard of it or touched it, that you get a liking for it. Therefore, the safest rule of human conduct is not to take, touch, or see whatever is likely to taint the imagination.[2]

Also, the spiritual seeker should never dwell on past failings. Dwelling on the dark memories of the past only stalls the seeker on the path. Instead, the seeker is advised to advance with the sincere practices of prayer and meditation with firm faith that such practices will destroy the results of all past mistakes and failings. Whatever they might have been, the more a seeker dwells upon past mistakes, the more these distracting thoughts assume power over the seeker. The remedy for impure thoughts is filling the mind with thoughts of holiness and purity. A seeker should always think of the omnipresence of God and remember that God is the ever-pure indweller seated in every human heart. In this sense, the system of nondualistic Vedanta does not recognize sins that permanently haunt a spiritual seeker. Vedanta only admits of error and mistakes. All past mistakes a seeker has made are said to be eradicated by chanting the name of God and having faith in the divinity of one's own Self.

In this regard, the seeker is advised to seek holy company. Holy company accelerates a seeker's spiritual progress. The company of those who are the very embodiment of purity and holiness gives the mind of the seeker faith, hope, courage, and spiritual inspiration. The spiritual journey of a seeker is always solitary. Every seeker has to journey alone, make mistakes alone, take risks alone, and reach the goal alone. It is often seen that a seeker, however adept, can lose sight of the goal, succumb to temptations, and become lost on the way. Company of the holy assures a seeker that he or she is on the right path and proceeding toward the goal.

A seeker should not only avoid bad company, but maintain a meditative state of mind by repeating the name of God as much as possible, by studying the sacred texts, and by serving the holy, so that the mind has no time to indulge in worldly thoughts. Many of the practices of bhakti-yoga are designed to keep the mind busy with the thought of God—since the mind is by nature always busy with something or other. As the *Panchadasi* says, "So long as you are not asleep or dead, pass your time in the study of *Vedanta*. Do not let lust have an opportunity to enter your mind."[3] The mind is often a slave of its past habits. Unless engaged in spiritual practices, it has the tendency to succumb to its old habits. If one is not proceeding and advancing on the path of yoga, one should know that one is receding.

IDLE GOSSIP

A seeker should scrupulously avoid all forms of idle gossip, fault-finding, and the habit of criticizing others for no purpose. It is not uncommon for seekers following the path of bhakti-yoga to succumb to this obstacle. By dwelling on the shortcomings of others, seekers themselves become infected by those shortcomings. Seekers of bhakti-yoga should avoid conversations and discussions that are unrelated to their spiritual goal and practice.

They should cultivate the habit of seeing the good qualities in every person. This is such an important aspect of the spiritual quest that Sri Sarada Devi, the Holy Mother advised in her last message, "My child, if you want peace, then do not look into anybody's faults. Look into your own faults. Learn to make the world your own. No one is a stranger, my child; the whole world is your own."[4]

DOGMATISM

Dogmatism is the strongest obstacle in the path of bhakti-yoga. A seeker often becomes dogmatic and justifies that dogmatism as one-pointed love for the Chosen Ideal. But all dogmatism leads to narrow-mindedness, sectarianism, and bigotry. Impelled by dogmatism, a seeker often becomes too concerned with literally adhering to every word of the scriptures, instead of taking the essence of the sacred texts and proceeding on the path. As Swami Vivekananda points out:

> The counting of beads, meditation, worship, offering oblations in the sacred fire—all these and such other things are the limbs of religion; they are but the means; and to attain to supreme devotion (Para-Bhakti) or to the highest realisation of Brahman is the pre-eminent end. If you look a little deeper you will understand what they are fighting about. One says, "If you pray to God facing the East, then you will reach Him." "No," says another, "you will have to sit facing the West, and then only you will see Him." Perhaps someone realised God in meditation, ages ago, by sitting with his face to the East, and his disciples at once began to preach this attitude, asserting that none can ever see God unless he assumes this position. Another party comes forward and inquires, "How is that? Such and such a person realised God while facing the West, and we have seen this ourselves." In this way all these sects have originated.[5]

To adhere to the study of scriptures and performance of rituals without trying to achieve the goal is like reading the same letter over and over again without assimilating the instructions embodied in the letter. The following parable of Sri Ramakrishna portrays the distinction between the letter and the spirit of the teachings:

> A man received a letter from home informing him that certain presents were to be sent to his relatives. The names of the articles were given in the letter. As he was about to go shopping for them, he found that the letter was missing. He began anxiously to search for it, several others joining in the search. For a long time they continued to search. When at last the letter was discovered, his joy knew no bounds. With great eagerness he opened the letter and read it. It said that he was to buy five seers of sweets, a piece of cloth, and a few other things. Then he did not need the letter anymore, for it had served its purpose. Putting it aside, he went out to buy the things. How long is such a letter necessary? As long as its contents are not known. When the contents are known one proceeds to carry out the directions.
>
> In the scriptures you will find the way to realize God. But after getting all the information about the path, you must begin to work. Only then can you attain your goal.[6]

Rituals and ceremonies are necessary insofar as they help the seeker to realize the goal. As the husk of rice protects the kernel, so rituals, mythology, and philosophy protect and preserve the spiritual truth. But as the sprout appears, the husk drops away; as the seeker develops a meditative mood, the external aids of rituals and ceremonies gradually become less significant.

From dogmatism springs tendencies toward exclusiveness and intolerance. Dogmatists claim that their God is the highest of all, their path the best of all paths, and their interpretation of religion the only interpretation. A seeker in the path of bhakti-yoga must see that having one-pointed love for the Chosen Ideal does not lead to dogmatism or sectarianism. The seeker must realize that he or she cannot hold hatred toward other religions and, at the same time, love his or her own Ideal. One should know that one's personal Chosen Ideal is also the all-pervading and all-loving God of all.

EMOTIONALISM

Emotions play an important part in the path of bhakti-yoga, but unless one's emotions are tempered by reason, they are an obstacle in the path of divine love. Mere emotion is not always a sign of devotion; in fact, tears of anguish, fear, and depression often pass as tears of devotion. Similarly, complacency and laziness are often taken as self-surrender to God. The emotions that lead a seeker upward can also lead downward. Swami Vivekananda's instructions in this regard are very important:

> During meditation, suppress the emotional side altogether. That is a great source of danger. Those that are very emotional have no doubt their Kundalini* rushing quickly upwards, but it is as quick to come down as to go up. And when it does come down, it leaves the devotee in a state of utter ruin. It is for this reason that Kirtanas [congregational singing] and other auxiliaries to emotional development have a great drawback. It is true that by dancing and jumping, etc. through a momentary impulse, that power is made to course upwards, but it is never enduring. On the contrary when it traces back its course, it rouses violent lust in the individual ... this happens simply owing to a lack of steady practice in meditation and concentration.[7]

---

*The kundalini is the spiritual energy lying coiled up, or dormant, at the base of the spine in all individuals. When consciously awakened through spiritual practice, it rises through the spinal column, passes through various centers, *chakras*, and at last reaches the brain, whereupon the yogi experiences *samadhi*.

A seeker following the path of bhakti-yoga is advised to control emotions with the help of reason and discrimination. The more one can overcome the outbursts of emotions, the more one's devotion grows, strengthens, and matures. A temporary upsurge of spiritual emotions can be followed by violent reactions that bring the seeker downward into the indulgence of gross desires. True love for God can only exist where there is not even the slightest trace of lust and greed in one's heart. So Swami Vivekananda warns seekers about the dangers of temporary emotions:

> There are ... certain great dangers in the way. There is, for instance, the danger to the receiving soul of its mistaking momentary emotions for real religious yearning. We may see this in ourselves. Many a time in our lives somebody dies whom we loved. We receive a blow; we feel that the world is slipping between our fingers, that we want something surer and higher, that we must become religious. In a few days that wave of feeling passes away, and we are left stranded exactly where we were before. All of us often mistake such impulses for real thirst after religion; but as long as these momentary emotions are thus mistaken, that continuous, real craving of the soul for religion will not come, and we shall not find the true transmitter of spirituality [the guru]. So whenever we are tempted to complain that our search after the truth that we desire so much is proving vain—instead of complaining, our first duty is to look into our own souls and find whether the craving in the heart is real. Then, in the vast majority of cases, it will be discovered that we were not fit to receive the truth, that there was no real thirst for spirituality.[8]

DISLOYALTY, OR LACK OF SPIRITUAL ROOT

Seekers lacking in loyalty to the Chosen Ideal inevitably find meditation very difficult. Such disloyalty stems from a deep inner restlessness that distracts the mind from the object of meditation.

There are seekers who justify themselves as being universal and harmonious in their spiritual outlook and who do not have a specific Chosen Ideal. They make no progress in the path because they have no spiritual root.

True harmony of religions is the harmony of realization and God-consciousness. It is not the harmony of paths. The goal is one but the paths are different. Unless seekers remain faithful and steadfast in their own path, they never experience the harmony of God-consciousness.

INDOLENCE

Indolence and dullness are great obstacles in the path of meditation, and a seeker on the path of bhakti-yoga should be particularly careful about them. Self-surrender is the bhakti-yogi's watchword, but unless one is careful, one may take laziness to be an expression of self-surrender to the will of God. True self-surrender never makes an aspirant inactive. Self-surrender is the effacement of the ego and not the giving up of activity. Self-surrender is attained only when one has exerted oneself to the utmost. True love of God is never passive. It is actively striving for the vision of God.

Lapsing into indolence and inertia, seekers often become irregular in their practice of meditation and hope for the grace of God for the realization of their spiritual goal. But grace does not come to those who do not make a sincere effort for it. Grace and self-effort are intimately related. There is no grace without self-effort. Only in the end do seekers realize that their self-effort was made possible due to grace. By the grace of God, seekers are drawn to the spiritual path and feel enthusiasm in their prayer and meditation. But seekers cannot realize this in the beginning. They must remain alert to avoid becoming deluded by a false sense of self-surrender and thus giving up faith in their self-effort.

GULLIBILITY

Seekers in the path of bhakti-yoga often develop an aversion toward reason and discrimination and fall victim to gullibility. Such persons fail to distinguish the true from the false and the rational from the superstitious in the realm of religion. Gullibility leads them to imitate others and follow mass thinking. Following the ways of holy persons is no doubt a means to acquire love of God, but persons who do not cultivate reason often merely imitate the dress and mannerisms of holy persons rather than their renunciation and love for God. Such thoughtless imitation eventually leads to hypocrisy and self-deception. Seekers must develop both reason and devotion if their love is to be true. The path of bhakti-yoga must be balanced by the study of scriptures, self-analysis, and knowledge (jnana).

FASTIDIOUSNESS AND OSTENTATION

Fastidiousness is another obstacle that besets the path of bhakti-yoga. Seekers unable to concentrate the mind often busy themselves with non-essential details, such as the purity of food, appropriateness of dress, or posture. Compliance with the injunctions of the scriptures with regard to such details does not serve any purpose unless inspired by true renunciation and dispassion. Those whose hearts are empty make an outer show of their spirituality to cover up their lack of faith. Such persons may attract the credulous adoration of others but soon lose sight of the goal and become more concerned with their own ego than their God. The deeper the seeker's love for God, the lesser the outer display of spiritual emotions. The true follower of bhakti-yoga practices charity, austerity, japa, and meditation privately and in an unostentatious manner. A seeker of bhakti-yoga is advised to be discriminating enough to distinguish the inner spirit of bhakti-yoga from the non-essential rituals and adhere to the essential spiritual practices while avoiding all outward display.

PART THREE

The Way of Raja-Yoga: The Path of Meditation

13
The Message of Raja-Yoga

*Placing the body in a straight posture, with the chest,
the neck, and the head held erect, making the organs
and the mind enter the heart, the sage crosses all the
fearful currents by means of the raft of Brahman.*
—SVETASVATARA UPANISHAD 2.8

Raja-yoga is a path to unify our apparent self, or individual consciousness, with our true Self, or absolute Pure Consciousness. It focuses on the infinite world within our own being that we have forgotten, having become lost in the external world of delusions and fantasies. Raja-yoga maintains a pragmatic, matter-of-fact attitude toward the meaning of truth and refuses to endorse any dogma or tradition based not on reason but on mere faith. Its philosophy is methodologically scientific, and its practice emphasizes the need of experimentation on the path of yoga toward its final demonstration of truth. The way of raja-yoga is to dig deep into the layers of our psychophysical being and discover our true Self, the realization of which alone can put an end to the sorrows and miseries of life. Nothing can help us in this task except our own disciplined and rigorous self-effort.

The seers of raja-yoga conclude that yoga is the search for unbounded existence, awareness, and joy that every human being will eventually be forced to undertake. When yoga is practiced consciously, we call it a spiritual quest; when practiced unconsciously, we call it evolution. The only requirement to practice raja-yoga is to have a tenacious will that can overcome all obstacles on the path. As Swami Vivekananda outlines:

> This is what Raja-yoga proposes to teach. The goal of all its teaching is to show how to concentrate the mind; then how to discover the innermost recesses of our own minds; then how to generalize their contents and form our own conclusions from them. It never asks what our belief is—whether we are deists, or atheists, whether Christians, Jews, or Buddhists. We are human beings, and that is sufficient. Every human being has the right and the power to seek religion; every human being has the right to ask the reason why and to have his question answered by himself—if he only takes the trouble.
>
> So far, then, we see that in the study of Raja-yoga no faith or belief is necessary. Believe nothing until you find it out for yourself; that is what it teaches us.[1]

The scientific practice of raja-yoga, as outlined by Patanjali, the founder of raja-yoga, is closely allied to the Samkhya system of Hindu philosophy. Generally speaking, Samkhya is yoga in theory, and raja-yoga is yoga in practice. The Samkhya system is often accused of atheism, since it believes that the existence of God cannot be proved; raja-yoga, however, believes in the existence of God, although its meaning of God radically differs from the conventional and traditional meanings of God as creator, father, mother, or divine person.

God, according to Patanjali, is a special being, the most perfect Purusha (Self), in whom all knowledge, power, and virtue find their supreme manifestation. Perfect in all respects, God is the ideal of perfection to be attained. Meditation on any form of God, therefore, is one way of attaining Self-realization. The goal of yoga, according to Patanjali, is neither communion with God nor union with the absolute, all-pervading Brahman; yoga is a relentless battle to manifest the perfection of the soul by consciously controlling the outward tendencies of the body, mind, and senses and by practicing right discrimination. While the system of Samkhya emphasizes right discrimination and knowledge for the realization of the Self, Patanjali advocates the persistent practice of meditation. Concentration and meditation are mentioned in the Upanishads as potent means to attain Self-realization, but Patanjali systematized the Upanishadic theory for the practice of meditation as raja-yoga.

The practice of meditation is supported by concentration of mind. Swami Vivekananda says, "It is impossible to find God outside ourselves. Our own souls contribute all the divinity that is outside us. We are the greatest temple. The objectification is only a faint imitation of what we see within ourselves."[2] Meditation leads to the state of *samadhi,* attaining which the soul crosses the boundaries of the mind and shines in its own glory in unbounded freedom.

Raja-yoga is never vague in its guidelines for reaching the goal of Self-realization. According to its tradition, focusing the mind on the same object for twelve seconds achieves one unit of concentration; twelve such units of concentration (two minutes and twenty-four seconds) make one unit of meditation; twelve such successive units of meditation (twenty-eight minutes and forty-eight seconds) make one unit of lower *samadhi*; twelve such successive units of lower *samadhi* (five hours, forty-five minutes and thirty-six seconds) then lead the meditator to *asamprajnata samadhi,* the highest *samadhi*—the final goal of spiritual quest.

Success in raja-yoga depends upon the moral fitness and earnestness of the seeker. Swami Vivekananda says:

Those who are ready advance very quickly and become yogis in six months. The less developed may take several years; and anyone, by faithful work and by giving up everything else

> and devoting himself solely to practice, can reach the goal in twelve years. Bhakti will bring you there without any of these mental gymnastics; but it is a slower way.[3]

Sincere and methodical practice of yoga proves its results. "By Yoga, Yoga must be known; through Yoga, Yoga advances. He who cares for Yoga, in Yoga rests forever."[4]

Patanjali presents the seeker with the eight-limbed practice to reach the goal of yoga. The first two limbs are *yama* and *niyama* for achieving moral purity through strict self-control. The third limb is *asana*, which constitutes directions for yogic posture in order to gain mastery over the body. The fourth limb, *pranayama*, is the control of breath, by which the yogi seeks to awaken the mind. The fifth limb is *pratyahara*, or the practice of withdrawing the mind from sense objects. The sixth limb of raja-yoga is *dharana*, or concentration, which focuses the awakened mind on a certain part of the body to the exclusion of all others. The seventh limb is *dhyana*, or meditation on one single thought to the exclusion of all other thoughts. The eighth limb of raja-yoga is *samadhi*, when the mind becomes completely absorbed in the object of meditation.

The greatest roadblock on the way to raja-yoga is restlessness of the mind. The mind, according to raja-yoga, remains in one of the following five states: darkened *(mudha)*, scattered *(kshipta)*, distracted *(vikshipta)*, one-pointed *(ekagra)*, or suspended *(niruddha)*. The darkened mind is inert, dull, and unfit to think of the subtle principles of yoga. People of this state of mind generally think only of worldly matters, and the concentration of a darkened mind is a concentration of infatuation. The scattered mind remains in a state of persistent restlessness and has neither the patience nor the intelligence to comprehend spiritual principles. Through intense jealousy or anger, a scattered mind may at times attain a state of concentration, but not yogic concentration. The distracted mind is different from a scattered mind. A distracted mind can remain calm at times but easily becomes disturbed. Such a mind may attain concentration, but it generally does not last very long. The one-pointed mind concentrates on one thought and one thought alone. Patanjali describes such a state of mind as that in which the same thought arises in unbroken succession. When a seeker becomes established in one-pointedness, the mind becomes wholly occupied with the same thought, even in the dream state. It is said in the Vedas that even if an undesirable, unconscious thought suddenly surfaces in a one-pointed mind, it cannot overcome and distract the seeker. The suspended mind remains absorbed in the thought of the Self.

There are four paths to achieve tranquility of mind: persuasion (jnana-yoga), purification (bhakti-yoga), eradication (karma-yoga), and confrontation (raja-yoga). Persuasion employs reason to convince the mind to give up all its attachments and desires for the sake of Self-realization. The way of purification asks for pouring only holy thoughts into the mind, which washes out all worldly thoughts. The way of eradication is the eradication of our attachments to all that is not-Self by way of selfless action. According to raja-yoga, persuasion generally fails because the mind is too weak and perverted to listen to reason; purification calls for faith in God, which many seekers lack; and eradication is a slow and often painful process. Raja-yoga chooses to confront the restless mind through the subjective practices of concentration and meditation, supported by the objective disciplines of right posture, right breathing, and the strength of an uncompromising will.

THE WISDOM OF RAJA-YOGA

A human individual is essentially a Purusha or Self. This Self residing within every human heart is immortal, infinite, ever pure, and ever blissful. Because of its forgetfulness, the Self becomes entangled with the world of matter and suffers from all its afflictions.

The world of matter, or Prakriti, is unconscious. Only by the proximity of the soul or Self does the world of matter appear conscious and living. The role of Prakriti is essentially to awaken the soul from its self-inflicted delusion.

Self-forgetfulness is the cause of all suffering. Self-forgetfulness is caused by ignorance, which gives rise to ego, attachment, aversion, and clinging to life. These five conditions of the mind constitute the bondage of the Self and can only be overcome by Self-realization.

Bondage creates samskaras. *Samskaras* are deep-seated tendencies of past actions and their results stored in the mind. *Samskaras* can only be overcome by counter-*samskaras*. Concentration and meditation on the Self supported by right posture and breath control is the only way to break the chain of bondage.

Meditation overcomes all obstacles. The process of meditation is to feed a single thought to the mind and make the mind continue to repeat that thought in a methodical and persistent way. Through such repetition with devotion and determination, the whole mind takes the form of that thought and overcomes all other undesirable thoughts. The essential teaching of raja-yoga is that the mind never becomes controlled unless we consciously control the *effects* of the mind's restlessness—and not only the *causes* of restlessness.

Awakening the spiritual consciousness is vital. Raja-yoga maintains that the awakening of spiritual consciousness (kundalini) is vital for success in yoga. Such spiritual awakening should be attempted after the development of a strong moral foundation and then strengthened through concentration and meditation.

In praise of yoga, Swami Vivekananda writes:

> The fire of yoga burns the cage of sin which imprisons a man.
> Knowledge becomes purified and Nirvana is directly obtained.
> From yoga comes knowledge; knowledge, again, helps the

yogi to obtain freedom. He who combines in himself both yoga and knowledge—with him the Lord is pleased. Those who practise maha-yoga either once a day, or twice, or thrice, or always—know them to be gods. Yoga is divided into two parts: one is called abhava-yoga, and the other, maha-yoga. That in which one's self is meditated upon as a void or without qualities is abhava-yoga. That in which one sees one's self as blissful, bereft of impurities, and as one with God is called maha-yoga. The yogi, by either of these, realizes the Self. The other yogas that we read and hear of do not deserve to be ranked with maha-yoga, in which the yogi finds himself and the whole universe to be God. This is the highest of yogas.[5]

14

The Philosophy and Psychology of Raja-Yoga

*Engaged in the yoga of constant practice and not
allowing the mind to wander away to anything else,
he who meditates on the supreme, resplendent
Purusha reaches Him.*

—BHAGAVAD GITA 8.8

THE NATURE OF ULTIMATE REALITY

According to Samkhya, inquiry about the nature of Ultimate Reality is an inquiry about the nature of human beings as individuals. That which is real in every individual is Purusha, or the indwelling Self, the immutable and incorporeal Pure Consciousness that remains hidden within the psychophysical layers of the intellect, mind, sense organs, vital forces, and body. These psychophysical components belong to Prakriti (nature), or the world of matter, the other aspect of Reality. Purusha and Prakriti are coeternal and coexistent but independent of one another.

According to both Samkhya and raja-yoga, Prakriti, the first cause of the universe, evolves itself into manifold beings and things for the fulfillment and eventual liberation of the Purusha. Purusha, although ever perfect, immortal, and ever free, wrongly identifies itself with its reflection in the intellect and mind due to indiscrimination and, therefore, attaches itself to Prakriti. The Purusha in bondage is the Purusha enchanted and deluded by Prakriti. Prakriti, therefore, plays a vital role in awakening the Purusha by presenting before it all that is enjoyable, so that the Purusha may realize in time that nothing in the realm of Prakriti endures eternally and nothing of the world of the senses can grant abiding happiness. True discrimination and sincere longing for liberation never dawn on a person until he or she is through with the material enjoyments provided by Prakriti and realizes the futility of such enjoyments.

THE MEANING OF CREATION

The Samkhya philosophy subscribes to the cyclical theory of creation and describes the world process as the evolution and involution of Prakriti. Prakriti is the uncaused cause of all objects. It is said to evolve itself into manifold objects, endure for a certain length of time, and again dissolve itself into its original matter. Furthermore, Prakriti evolves and devolves itself differently for different individuals according to their respective moral and spiritual development. Evolution is, therefore, the manifestation of the cause as the effect.

Although Prakriti is the original cause of evolution, being unconscious and devoid of intelligence, it cannot evolve by itself. It evolves into the world of plurality and diversity only when it comes into contact with the Purusha. The proximity of the Purusha activates Prakriti with consciousness and intelligence just as contact with an electric current causes a piece of iron to become electrically charged.

THE MEANING OF GOD

According to Samkhya and Patanjali's raja-yoga, there is no absolute creator known as God, since there is no act of creation.

Samkhya rejects the idea of God, because an eternal and immutable being cannot be the cause of the world of matter. The unchanging can never cause change.

Yet there are some commentators on Samkhya who believe in God the eternally perfect spirit, or witness consciousness of the universe, whose presence causes Prakriti to evolve and devolve, but they do not believe in God the creator. According to Patanjali, God is the supreme teacher of yoga. In God, knowledge is unlimited; in individual Purushas, it is limited. The vehicle of God's manifestation, according to Patanjali, is the word *Om* (or *Aum*). By meditating on the meaning of Om, one attains knowledge of the Purusha. Describing the meaning of Om, Sri Ramakrishna says:

> You explain "Aum" with reference to "a," "u," and "m"* only....
> But I give the illustration of the sound of a gong: "tom," t-o-m.
> It is the merging of the Lila in the Nitya [the relative in the
> Absolute]: the gross, the subtle, and the causal merge in the
> Great Cause; waking, dream, and deep sleep merge in Turiya.
> The striking of the gong is like the falling of a heavy weight
> into a big ocean. Waves begin to rise: the Relative rises from
> the Absolute; the causal, subtle, and gross bodies appear out
> of the Great Cause; from Turiya emerge the states of deep
> sleep, dream and waking. These waves arising from the Great
> Ocean merge again in the Great Ocean. From the Absolute to
> the Relative, and from the Relative to the Absolute.[1]

The concepts of Purusha and Prakriti in the Samkhya system are similar to, but also in many ways different from the concepts of Brahman, Atman, and maya in jnana-yoga (see chapter 19). The Atman, or Self, of jnana-yoga is one without a second, immutable, all-pervading, absolute Pure Consciousness, and also the common Self of all beings and things. This Atman or Brahman, though one without a second, appears as the manifold universe due to its inscrutable power, maya. Maya, which gives rise to the world of

---

* *A, u,* and *m* signify the processes of creation, preservation, and destruction.

multiplicity and change, has no reality outside the mind, which is a product of ignorance. The world of maya is an illusory superimposition on the Self, like a mirage in the desert. True liberation, according to jnana-yoga, is total absorption and union with the immutable and all-pervading Self. It is a complete unity, like the merging of a drop of water in the ocean. The Samkhya system, however, argues against these presuppositions of jnana-yoga on the following grounds:

- The indwelling Purusha, although immortal and incorporeal, is not one without a second. Purushas are many in number and each individual represents a Purusha.

- One's birth and death, inner disposition, physical form, and so forth, are different for each individual, and this presupposes that Purushas are many.

- Prakriti is constituted by the three *gunas*. If there is only one Purusha, then all individuals would be endowed with the same proportion and variety of *guna* components and all would have the same disposition of mind.

- If there is one Purusha or Self for all living beings, then the liberation of one being would be the liberation of all beings.

- The concept of one Purusha—one without a second—of all beings cannot account for the diversities or pluralities of individual intellects, egos, and minds.

- According to jnana-yoga, all that is not-Self—including the intellect and mind—is a mere illusory superimposition and, therefore, the individual personality or ego is also illusory. But Prakriti is not illusory or unreal, nor is the ego or the intellect of the knower of Prakriti.

- The maya of jnana-yoga is inscrutable. It is neither real nor unreal but a fact. Maya also has an end with regard to the soul attaining liberation. But Prakriti is both beginningless and endless. It does not become nonexistent for a soul who attains to liberation; it only ceases to evolve for that soul.

• While the influence of Prakriti ceases for one who is liberated, it continues to evolve for other Purushas still in bondage.

According to the Samkhya and Yoga systems, the reality of Prakriti exists outside our mental experiences and stands before us by its own power. The beings and things of the external world remain the same even though different persons feel differently about them. No two persons see the same object in the same way, nor do they have the same reaction to it. The external world of Prakriti cannot, therefore, owe its origin to our imagination but must exist independently of our feelings and perceptions of it.

BONDAGE AND LIBERATION

The bondage of the Purusha, according to Patanjali, is due to indiscrimination *(aviveka)*. Such bondage generates the five kinds of misery: ignorance, egotism, attachment, aversion, and clinging to life. The Purusha suffers from this fivefold bondage due to its mistaken identification with the components of Prakriti, especially the intellect, ego, and mind. Taking the modifications of these three to be its own, the Purusha is bound to experience suffering and transmigration.

Liberation of the Purusha is freedom from Prakriti. It is the state of *kaivalya,* where Purusha shines in its own light. The means to attain this state, according to Patanjali, is yoga.

Yoga begins with a sense of disillusionment about Prakriti; the individual realizes that most of the experiences of the world are sorrowful and that moments of happiness are inevitably followed by sorrow. A person feels sorrowful while seeking pleasure, because of the pain of separation from the desired object; again, a person feels sorrowful even after getting the object for fear of losing it. The pleasures of life only accentuate the experiences of sorrow. There is no striving for liberation, according to raja-yoga, until a person is convinced of this mysterious truth that no pleasure, worldly or heavenly, can put an end to the cause of sorrow— not even death. In search of fulfilling these desires, a person is reborn on earth again and again.

Raja-yoga pointedly reminds an aspirant of the extensive nature of sorrow, the root cause of sorrow, the decisive way to uproot the cause of sorrow, and the way to freedom. The state of liberation is not a state of bliss, because all notions of experience and experiencer belong to the realm of Prakriti. Liberation is freedom from all experiences, and the way to liberation is through the practice of discriminative knowledge (*vivekakhyati*). With the dawning of discriminative knowledge, the Purusha realizes its separateness from Prakriti. Devoid of the Purusha's light, Prakriti drops off from the Purusha and falls to the ground, never to rise again.

In this regard, raja-yoga is a system of conscious, intense, and decisive living. It is compressing many cycles of birth and death into one and undergoing all possible experiences in this very life.

The goal of raja-yoga is Self-realization attained in *samadhi*. *Samadhi* is a prolonged state of meditation. As meditation becomes absorbing, the meditator, the object of meditation, and the process of meditation begin to converge, and the mind enters the first stage of *samadhi*, known as *samprajnata samadhi*, where the meditator still remains conscious of the object of meditation.

Prolongation of *samprajnata samadhi* culminates in the second stage, *asamprajnata samadhi*. It is the state of absolute transcendence. Whereas the state of meditation is intensely active, with the rising of thought-waves reminiscent of the object of meditation, *asamprajnata samadhi* is neither passive nor active. In this state, all thought-waves—good or bad, with their potencies (*samskaras*)—are completely destroyed. The state of ignorance is a flaming fire fed by the fuel of countless desires; the state of meditation is also a burning fire, but restricted to a particular kind of fuel—that is to say, the desire for liberation; and the state of *asamprajnata samadhi,* or final liberation, is like the glowing fire that has consumed all its fuel. Swami Vivekananda describes the nature of *asamprajnata samadhi*:

> In a concentration where there is consciousness, where the mind succeeds only in quelling the waves in the chitta and holding them down, the waves remain in the form of tendencies. These tendencies, or seeds, become waves again when the opportunity comes. But when you have destroyed all these tendencies, almost destroyed the mind, then the samadhi becomes seedless; there are no more seeds in the mind out of which to manufacture again and again this plant of life, this ceaseless round of birth and death.
>
> You may ask what that state would be in which there is no mind, no knowledge. What we call knowledge is a lower state than the one beyond knowledge. You must always bear in mind that the extremes look very much alike. If a very low vibration of ether is taken as darkness, and an intermediate state as light, a very high vibration will be darkness again. Similarly, ignorance is the lowest state, knowledge is the middle state, and beyond knowledge is the highest state; the two extremes seem the same. Knowledge itself is a manufactured something, a combination; it is not Reality.[2]

Patanjali describes final liberation as the complete cessation of the modifications of *chitta* (the mind and mind-stuff). The *chitta* acts as the storehouse of all of our past memories. The Purusha mistakenly looks upon its reflection in the *chitta* as its own self, becomes identified with it, and consequently undergoes suffering.

The *chitta* is compared to a lake constantly troubled by countless waves and ripples, by the agitating force of sense perceptions. The bottom of the lake, which is compared to the Self, remains unperceived because of the waves and ripples on the surface. These waves are called *vrittis,* or thought-waves of the mind; countless sense perceptions are like pebbles thrown into the lake creating countless waves. When a wave subsides, however, it is never altogether lost. It resides in the *chitta* in a potential form as a *samskara,* or a deep-seated tendency developed by our repeated habits. These potential thought-forces, or *samskaras,* manifest themselves into thought-waves whenever they meet with favorable circumstances. Each thought-wave creates a *samskara,* which intensifies similar thought-waves. It is a vicious circle of thoughts depositing *samskaras,* which again manifest into thoughts. Each such repetition of a thought makes the *samskara* stronger. The inherent tendency of the *chitta* is to preserve its natural calmness, but it remains disturbed because of the outward tendencies of the senses. As soon as the waves stop, the lake becomes calm and the bottom of the lake becomes visible. So it is with the mind: when it becomes calm and free from the disturbances of all thought-waves, the presence of the Purusha, the indwelling Self, becomes evident.

The complete cessation of the modifications of the *chitta* involves not merely the cessation of thought-waves but also of their potencies or *samskaras.* Such cessation is generally achieved by first weakening the *samskaras,* then overcoming them, and finally destroying them. All thought-waves, Patanjali points out, come under two categories: *klista,* or painful, and *aklista,* or non-painful. A painful thought-wave dies down or passes into another thought-wave, leaving a deposit of darkness on the mind, thereby adding to our bondage and suffering. The deposits of *samskara* left by a non-painful thought-wave bring light to the darkness of the mind and lead us to the knowledge of the Purusha; therefore, all non-painful thought-waves reduce the causes of bondage and suffering. A lustful thought-wave, for example, is considered painful because it creates either restlessness *(rajas)* or darkness *(tamas)* in the mind. A compassionate thought-wave is non-painful because it creates tranquility *(sattva)* and adds to the steadiness of the mind.

The technique for eradicating unfavorable thoughts is the deliberate cultivation of favorable thoughts. *Samskaras* are overcome only by counter-*samskaras*. Bad thoughts are subdued only by good thoughts.

All one's *samskaras* taken together constitute one's personality. A person's character is shaped only by his or her habits. A person often becomes addicted to particular actions, which become habitual and impel that person to act and react in a certain way. But we need not become victims of ourselves. Habits constitute the whole nature of the individual, and as Swami Vivekananda says:

> That gives us consolation; for if it is only habit, we can make and unmake it at any time. The samskaras are left by these vibrations, which pass out of our mind, each one of them leaving its result. Our character is the sum total of these impressions, and according as a particular wave prevails one takes that tone. If good prevails, one becomes good; if wickedness, one becomes wicked; if joyfulness, one becomes happy. The only remedy for bad habits is counter-habits; all the bad habits that have left their impressions are to be controlled by good habits. Go on doing good, thinking holy thoughts, continuously; that is the only way to suppress base impressions. Never say any man is hopeless, because he only represents a character, a bundle of habits, which can be checked by new and better ones. Character is repeated habits, and repeated habits alone can reform character.[3]

Meditation is the practice of deliberately concentrating on one supremely good thought, which in time naturally creates a huge wave of that thought in the mind and drowns all the other *samskaras* of bad thoughts dormant in the mind. Swami Vivekananda says:

What is the result of constant practice of this higher concentration? All old tendencies of restlessness and dullness will be destroyed, as well as the tendencies of goodness too. The case is similar to that of the chemicals used to take the dross from gold ore. When the ore is smelted, the dross is burnt along with the chemicals. So this constant controlling power will destroy the previous bad tendencies, and eventually the good ones also. Those good and evil tendencies will destroy each other, leaving alone the Soul in Its own splendour, untrammeled by either good or bad, omnipresent, omnipotent, and omniscient.[4]

It has often been asked, If we are the products of our past tendencies or *samskaras,* are we not merely victims of fate? Isn't the doctrine of *samskaras* fatalistic? What is our incentive, then, to change our habits?

Patanjali reminds us that there are two tendencies in every individual that operate simultaneously: one is the will to attachment and the other is the will to freedom. Intense longing for liberation is the victory of the latter over the former, accomplished through conscious, persistent, and prolonged efforts in counteracting our past bad habits. The will to freedom, according to Patanjali, is natural in every individual; the will to attachment is a kind of perversion. The goal of raja-yoga is to cultivate and strengthen this will to freedom by the conscious practice of yoga.

The state of *kaivalya,* or final liberation, results from perfect knowledge, and the keynote of perfect knowledge is perfect nonattachment. Perfect nonattachment is attained through undeviating practice of the eight-limbed yoga, which is the principal contribution of raja-yoga. The practice of raja-yoga is impossible unless one practices the spirit of nonattachment. In this context, Patanjali stresses three vital points: (1) practice must be steady and continuous; (2) practice must be uninterrupted; and (3) practice must be conducted with undaunted enthusiasm and devotion.

Progress toward the goal of yoga is measured by the degree of the seeker's nonattachment, which, according to raja-yoga, has four stages: *yatamana, vyatireka, ekendriya,* and *vasikara.*

In the *yatamana* stage, the seeker first develops distaste for sense pleasures and their enjoyment and begins to recoil from them; in the *vyatireka* stage, the seeker struggles to conquer and subdue the senses and their outgoing habits; in the *ekendriya* stage, the seeker is able to conquer the desire for the objects of enjoyment but not, as yet, the subtle longing for them; and, finally, in the *vasikara* stage, the seeker is able to overcome the root longing for sense enjoyment, feeling no attraction or aversion toward objects of enjoyment—gross or subtle—especially when perceiving them.

SUCCESS IN THE PATH OF RAJA-YOGA

Success in the path of raja-yoga depends solely on the sincerity and will of the seeker. The teachings of raja-yoga shun all supernaturalism and false optimism. The state of superconsciousness is attained by conscious endeavor supported by a determined will. The attainments at different stages of progress in this path appear supernatural only to those who lack faith in themselves and in the possibilities of human endeavor. The final stage in yoga is knowing that knowledge comes from within one's own Self and not from the outside world. In the words of Swami Vivekananda:

> After long searches here and there, in temples and in churches, on earth and in heaven, at last you come back to your own soul, completing the circle from where you started, and find that He whom you have been seeking all over the world, for whom you have been weeping and praying in churches and temples, on whom you were looking as the mystery of all mysteries, shrouded in the clouds, is the nearest of the near, is your own Self, the reality of your life, body, and soul. That Self is your own nature.[5]

In the path of raja-yoga, a seeker is required to have faith, willpower, sharp memory, and discriminating intellect. Faith is the firm conviction about the path and its goal. The difference between beginners and adepts in yoga is the degree of their spiritual conviction. Seekers on the path of raja-yoga must have unshakable faith in their inner spiritual potentiality, the effectiveness of the teaching, reality of the goal, and guidance of the teacher. They must be ready to persevere in their endeavor up to the very end.

Seekers are also required to have indomitable will that refuses to give in, accept defeat, or retreat. Inspired by such will, they should be ready to die on the path of yoga rather than give up their practice.

A spiritual memory helps seekers avoid many roadblocks that are common on the path of yoga. Life is short and the obstacles many. Seekers, therefore, must hasten their steps to reach the goal by any and all means. They cannot afford to waste a single moment of their lives in depression or frustration. They must continue their practice in the face of all obstacles.

The path of raja-yoga is a tremendous spiritual adventure. It is dealing with one's own mind and its countless thoughts, memories, volitions, emotions, habits, and tendencies. Seekers are to remain firmly anchored in their discrimination and not be swept away by distractions of their own minds. Discrimination will enable them to distinguish the real from the unreal and help them maintain a high intensity of spiritual longing, purity of character, and loyalty to yoga.

15

Preparatory Practices in Raja-Yoga

Unless the mind becomes steady there cannot be yoga.
It is the wind of worldliness that always disturbs the
mind, which may be likened to a candle flame. If that
flame doesn't flicker at all, then one is said to have
attained yoga.

—SRI RAMAKRISHNA

The practice of raja-yoga is a twofold process: (1) to discard the small and egotistic old self and, at the same time, (2) to recognize and grow into one's new Self. The practice of raja-yoga completely transforms an aspirant's life. Yoga is not possible for the halfhearted, curious, or casual. It requires changing oneself entirely by changing one's aspirations, thoughts, habits, and tendencies through persistent and conscious self-effort. Swami Vivekananda says:

> Those who really want to be yogis must give up, once for all, this nibbling at things. Take up one idea; make that idea your life. Think of it, dream of it, live on that idea. Let the brain, muscles, nerves, every part of your body, be full of that idea, and just leave all other ideas alone. This is the way to success and

this is the way great spiritual giants are produced. Others are mere talking-machines. If we really want to be blessed and make others blessed, we must go deeper.[1]

The principal practice in this path is that of concentration and meditation. The average mind, accustomed to dwell on varieties of external objects, finds it extremely difficult to concentrate on a single thought for more than a few moments. It has become pampered and restless. Many people have allowed themselves to become slaves of their own minds. There are some aspirants who become fascinated with the teachings of raja-yoga and begin practicing it without making the necessary preparations. Eventually, however, they find it too hard to stay on the path, and give up.

To prepare for the eight-limbed practice of raja-yoga, aspirants are guided to begin with the three foundational disciplines of kriya-yoga: austerity, study, and surrendering the results of one's work to God.

AUSTERITY

The Sanskrit word for austerity is *tapas,* which literally means "heating." As gold becomes purified in fire, our psychophysical system becomes purified in the fire of austerity. Austerity is not mortification or self-torture. It is not mere abstinence. Austerity is the practice of self-control for the sake of the realization of the truth. Love for truth in raja-yoga is measured by the amount of self-sacrifice made for its sake. The sufferings of life in themselves are degrading and degenerating, but when a person voluntarily undergoes suffering for the sake of a spiritual goal, such endurance is *tapas,* or austerity. Practice of austerity generates strength of mind and moderation in one's habits. *Tapas* is the only means to Self-realization, which puts an end to all suffering.

The Bhagavad Gita speaks of austerities of the body, of speech, and of the mind:

Worship of the gods, of the twice-born, of teachers, and of the wise; cleanliness, uprightness, continence, and non-violence—these are said to be the austerity of the body.

Words that do not give offence and that are truthful, pleasant, and beneficial, and also the regular recitation of the Vedas—these are said to be the austerity of speech.

Serenity of mind, gentleness, silence, self-control, and purity of heart—these constitute the austerity of the mind.[2]

Through these three austerities, aspirants seek to unify their thoughts, words, and deeds. In addition to the above, austerity of the body also includes cultivation of reverence for holy persons and service to them. These practices generate an ennobling love in the hearts of aspirants.

Austerity of speech is vital for the practice of raja-yoga. Restlessness of mind manifests itself in the restlessness of body and of speech. But control of speech is not just forced silence. It is eliminating inner restlessness and empty noise. There are many who cannot remain still or quiet even for one moment. They seek conversation, controversy, and argument. They chat with everyone they meet, and when alone, they continue a monologue within their own mind—and sometimes aloud. There is no greater distraction in the path of yoga than idle controversy and impulsive speech. Aspirants, in order to control their speech, are advised to talk only of spiritual matters, be measured in their speech, and regular in their vow of silence.

Austerity of the mind is essentially the practice of controlling the outward tendencies of the sense organs. It is focusing and concentrating one's mind on the chosen object of meditation by reducing stray thoughts that distract the mind for no purpose.

The keynote of austerity is the subordination of all our aspirations, activities, thoughts, and habits to the realization of the goal. Austerity is the very foundation of yoga. According to the

Katha Upanishad, the secret of the Self cannot be mastered by one who is devoid of austerity; nor can it be taught by one who is without austerity.[3]

STUDY

Study in the path of raja-yoga indicates reading and hearing texts that encourage control of the mind and knowledge of the Self. The purpose of study is to intensify the aspirant's conviction in the rewards of yoga.

Spiritual study also includes the practice of *japa. Japa* keeps the mind occupied with one spiritual thought and replaces the mind's brooding on objects of gross enjoyment.

SURRENDERING THE RESULTS OF ACTION

The third aspect of kriya-yoga is surrendering the fruits of one's work to God. The aspirant must practice devotion to God to become selfless and egoless. All spiritual practices are to be performed as sacred offerings at the altar of truth.

Knowledge of Ultimate Reality cannot be attained by mere austerity or spiritual practice. An aspirant must exert all available efforts in the path of yoga and then offer them all in the fire of the Supreme Self.

16
The Eight-Limbed Practice

*This Atman, resplendent and pure, whom the sinless
sannyasins behold residing within the body, is
attained by unceasing practice of truthfulness,
austerity, right knowledge, and continence.*
—MUNDAKA UPANISHAD 3.1.5

The eight limbs of raja-yoga are *yama* (five abstentions), *niyama* (five observances), *asana* (posture), *pranayama* (control of breath), *pratyahara* (withdrawal of the mind), *dharana* (concentration), *dhyana* (meditation), and *samadhi* (absorption in the Self). Of the eight, the first five limbs are external practices *(bahiranga)* and the last three internal *(antaranga)*.

YAMA

Yama constitutes the following five practices: *satya* (truthfulness), ahimsa (nonviolence), *asteya* (abstention from stealing), *brahmacharya* (continence), and *aparigraha* (non-covetousness).

Satya is the practice of truthfulness in our thoughts, speech, and actions. There should be absolutely no compromise in this respect. Sri Ramakrishna says, "If a man clings tenaciously to truth he ultimately realizes God. Without this regard for truth, one gradually loses everything."[1] Falsehood cannot be justified even if it is meant for a good purpose. According to raja-yoga, any deviation from truth, no matter to what extent or for what purpose, is a deviation from yoga. The aspirant is advised to remain steadfast in the practice of truthfulness at the sacrifice of everything.

But truthfulness is not just being literally true. One should speak truthfully without causing pain or injury to any other being, for the motive of truthfulness must be the welfare of all beings. One should not unnecessarily speak the unpleasant truth or cause harm to others by speech or action—or even thought. One should rather remain silent. In order to practice truthfulness, an aspirant should avoid controversies and arguments, speak only when necessary, and otherwise maintain silence, keeping occupied in thoughts that are conducive to the realization of the goal. An unrestrained tongue is evidence of a restless mind.

Ahimsa is nonviolence in thought, word, and deed. An aspirant must not directly or indirectly injure any living being. Even if a person induces others to violence, grants consent to, or merely condones violence, he or she is far from ahimsa. An aspirant must cultivate love, compassion, and reverence for all living beings.

There are certain practical limitations of ahimsa. No one can live without being the cause of some injury to others. Our food is procured by causing injury to many other living beings; even drinking a glass of water involves harm to millions of microbes we do not perceive. Despite such limitations, an aspirant should never consciously or deliberately injure anything. The test of perfect nonviolence is said to be the absence of jealousy. As long as jealousy remains in one's heart, one cannot become established in nonviolence. In the presence of a yogi who is established in perfect nonviolence, all creatures give up their violence and become peaceful.

Asteya is the practice of non-appropriation of anything that belongs to another person—whether it is a material object, a privilege, or an opportunity. Misappropriation is taking something that does not belong to one or that has not been duly given to one. An aspirant must scrupulously desist from such misappropriation and acquisitiveness. All the wealth of nature comes to the yogi who is established in the practice of *asteya*. As Swami Vivekananda points out, nature does not care to serve one who is a slave of desires.[2]

Brahmacharya is the practice of continence, the most important of all virtues. No one can succeed in the path of any yoga without being established in this virtue. The practice of *brahmacharya* has a negative aspect and a positive one. Negatively, *brahmacharya* requires abstention from unchastity, both physical and mental. An unchaste imagination or desire is equivalent to an unchaste act. An aspirant is required to abstain in every possible way from all unchaste indulgences—gross or subtle, direct or indirect. The sense organs should be withdrawn from everything unchaste, immoral, and impure. Such withdrawal is never possible unless the aspirant is devoted to the positive practice of "dwelling on Brahman," which is the literal meaning of the Sanskrit word *brahmacharya*. The positive aspect is dwelling on purity and truth. The orthodox view is that the vow of *brahmacharya* cannot be maintained without being a *japaka*, or one adept in *japa*. If the aspirant continually contemplates God and develops a liking for repeating God's name, the desires for gross pleasures will naturally become less and less enjoyable until they become utterly repulsive in comparison to the bliss of repeating God's name.

The twofold process of "withdrawing from" and at the same time "dwelling on" applies to all the other practices of *yama* as well. Any of these practices is bound to become inhibitive unless motivated by a spiritual goal. When the mind is not spiritually inspired and the aspirant is casual in yoga, the restraints of *yama* prove to be blind, mechanical, and futile, if not utterly destructive.

Steadfastness in *brahmacharya* endows aspirants with physical, mental, and spiritual vigor. They develop good health, mastery over their senses, and steady concentration of mind. *Brahmacharya* has no alternative or substitute. The door to the inner recess of the heart never opens to aspirants who are not established in this practice.

The practice of *brahmacharya* is considered indispensable in any of the paths of yoga but is the most vital prerequisite for an aspirant following the path of raja-yoga. Swami Vivekananda writes on the meaning and significance of *brahmacharya* in raja-yoga:

> The yogis claim that, of all the energies that are in the human body, the highest is what they call ojas. Now, this ojas is stored up in the brain, and the more ojas a man has, the more powerful he is, the more intellectual, the more spiritually strong. One man may express beautiful thoughts in beautiful language, but cannot impress people. Another man may not be able to give beautiful expression to his thoughts, yet his words charm; every movement of his is powerful. That is the power of ojas.
>
> Now, in every man there is stored up more or less of this ojas. The highest form of all the forces that are working in the body is ojas. You must remember that it is only a question of transformation of one force into another. The same force which is working outside as electricity or magnetism will be changed into inner force; the same force that is working as muscular energy will be changed into ojas. The yogis say that the part of the human energy which is expressed through sexual action and sexual thought, when checked and controlled, easily becomes changed into ojas; and since the Muladhara [the lowest center of consciousness] guides these, the yogi pays particular attention to that center. He tries to convert all his sexual energy into ojas. It is only the chaste man or woman who can create ojas and store it in the brain; that is why chastity has always been considered the highest virtue. A man feels that if he is unchaste, his spirituality goes away; he loses mental vigour and moral stamina. That is why, in all the religious orders in the world which have produced spiritual giants,

you will always find absolute chastity insisted upon. That is why there came into existence monks, who gave up marriage. There must be perfect chastity in thought, word, and deed. Without it the practice of raja-yoga is dangerous and may lead to insanity.[3]

Steadfastness in *brahmacharya* is especially necessary for a spiritual teacher. Spiritual teaching is not the mere intellectual elaboration of dogma. It is the transmission of truth from the teacher to the aspirant, and such transmission is possible only through the power of *brahmacharya* by a teacher who has controlled all gross desires and actions.

The fifth aspect of the practice of *yama* is *aparigraha,* or non-covetousness. An aspirant must be free from all acquisitiveness. *Aparigraha* literally means abstaining from receiving gifts or favors. The psychology behind this injunction is that a gift is often given with selfish motives. The acceptance of such gifts then binds the receiver with a sense of obligation. The receiver becomes exposed to and contaminated by the thoughts and desires of the giver. The receiver may then lose his or her sense of freedom.

Steadfastness in *aparigraha* is achieved when aspirants not only do not receive gifts or favors but no longer plan for the future. The more they develop non-covetousness toward physical comforts and pleasures, the more they become free from the idea of embodiment itself.

NIYAMA

Niyama constitutes the following five observances: *soucha* (internal and external cleanliness), *santosha* (contentment), *tapas* (austerity), *svadhyaya* (study of the sacred texts), and *iswara-pranidhana* (worship of God).

Soucha is cleanliness of the mind and the body. External cleanliness is keeping the body clean by such processes as bathing in water and performing ceremonial ablutions. But the raja-yogi cannot feel fully pure until the mind is pure. Internal *soucha* is cleansing the mind of such thoughts as jealousy, hatred, egotism, and attachment by cultivating counter-thoughts of purity, renunciation, humility, and devotion to God.

The keynote of inner cleanliness is eliminating the elements of inertia *(tamas)* and restlessness *(rajas)* from the mind with the help of tranquility *(sattva)*. Such tranquility must be physical as well as mental. The psychology behind *soucha* is that it endows the seeker with a spirit of non-dependence on the external world and a spirit of faith in himself or herself. Cleanliness, when adhered to both externally and internally, endows one with a feeling of purity that brings in its wake a sense of aversion for one's own body and a disinclination to come into physical contact with others.

Santosha is contentment. To achieve *santosha*, a seeker must not only give up the fulfillment of desires but the desires themselves, reducing the necessities of life to a minimum. *Santosha* is remaining satisfied with few material necessities procured without great effort and decreasing our desires to meet only those needs that are conducive to self-control. True contentment is found in detaching oneself from the sufferings caused by Prakriti and attaching oneself to the purity of Purusha. The perfect yogi entertains only one thought in meditation, renouncing all distracting thoughts and temptations.

The *Srimad Bhagavatam* tells the story of a wandering ascetic who derived a great lesson from observing a crow. One day, this crow sitting on a tree felt hungry and saw a piece of meat down below on the ground. It swiftly dove down, grabbed the piece of meat in its beak, and flew away. But as soon as it flew away, hundreds of other crows began to fly after it. The crow could not understand why all the crows were chasing it. It flew from one tree to another, thinking that if it could only find a suitable, peaceful place, the other crows would leave it alone. But this change of place did not eliminate the crow's cause of worry and misery.

The other crows still pursued it. It flew high and low, north and south, fast and slow, through city streets and dense forests—but the other crows pursued it all the same. Finally, feeling tired and sick, it perched on a branch and the piece of meat accidentally fell from its beak. Immediately the hundreds of other crows flew toward the piece of meat. The crow was left in peace. This incident served as a great revelation to the wandering ascetic, and he understood that one becomes established in contentment only by giving up desire itself. By being established in *santosha*, the seeker achieves supreme happiness.

Tapas, as previously discussed in the context of kriya-yoga, is the capacity and willingness to cheerfully endure the pairs of opposites in life, such as pain and pleasure, happiness and misery, heat and cold, and all physical and mental sufferings that are a part of our everyday lives. *Tapas* is not suffering for the sake of suffering but suffering for the sake of yoga, or the realization of one's goal. Instead of becoming frustrated, angry, or depressed, the raja-yogi faces the harsh realities of life with calmness. Controlling the palate, minimizing personal needs, reducing the hours of sleep, sacrificing luxuries, vowing silence, engaging in selfless activity, seeking solitude, and devoting time to spiritual practices—these are some of the practices of *tapas*. *Tapas* is essentially reducing one's ego and desires and has been compared to a fire that burns to ashes the harmful habits we have cultivated by reckless living.

Svadyaya is the study of sacred texts to develop devotion and concentration. *Svadyaya* also includes repetition of a sacred word, or mantra, by which the yogi purifies the body and mind. Repetition of the mantra is considered the most purifying preparatory practice for concentration and meditation in yoga. The companion practice of *iswarapranidhana,* or worship of the Lord, also allows a seeker to grow in devotion and concentration on the Chosen Ideal and the Self.

ASANA

Asana is the practice of right posture. Posture that is steady and restful is conducive for concentration and meditation. The follower of meditation is advised to sit erect, holding the back, neck, and head in a straight line. The entire weight of the upper body should rest on the ribs. With the chest out, one finds it easy to concentrate.

In his *Yoga Aphorisms*, Patanjali points out the way to achieve firmness of posture: "Through the lessening of the natural tendency [for activity, caused by identification with the body] and through meditation on the Infinite, [posture becomes firm and pleasant]." Commenting on the meaning of this aphorism, Swami Vivekananda says, "We can make the posture firm by thinking of the Infinite. We cannot actually think of the transcendental Infinite, but we can think of the infinite sky." The next aphorism of Patanjali says, "Posture being conquered, the dualities do not obstruct."[4] That is to say, when posture is conquered, the seeker overcomes all dualities, such as good and bad, heat and cold, pain and pleasure, and various other pairs of opposites.

PRANAYAMA

Pranayama is a proven way to control the restless mind and invoke the right mood for concentration. Generally speaking, *pranayama* is the control and regulation of the breathing process, through which the seeker strives to mobilize and stabilize the vital force within. According to Swami Vivekananda:

> These various breathing exercises are a great help in regulating the different parts of the body. All the different parts are inundated with breath. It is through breath that we gain control of them all. Disharmony in parts of the body is controlled by more flow of the nerve currents towards them.... People who work with their brains are the longest-lived people.... Do

not burn the lamp quickly. Let it burn slowly and gently....
Every anxiety, every violent exercise—physical and mental—
[means] you are burning the lamp.[5]

Raja-yoga says that breathing is the clearest indicator of the actual condition of the mind and that restlessness of the mind is reflected in our breathing. If we become excited, angry, fearful, depressed, or passionate, we notice that our breathing becomes rapid, shallow, and irregular. At these times, raja-yoga says, our breath generally flows through only one nostril. On the other hand, when the mind is calm, collected, and controlled, our breathing is steady and light. At such times, our breath naturally flows through both nostrils. When the mind is calm, our breathing is calm; when the mind is restless, our breathing is restless. *Pranayama* seeks to make the mind tranquil by controlling and regulating our breathing.

In a deeper and truer sense, *pranayama* is more than regulation of our breath. The Sanskrit word *pranayama* is a compound word: *prana* means the vital force, and *ayama* indicates restraint. *Prana* is therefore not just breath: the *prana* in each of us is a manifestation of the cosmic life force. And our breath is the gross manifestation of *prana*, which is subtle, ever awake, and ever active in us.

Pranayama forms an important part of raja-yoga for controlling the mind and awakening our spiritual consciousness. Proper *pranayama* is a cessation of breath for a specified period of time between inhalation and exhalation. When the air is retained within after inhalation, this is one form of *pranayama*. If the breath is held after exhalation of air, this is the complementary form of *pranayama*. It is the retention of breath (*kumbhaka*)—following either inhalation (*puraka*) or exhalation (*rechaka*)—that constitutes *pranayama*.

Kumbhaka is of three kinds: retaining the breath inside the lungs; keeping the breath outside; and gradually stopping the breath. *Kumbhaka* is the most essential component of *pranayama*. Since it involves stopping and regulating the breath, there are many dangers and risks in its practice and should, therefore, be learned from an illumined teacher.

There are many other risks in the practice of *pranayama*. *Pranayama* forcibly rouses the unconscious mind. Unless the seeker is already established in the practice of moral purity, *pranayama* may produce a violent reaction from the mind and create confusion instead of tranquility. There are many latent non-spiritual tendencies in us. When forced up to the conscious level, they may destroy our spiritual practice, and if we are not established in self-control, we may be unable to restrain such powerful tendencies. *Pranayama* can awaken not only the angels in us but also the devils.

Conditions essential for the success of *pranayama* are often ignored. Excited by the promises of *pranayama,* many forget that it is the mind that controls the body—control of the body can never guarantee control of the mind. Raja-yoga specifically warns that *pranayama* should never be practiced without the observance of *brahmacharya*. Seekers may become preoccupied with the physical benefits of the practice of *pranayama* and forget its supreme goal of transcending body-consciousness in order to contact the pure Self within. *Pranayama* can also open the door to the untimely experience of occult phenomena, the lure of which may lead the seeker off the path of yoga.

There is an element of fascination about the practice of *pranayama*. It is sometimes considered a quick and easy means of attaining the spiritual goal, a form of mechanical spirituality. But raja-yoga is not a mechanical means to attain Self-realization. Those who resort to the practice of *pranayama* without having genuine spiritual longing only harm themselves. Shankaracharya says:

> The conviction of the Truth is seen to proceed from reasoning
> upon the salutary counsel of the wise, and not by bathing

in the sacred waters, nor by gifts, nor by a hundred
Pranayamas.[6]

Spiritual longing cannot be generated by mere rhythmic breathing. The mind can refuse to yield to such mechanical exercises.
This is why *pranayama* should be practiced within the context of
the other seven limbs of raja-yoga. Unless there is a strong spiritual motivation for this upward journey, the awakened spiritual
consciousness (kundalini) has every chance of falling; and when
it falls, it falls fast and violently down to the lowest depths of the
unconscious. Once awakened, the kundalini must be led upward.

Six Centers of Spiritual Consciousness

In symbolic language, the Yoga system speaks of the six centers of
consciousness. The awakened kundalini rises and passes through
six centers of consciousness located in the vicinity of the spinal
column, where there are three subtle nerve channels known as
ida, pingala, and *sushumna.* The *sushumna,* the central and most important nerve channel, is, as it were, inside the spinal cord; *ida* is
to the left of the *sushumna;* and *pingala* is to its right. The centers
of consciousness are arranged in the form of figure eights placed
horizontally one on top of the other, and the three nerve channels
have their meeting point near the base of the spine.

The *sushumna* channel begins at the lower extremity of the
spine, runs up along the spine itself, and extends to the top of the
head. Contained within the *sushumna* channel are the six centers
of consciousness, described as six lotuses. For ordinary persons,
the *sushumna* channel remains closed at the bottom, and the
petals of each lotus are hanging down.

According to Yoga, these six centers and lotuses range from
the lowest plane of gross impulses to the highest plane of pure
bliss. The first center is called *muladhara* (root support). Located
at the base of the spine, it has four petals and manifests the earth

aspect of matter, governs gross physical urges, and controls the sense of smell. Dwelling on this level of consciousness, a human individual is guided by gross, subconscious desires.

The second center is called *svadhisthana* (own abode). It is located at the base of the organ of generation and has six petals. This center manifests the water aspect of matter, governs the sense of taste, and controls the sense organ of the palate. Remaining at this center, an individual is constantly swayed by gross impulses, imaginations, and animal propensities.

The third center is known as *manipura* (city of jewels). It is situated in the region of the navel and has ten petals. This center manifests the fire aspect of matter and especially controls the sense of sight. As clouds obstruct the vision of the sun, so do the clouds of gross urges and impulses obstruct the clear vision of truth.

The fourth center, known as *anahata* (unobstructed), is located at the level of the heart and has twelve petals. It manifests the air aspect of matter, governs the perception of touch, and controls the expression of our emotions. This center is characterized by subtle and spiritual experiences, as opposed to gross and material experiences. One distinctive feature of this lotus is that its filaments are tinged with the rays of the sun.

This fourth center is different from the "lotus of the heart," a plane of consciousness described in the Vedas, which is eight-petaled and located below the *anahata*. The lotus of the heart is not a center of consciousness, per se, but an inner recess resembling a lotus with its petals turning upward. This inner recess has been compared to a lotus because many nerve channels *(nadis)* proceed from the heart and spread throughout the body like the rays of the sun. The lotus of the heart, also known as *anandakanda* (root of bliss), is where concentration upon one's Chosen Ideal is usually practiced.

The fifth center of consciousness is called *visuddha* (pure) and is located in the region of the throat with sixteen petals. The fifth center manifests the spatial aspect of matter and influences our perception of sound. Existence at this center is marked by complete purity.

The sixth center is known as *ajna* (command, where the command of the Divine is received). The lotus of this center is situated in the region between the eyebrows and has two petals. The sixth center is the actual seat of the mind and controls all our thoughts and volitions. By reaching this center of consciousness, one attains a vision of truth that is almost absolute in nature. Beyond the six centers there is a plane described in Vedanta as *sahasrara*. It is located at the crown of the head and has a thousand petals. The *sahasrara* is the summit where one's individual consciousness meets with the all-pervading Universal Consciousness.

Through the practice of prayer and meditation, the inner consciousness becomes awakened and gradually travels upward, following the *sushumna* channel from the lowest center *(muladhara)*, through the next five centers, and finally reaching the highest point *(sahasrara)* at the crown of the head. The awakening of the first center activates the memories of our past; the second, gross impulses; and the third, awareness of the sense of individuality. The awakening of the fourth center brings spiritual experiences and visions; the fifth, partial spiritual absorption; and the sixth, deep spiritual absorption, but still with a faint sense of I-consciousness *(savikalpa samadhi)*. At the *sahasrara*, one attains total spiritual absorption *(nirvikalpa samadhi)*.

For most persons, the mind is forced to travel between the three lower centers. At these stages, a person's mind remains immersed in gross pleasures. It constantly broods over the cravings of lust and greed; eating, sleeping, and procreation are its dominant preoccupations. All perception and cognition of the mind at these three centers are influenced by animal propensities.

But when the mind reaches the fourth center, seekers experience spiritual awakening. New vistas open up before them—they see the same world but in its fine and spiritual form; they see light all around and visualize the individual soul as a flame. When their minds reach the fifth center, they want to talk and hear only about God and do not enjoy anything else. Conversations on worldly subjects cause them great pain, and they immediately leave a place where people are talking of these matters. Reaching the sixth center, their minds are taken over by a deep spiritual absorption, not only spontaneous but also continuous. They see the living form of God like a light inside a lantern; they want to touch the form but are unable to do so. Finally, when their minds reach the crown of the head, they attain total absorption. Overcome by the intense inebriation of pure bliss, they lose all outer consciousness. The mind no longer wants to come back to the level of body-consciousness. Only extraordinary souls can come down from that exalted state—and then with great effort.

PRATYAHARA

Pratyahara is preventing the sense organs from becoming identified with their external objects, which cause the mind to become restless. By the practice of *pratyahara,* the outgoing tendencies of the sense organs are brought under control. Swami Hariharananda Aranya explains, "Just as bees follow the course of the queen bee and rest when the latter rests, so when the mind stops the senses also stop their activities."[7]

Swami Vivekananda describes one method of practicing *pratyahara*:

> The first lesson, then, is to sit for some time and let the mind run on. The mind is bubbling up all the time. It is like that monkey jumping about. Let the monkey jump as much as he can; you simply wait and watch. Knowledge is power, says the proverb, and that is true. Until you know what the mind is doing you cannot control it. Give it the rein. Many hideous thoughts may come into it; you will be astonished that it was

possible for you to harbour such thoughts; but you will find that each day the mind's vagaries are becoming less and less violent, that each day it is becoming calmer. In the first few months you will find that the mind has a great many thoughts; later you will find that they have somewhat decreased, and in a few more months they will be fewer and fewer, until at last the mind is under perfect control.[8]

The second method is to control restlessness of the mind and the sense organs by sheer willpower. According to Patanjali, the effect of practicing *pratyahara* is that the sense organs no longer focus outward but inward, and they follow the nature of the mind; "Thence arises supreme control of the organs."[9] Commenting upon *pratyahara*, Swami Vivekananda writes:

He who has succeeded in attaching or detaching his mind to or from the centres [of sense perception] at will has succeeded in pratyahara, which means "gathering towards," checking the outgoing powers of the mind, freeing it from the thraldom of the senses. When we can do this we shall really possess character. Then we shall have taken a long step towards freedom; before that we are mere machines.[10]

THE INTERNAL PRACTICES: DHARANA, DHYANA, SAMADHI

These last three limbs of raja-yoga are internal practices. *Dharana* (concentration) is keeping the mind focused on an object for a certain length of time without interruption. The object may be internal or external. *Dhyana* (meditation) in raja-yoga is effortless and continuous concentration of thought on its object. This itself turns into *samadhi* (absorption) when the object alone shines and the thought of meditation and meditator is lost.[11] *Samadhi* is attained when meditation becomes constant and continuous and the mind merges in the object of meditation.

The process of *dharana, dhyana,* and *samadhi* has several stages. This process has been beautifully explained by Swami Vivekananda in his commentary on the *Yoga Aphorisms* of Patanjali:

> *The samadhi endowed with right knowledge is that which is attended by reasoning, discrimination, bliss, and unqualified ego.*
>
> Samadhi is divided into two kinds: one is called samprajnata, and the other, asamprajnata. In samprajnata samadhi come all the powers of controlling nature. It is of four varieties. The first variety is called savitarka, when the mind meditates upon an object again and again, by isolating it from other objects.... That sort of meditation where the external gross elements are the objects is called savitarka. Vitarka means "question"; savitarka, "with question." This samadhi implies the questioning of the elements, as it were, that they may yield their powers to the man who meditates upon them. There is no liberation in getting powers. It is a search after worldly enjoyments, and there is no real enjoyment in this life. All search for enjoyment is vain; this is the old, old lesson which man finds so hard to learn. When he does learn it, he gets out of the universe and becomes free. The possession of what are called occult powers only intensifies worldliness, and, in the end, intensifies suffering. Though as a scientist Patanjali is bound to point out the possibilities of his science, he never misses an opportunity to warn us against these powers.
>
> Again, in the very same meditation, when one struggles to take the elements out of time and space, and thinks of them as they are, it is called nirvitarka samadhi, "samadhi without question." When the meditation goes a step higher and takes the tanmatras* as its object, and thinks of them as within time and space, it is called savichara samadhi, "samadhi with dis-

---

*The subtle elements of matter.

crimination"; and when in the same meditation one eliminates time and space and thinks of the fine elements as they are, it is called nirvichara samadhi, "samadhi without discrimination."

In the next step the elements, both gross and fine, are given up and the object of meditation is the interior organ, the thinking organ. When the thinking organ is thought of as bereft of the qualities of activity and dullness, then follows the sananda or blissful samadhi. When the mind itself, free from the impurity of rajas and tamas, is the object of meditation, when meditation becomes very ripe and concentrated, when all ideas of the gross and fine materials are given up, when only the sattva state of the ego remains, but differentiated from all other objects, it is called asmita samadhi. Even in this state one does not completely transcend the mind. The man who has attained it is called in the Vedas videha, or "bereft of body." He can think of himself as without his gross body; but he will have to think of himself as having a fine body. Those who in this state get merged in nature without attaining the goal are called prakritilinas; but those who do not stop even here reach the goal, which is freedom.

There is another samadhi, which is attained by constant practice of the cessation of all mental activity, and in which the chitta retains only the unmanifested impressions.

This is the perfect superconscious asamprajnata samadhi, the state which gives us freedom. The first state does not give us freedom, does not liberate the soul. A man may attain all the powers and yet fall again. There is no safeguard until the soul goes beyond nature. It is very difficult to do so although the method seems easy. The method is to meditate on the mind itself, and whenever any thought comes, to strike it down, allowing no thought to come into the mind, thus making it an entire vacuum. When we can really do this, that very moment we shall attain liberation. When persons without training and preparation try to make their minds vacant, they are likely to succeed only in covering themselves with tamas, the material of ignorance, which makes the mind dull and stupid and leads them to think that they are making a vacuum of the mind. To be able to really do that is to manifest the greatest strength, the highest control.

When this state, asamprajnata, or superconsciousness, is reached, the samadhi becomes seedless. What is meant by that? In a concentration where there is consciousness, where the mind succeeds only in quelling the waves in the chitta and holding them down, the waves remain in the form of tendencies. These tendencies, or seeds, become waves again when the opportunity comes. But when you have destroyed all these tendencies, almost destroyed the mind, then the samadhi becomes seedless; there are no more seeds in the mind out of which to manufacture again and again this plant of life, this ceaseless round of birth and death.[12]

Each one of the steps to attain samadhi has been reasoned out, properly adjusted, and scientifically organized. When faithfully practised, they will surely lead to the desired end. Then will all sorrows cease, all miseries vanish. The seeds of action will be burnt, and the Soul will be free for ever.[13]

SIGNS OF PROGRESS

Regarding the signs of progress in the eight-limbed practice, Swami Vivekananda says:

The first effect of this practice [*pranayama*] is perceived in a change of expression in one's face. Harsh lines disappear; with calm thought, calmness comes over the face. Next comes a beautiful voice. I never saw a yogi with a croaking voice. These signs come after a few months' practice.[14]

Such is the power of yoga that even the least of it will bring a great amount of benefit. It will not hurt anyone but will benefit everyone. First of all, it will calm down nervous excitement, bring peace, and enable us to see things more clearly. The temperament will be better and the health will be better.... Those who practice hard will get many other signs. Sometimes there will be sounds, as of a peal of bells heard at a distance, commingling and falling on the ear as one continuous sound. Sometimes things will be seen—little specks of light floating and becoming bigger and bigger; and when these things appear, know that you are progressing fast.[15]

With practice, within a few days, a little glimpse will come, enough to give one encouragement and hope. As a certain commentator on Yoga philosophy says: "When one proof is obtained, however little that may be, it will give us faith in the whole teaching of Yoga." For instance, after the first few months of practice you will begin to find you can read another's thoughts; they will come to you in a picture form. Perhaps you will hear something happening at a long distance when you concentrate your mind with a wish to hear. These glimpses will come, by little bits at first, but enough to give you faith and strength and hope.[16]

[The seer's] knowledge is attained in seven supreme steps.

When this knowledge comes, it comes, as it were, in seven steps, one after another; as we attain one of these we know that we are getting knowledge. The first step will make us feel that we have known what is to be known. The mind will cease to be dissatisfied. As long as we are aware of a thirst after knowledge we seek it here and there, wherever we think we can get some truth, and failing to find it we become dissatisfied and seek in a fresh direction. All search is vain until we begin to perceive that knowledge is within ourselves, that no one can help us, that we must help ourselves. When we begin to develop the power of discrimination, the first sign that we are getting near truth will be that this dissatisfied state will vanish. We shall feel quite sure that we have found the truth and that it cannot be anything else but the truth. Then we may know that the sun is rising, that the morning is breaking for us; and taking courage, we must persevere until the goal is reached.

The second step will be the absence of all pain. It will be impossible for anything in the universe, external or internal, to give us pain. The third will be the attainment of full knowledge. Omniscience will be ours. The fourth will be the attainment, through discrimination, of the end of all duties. Next will come what is called freedom of the chitta. We shall realize that all difficulties and struggles, all vacillations of the mind, have fallen away, just like a stone rolling from the mountain top into the valley and never coming up again. The next will be that the chitta will realize that it can melt away into its causes whenever we so desire.

Lastly, we shall find that we are established in our true Self, that the Self in us has been alone throughout the universe, and that neither body nor mind has ever been related, much less joined, to It. They were working their own way, and we, through ignorance, joined the Self to them. But we have been alone, omnipotent, omnipresent, ever blessed; our own Self was so pure and perfect that we required none else. We required none else to make us happy, for we are happiness itself. We shall find that this knowledge does not depend on anything else. Throughout the universe there can be nothing that will not become effulgent before this knowledge. This will be the last step, and the yogi will become peaceful and calm, never to feel any more pain, never again to be deluded, never to be touched by misery. He will know that he is ever blessed, ever perfect, almighty.[17]

17
Obstacles in Raja-Yoga

*When thoughts obstructive to yoga arise, contrary
thoughts should be employed.*

—PATANJALI

P atanjali identifies nine obstacles in the path of raja-yoga:
"Disease, mental laziness, doubt, lack of enthusiasm, lethargy,
clinging to sense enjoyments, false perception, non-attaining of
concentration, and falling away from concentration when attained—these are the obstructing distractions."[1] Commenting on
these obstacles, Swami Vivekananda writes:

> *Disease*: This body is the boat which will carry us to the other
> shore of the ocean of life. It must be taken care of. Unhealthy
> persons cannot be yogis. *Mental laziness* makes us lose all
> lively interest in the subject, without which there will be nei-
> ther the will nor the energy to practice. *Doubts* will arise in the
> mind about the truth of the science of Yoga, however strong
> one's intellectual conviction may be, until certain peculiar psy-
> chic experiences come, such as hearing or seeing at a dis-
> tance. These glimpses strengthen the mind and make the
> student persevere. *Falling away from concentration when*

attained: Some days or weeks, when you are practicing, the mind will be calm and easily concentrated and you will find yourself progressing fast. All of a sudden, one day, the progress will stop and you will find yourself, as it were, stranded. But persevere. All progress proceeds by such rise and fall.

Grief, mental distress, tremor of the body, and irregular breathing accompany non-retention of concentration.

Concentration will bring perfect repose to mind and body every time it is practiced. When the practice has been misdirected or the mind not well controlled, these disturbances come. Repetition of Om and self-surrender to the Lord will strengthen the mind and bring fresh energy. The nervous shaking will come to almost everyone. Do not mind them at all, but keep on practicing. Practice will cure them and make the seat firm.

To remedy this [one should] practice on one object.

Making the mind take the form of one object for some time will destroy these obstacles. This is general advice. In the following aphorisms it will be expanded and particularized. As one practice cannot suit everyone, various methods will be advanced, and everyone by actual experience will find out that which helps him most.

The feelings of friendship, mercy, gladness, and indifference, in regard to objects happy, unhappy, good, and evil, respectively, pacify the chitta.

We must have these four kinds of attitudes. We must have friendship for all; we must be merciful towards those that are in misery; when people are happy we ought to be happy; and to the wicked we must be indifferent. So with all objects that come before us. If the object is a good one, we must feel friendly towards it; if the object of thought is one that is miserable, we must be merciful towards the object. If it is good we must be glad; and if it is evil we must be indifferent. These attitudes of mind toward different objects that come before it will make the mind peaceful.[2]

In addition to the above, there are several other obstacles that are encountered on the path of raja-yoga: attraction for yogic powers, a mechanical view toward meditation, overemphasis or oversimplification of certain limbs of yoga, sharp turns of the mind, irregularity of practice, aimless wandering of the mind, and egotism. Swami Vivekananda reminds us that a raja-yogi must be vigilant in yoga and never give in to shortcuts out of laziness. If one faithfully stays on the path of yoga, one receives the highest reward. If, however, one does not practice raja-yoga in a disciplined way, one forfeits the attainment of eternal peace and happiness for a few cheap, worldly amusements:

Practice hard; whether you live or die does not matter. You have to plunge in and work without thinking of the result. If you are brave enough, in six months you will be a perfect yogi. But those who take up just a bit of it and a little of everything else make no progress. It is of no use simply to take a course of lessons. To those who are full of tamas, ignorant and dull—those whose minds never get fixed on any idea, who only crave for something to amuse them—religion and philosophy are simply objects of entertainment. These are the unpersevering. They hear a talk, think it very nice, and then go home and forget all about it. To succeed you must have tremendous perseverance, tremendous will. "I will drink the ocean," says the persevering will, "and at my will mountains will crumble." Have that sort of energy, that sort of will, work hard, and you will reach the goal.[3]

ATTRACTION FOR YOGIC POWERS

Many become fascinated by reading the teachings of raja-yoga and step onto the spiritual path without first developing a strong moral foundation. Such aspirants very soon realize the immensity of the task and abandon the path of raja-yoga in complete frustration or humiliation. Some become hypocrites. Others are attracted to this path for achieving a healthy body and long life. There are many who, in spite of their considerable advancement on this path, succumb to the temptations of yogic powers and psychic visions that may come to them, and they fail to reach the goal. Overemphasis on psychic attainments weakens the mind and eventually destroys the moral and spiritual foundations of the raja-yogi. Swami Vivekananda says:

> Anything that is secret and mysterious in this system of Yoga should be at once rejected. The best guide in life is strength. In religion, as in all other matters, discard everything that weakens you; have nothing to do with it....
>
> It is wrong to blindly believe. You must exercise your own reason and judgement; you must learn from experience whether these things happen or not. Just as you would take up any other science, exactly in the same manner you should take up this science for study. There is neither mystery nor danger in it. So far as it is true it ought to be preached in the public streets in broad daylight. Any attempt to mystify these things is productive of great danger.[4]

A MECHANICAL VIEW TOWARD MEDITATION

Progress on the path of raja-yoga mainly depends on one's self-effort. It is a path of strict discipline and self-control. It is often seen that aspirants take a mechanical view of the spiritual disciplines they practice. They forget their primary goal and become obsessed with the secondary details. They believe that eating a certain kind of food, sitting in a particular posture, and breathing in a specific way will lead them to liberation. To such aspirants, the goal of meditation is not liberation of the soul but peace of mind. They become fanatical about their dogma, pose, and posture and feel frustrated when the desired results are not realized.

Having a mechanical view of meditation defeats the very purpose of raja-yoga. It reduces spiritual knowledge to something that can be purchased by closing one's eyes and sitting in a certain way. Any peace and happiness that ensues from such mechanical meditation is short-lived. Liberation cannot be bought. One must really believe that one is the ever-free Purusha and not just say this. The secret of yoga lies not in the practice but in the motive. If one has faith in oneself and in one's goal, one is certain to reach the goal.

OVEREMPHASIS OR OVERSIMPLIFICATION

The third obstacle is overemphasis or oversimplification of one particular limb of yoga to the detriment of the others. Most aspirants overemphasize the aspect of *pranayama* (control of the breath) and oversimplify the steps preceding it. As a result, they suffer from violent reactions of the body that is not yet under the firm control of the mind. *Pranayama* itself cannot create spiritual longing. Mechanical restraint of breath, unaccompanied by a genuine spiritual longing, can result in harmful effects that, in the end, produce aversion to raja-yoga. Swami Vivekananda observes that raja-yoga practiced improperly or casually may even lead to insanity.[5] *Pranayama* practiced prematurely or in imitation of others may confer temporary peace of mind but is not considered a spiritual practice.

The aspirant may also develop a tendency to oversimplify the basic moral and spiritual disciplines (*yama* and *niyama*) in haste to attain *samadhi*. The five restraints of *yama* and five observances of *niyama* are to be practiced in the aspirant's every thought and action. Laziness in such practices makes concentration and meditation impossible. Such laziness lurks in the unconscious mind and comes back to haunt the aspirant. Swami Vivekananda says:

> Every vicious thought will rebound, every thought of hatred which you may have cherished, even in a cave, is stored up and will one day come back to you with tremendous power in the form of some misery here. If you project hatred and jealousy, they will rebound on you with compound interest. No power can avert them; when once you have put them in motion you will have to bear their fruit. Remembering this will prevent you from doing wicked things.[6]

Aspirants must be very careful not to oversimplify the rules of yoga. They must not be dogmatic about their disciplines in order to just follow the letter of the law. They should always remember the true spirit of the injunctions, their deeper meaning and spiritual purpose.

SHARP TURNS OF THE MIND

The mind of an aspirant practicing meditation and concentration for a length of time becomes razor sharp and highly sensitive. Such a concentrated mind may easily take a sudden and extreme turn upward or downward. Unable to curb sharp turns of the mind toward sense pleasures—especially lust, greed, and anger—some aspirants meet with a violent fall in the path of raja-yoga. One who rises high has the fear of falling very low. Aspirants should, therefore, proceed systematically in practice with care, caution, and purpose.

IRREGULARITY OF PRACTICE

In order to be effective, the aspirant's meditation must be regular. The aspirant may become complacent and justify irregularity in practice by claiming to be waiting for the right mood for meditation or inspiration to practice contemplation. Irregularity, if overlooked or condoned, soon becomes a habit and the aspirant slowly and imperceptibly gets lost on the path of yoga. Swami Vivekananda warns us:

> Practice is absolutely necessary. You may sit down and listen to me by the hour everyday, but if you do not practice, you will not get one step farther. It all depends on practice. We never understand these things until we experience them. We have to see and feel them for ourselves. Simply listening to explanations and theories will not do.[7]

Aspirants of raja-yoga must continue their practices without regard for their bodies, minds, changing moods, or general sluggishness. They must always think that it is only meditation that will ultimately save them from all suffering and misery. At risk is the liberation of one's soul from the bondage of countless desires. One's meditation is one's truest friend—the only friend who really attends to the needs of the soul and not merely the body and mind.

AIMLESS WANDERING OF THE MIND

An aspirant must be adept not merely in the firmness of posture but also in the ability to desist from aimless wandering. The tendency to wander from place to place, with the pretext of going on pilgrimage, seeking holy company, and other excuses always stems from inner restlessness. It is said that an aspirant must remain fixed in one place for at least twelve years in order to conquer that place.

The aspirant should also restrain aimless wanderings of the mind, avoiding all futile debates and idle discussion. He or she must practice concentration in all aspects of life, wholeheartedly thinking of one thought only. Swami Vivekananda describes the dedication aspiring raja-yogis must have toward their goal:

Give up all argumentation and other distractions. Is there anything in dry, intellectual jargon? It only throws the mind off its balance and disturbs it. The things of the subtler planes have to be realized. Will talking do that? So give up all vain talk. Read only those books which have been written by persons who have had spiritual experiences.

Be like the pearl-oyster. There is a pretty Indian fable to the effect that if it rains when the star Svati is in the ascendant, and a drop of rain falls into an oyster, that drop becomes a pearl. The oysters know this; so they come to the surface when the star appears, and wait to catch the precious raindrops. When the drops fall into them, quickly the oysters close their shells and dive down to the bottom of the sea, there patiently to develop the raindrops into pearls. You should be like that. First hear, then understand, and then, leaving all distractions, shut your minds to outside influences and devote yourselves to developing the truth within you. There is a danger of frittering away your energies by taking up an idea only for its novelty and then giving it up for another that is newer. Take one thing up and follow it, and see the end of it, and before you have seen the end, do not give up. He who can become mad with an idea, he alone sees the light. Those who only take a nibble here and a nibble there will never attain anything. They may titillate the nerves for a moment, but there it will end. They will be slaves in the hands of nature and will never go beyond the senses.[8]

EGOTISM

Egotism is the last obstacle that makes the path of raja-yoga very difficult for most aspirants. Aspirants may develop one of two tendencies: either they indiscriminately accept anything and become dependent on a temple, book, or person, or they become too independent and refuse to seek guidance when guidance from an illumined soul is necessary. Egotistic persons often take pride in their own abilities and ignore the rules that govern the practice of meditation. They fail to realize that they also have faults and that it is not demeaning but a sign of maturity to seek guidance.

In any path of yoga, there are some aspirants who only follow their own emotions and so-called mystic visions. They refuse to learn from others—especially those whom they know are more advanced. Preoccupied with their own attainments and salvation, such aspirants become selfish and isolated. They are prone to mistake their dreams and temporary emotions for real signs of spiritual progress. Therefore, an aspirant of meditation is advised to follow the time-tested eight-limbed practice of raja-yoga. Most importantly, an aspirant should follow the words of an illumined teacher. Such an illumined soul will guide the aspirant in accordance with what is best for the aspirant and in keeping with his or her natural disposition.

PART FOUR

The Way of Jnana-Yoga:
The Path of Knowledge

18

The Message of
Jnana-Yoga

*The man whose mind is not under his control has no
Self-knowledge and no contemplation either. Without
contemplation he can have no peace; and without
peace, how can he have happiness?*
—BHAGAVAD GITA 2.66

Jnana-yoga is fundamentally different from all other yogas. It is
worship of God as one's own inmost Self—the focus of the all-
pervading infinite Self, immortal and immutable. The goal of
jnana-yoga is the realization of the true nature of the Atman
(Self), which is identical with Brahman, or the Ultimate Reality,
absolute Pure Consciousness. All the things of this world that appear dear to us are for the sake of the Self alone. The Self is the
only reality in the universe. "This [Self] is dearer than a son,
dearer than wealth, dearer than everything else, [because] It is innermost.... One should meditate upon the Self alone as dear. He
who meditates upon the Self alone as dear—what he holds dear
will not perish."[1] Anything that is not-Self or does not reflect the
light of the Self is a figment of imagination. Life becomes a
tragedy when this Self is ignored or neglected.

According to jnana-yoga, Ultimate Reality has two faces: absolute reality, which is real for all time and under all conditions, and relative reality. When the Absolute is not realized, the world of relative values becomes delusive and self-destructive. The universe of beings and things appears real only because it reflects the light of the Absolute.

Jnana-yoga is the direct path to knowledge of the Self. The Self has no name, no form, and no attributes. It is Nirguna Brahman rather than Saguna Brahman, or Brahman with name, form, and attributes. Worship of Saguna Brahman as a personal God is merely the human mind superimposing various epithets on Nirguna Brahman. However, this is recommended for those who find the direct path too difficult, too demanding, and too uncompromising.

The path of jnana-yoga cuts through all symbols, images, philosophical speculations, and all superimpositions of the human mind on Ultimate Reality. The central message of jnana-yoga is "What has been described in millions of scriptures can be expressed in half a verse: Brahman alone is real; the world is illusory; and the individual soul and supreme soul are identical in essence."[2] The followers of this path, generally the *sannyasins,* rise above the awareness of the body and mind and seek to reach the pure Self. The Self in the inner recess of every heart is the greatest shrine of truth. The pursuit of this Self is the highest form of austerity. Meditation is taking a dip in the river of the Self. Contemplation of the Self is the greatest pilgrimage. In this path, one's personal experiences are the true scriptures, and self-control is the highest virtue.

The path of jnana-yoga gives a spiritual interpretation of truth, the world, creation, and the human individual. Its conclusions are verifiable, and the immortality it promises is attainable. Self-knowledge, the goal of jnana-yoga, alone can overcome the fear of death, guarantee us certainty of faith, and disclose the meaning of life. The *Katha Upanishad* aptly describes:

The wise man who, by means of concentration on the Self, realizes that ancient, effulgent One, who is hard to be seen, unmanifest, hidden, and who dwells in the buddhi [intellect] and rests in the body—he, indeed, leaves joy and sorrow far behind.[3]

19
The Philosophy and Psychology of Jnana-Yoga

There is One who is the eternal Reality among non-eternal objects, the one [truly] conscious Entity among conscious objects, and who, though non-dual, fulfils the desires of many. Eternal peace belongs to the wise, who perceive Him within themselves—not to others.

—Katha Upanishad 2.2.13

NATURE OF ULTIMATE REALITY

According to the philosophy of jnana-yoga, all things of the universe are really one—the infinite, immutable, Pure Consciousness, or Brahman. The world of diversity exists only in name and form through the inscrutable power of maya. The nature of Brahman is described as Sat-Chit-Ananda, or Existence-Knowledge-Bliss Absolute. The Reality is nondual yet appears to be many; immortal yet appears to undergo birth and death; ever blissful yet appears sometimes as pain and sometimes as pleasure. These appearances as a whole constitute what is called maya.

MEANING OF CREATION

The manifold universe is neither an absolute act of creation by God, nor a modification of nature, nor a transformation of the Ultimate—the one—into many, which is impossible. Ultimate Reality, one without a second, appears as manifold because of the illusory power of maya. Maya, the inscrutable power of the Ultimate, not only conceals the Ultimate but projects an apparent reality in its place. Ultimate Reality remains shrouded in the mist of maya, and we mistake the mist for reality. The illusory nature of maya is evident from everyday experiences; we find that what maya promises it cannot give and what it does give invariably disappoints us. We desire something more and yet do not know what we ultimately desire.

This veil of maya, according to jnana-yoga, cannot be explained away in disgust. Maya is a statement of fact, and the goal is to know that maya is really the power of Brahman. Maya resides in the individual mind. It is the individual mind that makes value judgments, such as what is pleasurable or painful, good or evil. But such value judgments do not affect Reality at all. Maya is delusive and destructive so long as it remains unknown. But when maya is known, maya is Brahman.

Maya has two modes: *vidyamaya* and *avidyamaya*. *Avidyamaya* binds the soul to the world; *vidyamaya* leads the soul to freedom. As Sri Ramakrishna describes:

> This universe is created by the Mahamaya [the inscrutable power of illusion] of God. Mahamaya contains both vidyamaya, the illusion of knowledge, and avidyamaya, the illusion of ignorance. Through the help of vidyamaya one cultivates such virtues as the taste for holy company, knowledge, devotion, love, and renunciation. Avidyamaya consists of the five elements and the objects of the five senses—form, flavour, smell, touch, and sound. These make one forget God.[1]

THE INDIVIDUAL

According to jnana-yoga, the microcosm and the macrocosm are built on the same plan. The Atman, or the individual soul, and Brahman, or the universal soul, are non-different in essence. The apparent separateness of the individual is due to time, space, and causation—the categories of maya. The individual (the microcosm) is like a bubble on the infinite ocean (the macrocosm). The two are identical in essence but different in name and form.

THE CAUSE OF SUFFERING

Suffering, according to jnana-yoga, is the result of embodiment. Embodiment is the result of one's previously acquired merits and demerits of karma that cause the attraction, aversion, and clinging of the mind. Knowledge of the Self alone can remove this ignorance and bondage of embodiment—not action, not prayer, not austerity, and not worship, which only purify the mind. Knowledge of the Self is revealed in the mirror of the pure heart.

Jnana-yoga is diving into the depths of the Self and not just floating on its surface. It is a yoga based upon unshakable faith in our divine destiny. To be a jnana-yogi is to discover the one, infinite Self common to all. The finite mind can never realize the infinite. The finite mind that intends to define and objectify Brahman is, as Sri Ramakrishna says, like a salt doll entering the waters of the ocean in order to measure its depths.

THE CAUSE OF BONDAGE

Bondage is due to the ego of the individual Self identifying itself with the body and mind out of ignorance. According to jnana-yoga, ignorance is born of selfish action, and so mere action (karma) is too weak to destroy ignorance. If a person mistakes a piece of rope for a snake in darkness, the darkness cannot be removed by further darkness.

This ignorance is not a positive entity. It is merely the absence of knowledge. Ignorance is like darkness, which is nothing but the absence of light. Due to ignorance, the *jiva,* or the individual, whose essential nature is Existence-Knowledge-Bliss Absolute imagines itself limited, small, and subject to birth and rebirth. Yet its real nature does not let it remain at rest. It is never happy being limited and perishable. It cannot accept the law of karma or the pairs of opposites as its ultimate destiny. Since its real nature is Existence-Knowledge-Bliss Absolute, it longs for immortal life, absolute joy, and all-embracing awareness. The only way to overcome ignorance is to focus the light of knowledge upon it. The only remedy for a nightmare is waking up from sleep.

THE WAY TO LIBERATION

According to jnana-yoga, liberation is Self-knowledge. Self-knowledge is knowledge of the identity between the individual Self and the Supreme Self. It is realizing "I am Brahman." As darkness lingering in a room for thousands of years becomes dispelled the moment light is brought in, all darkness of ignorance vanishes as soon as one's mind turns inward and discovers the light of knowledge. In the state of ignorance, an individual remains hypnotized, as it were, by ideas of diversity, separateness, and variety. The bound soul remains deluded by appearance. Jnana-yoga is a process of de-hypnotization.

Liberation is freeing our consciousness from the ego and eradicating the emotional biases of our mind and senses, so that we may directly perceive Reality as it really is—not how it appears to our prejudiced minds. The jnana-yogi's liberation is an all-embracing expansion. It is not gaining something we never had, enjoying something never enjoyed, or attaining something previously unattained. The jnana-yogi's relentless pursuit of Self-knowledge is one long and continuous meditation, a raging inner fire that steadily consumes all that is not-Self. In the end, only the Self remains—Self within and without.

THE TECHNIQUE OF JNANA-YOGA

The emphasis of the technique of jnana-yoga is less on controlling the mind than it is on deepening, widening, strengthening, and heightening one's consciousness of the Self. This is a technique of constant discrimination in which everything that is not-Self is dissolved into Self. The jnana-yogi's practice of discrimination is focusing the searchlight of knowledge on everything everywhere.

In order to control the mind, the jnana-yogi chooses the path of persuasion. To transcend the barriers imposed by the body and mind, which are products of maya, one has to rely not upon maya but upon Brahman, the controller of maya. Again, one cannot fight ignorance piecemeal. The jnana-yogi wants to go to the very root of ignorance and burn it in the fire of knowledge. Complete control of the mind is impossible until the mind is convinced that Self-knowledge is the goal of all goals. But then, one has to control the mind with the cooperation of the mind. By its very nature, the mind rebels against anything that is forced upon it. One need not adopt the method of force as long as there is room for persuasion. One may overcome the reasonable mind through the practices of discrimination, renunciation, and austerity, and by keeping holy company. This is why jnana-yoga agrees with raja-yoga that one must be decisive and resolute in the spiritual quest but believes raja-yoga to be unnecessarily confrontational in its technique.

The jnana-yogi counters the false desires of the unconscious mind with conscious detachment and repeated counter-suggestions about the reality of the Self as the ultimate source of power behind the facade of our apparent personality. The raja-yogi controls the mind by controlling the body and sense organs. The jnana-yogi controls gross sense urges by controlling the mind and controls the mind with the help of the intellect or understanding. This may be a less dramatic strategy; it is certainly, however, a more effective and permanent solution. If one can realize the reality of the Self, all that is not-Self vanishes into nothingness. To get rid of the false ego, the jnana-yogi says, one should not encourage it by responding to its challenges. One should ignore the ego and think only of the Self. Absorbed in the Self, the seeker is taken over by a meditative mood without being aware of it, just as a person is unconsciously taken over by deep sleep.

20

The Goal of Jnana-Yoga: Self-Knowledge

Therefore with the sword of Knowledge cut asunder
this doubt about the Self, born of ignorance and
residing in your heart, and devote yourself to yoga.
Arise, O Bharata!
—BHAGAVAD GITA 4.42

The highest realization of the jnana-yogi is *nirvikalpa samadhi* (oneness with Pure Consciousness)—the last word of all spiritual realizations attainable by the human mind. The liberation of the jnana-yogi is regarded as the most universal, unifying, and unqualified liberation. But first, let us look comparatively at the different depths of inner realization an aspirant may attain following the other three paths of yoga: raja-yoga, bhakti-yoga, and karma-yoga.

The crowning realization of the raja-yogi is *asamprajnata samadhi,* or the state of unqualified transcendence. *Asamprajnata samadhi* is the culmination of another state, known as *samprajnata samadhi,* which again has six levels: *savitarka samadhi,* or *samadhi* "with question"; *nirvitarka samadhi,* or *samadhi* "without question"; *savicara samadhi,* or *samadhi* with discrimination;

nirvicara samadhi, or *samadhi* without discrimination; *sananda samadhi,* or *samadhi* of supreme blissfulness; and *asmita samadhi,* or *samadhi* that transcends all body consciousness. The state of final liberation is achieved only when the aspirant attains *asamprajnata samadhi* by making the mind completely "seedless." In the former stages of *samadhi,* the mind struggles to subdue its countless thought-waves—gross and subtle. These suppressed thought-waves, however, continue to vibrate in the mind as unconscious tendencies—the "seeds" waiting for a favorable condition to arise once again. Through the practice of the six stages of *samprajnata samadhi,* the aspirant consciously feeds one steady thought-wave of the Self, which grows stronger and stronger and engulfs all the other waves until it, too, dissolves itself. Thus, no new desires inflame the liberated raja-yogi's mind, and the aspirant enters into the state of *asamprajnata samadhi,* where pure mind becomes one with the tranquil Self. The goal of raja-yoga, *kaivalya,* or aloneness of the Purusha, is liberation from the bounds of the false and fleeting world.

According to bhakti-yoga, liberation is neither withdrawal into the Self nor union with Brahman, the Absolute, but communion with a personal, all-loving God. A bhakti-yogi attains liberation when God becomes the sole object of love.

The karma-yogi may be a worshiper of the personal God or follower of nondualism, aspiring to the realization of the nondual Self in all. Depending on the karma-yogi's faith, he or she follows the disciplines of bhakti-yoga or jnana-yoga and in the end attains communion with God or realization of the Self. As a worshiper of the personal God, the karma-yogi is an instrument in the hand of God. To the karma-yogi, all activities are various forms of worship of the beloved Lord. There is no distinction between meditating upon God and serving God in all living beings. All spiritual practices—worship, contemplation, self-analysis, and service—are practices of karma-yoga. As an aspirant of Self-realization, the karma-yogi performs all activities in the spirit of yoga. The karma-yogi sees the Self as one in meditation and as many in the midst of activity. For a karma-yogi, the battlefield or marketplace is as sacred as the temple or church. The final liberation of karma-yoga is the transcendence of all ideas of action and non-action. The yogi of action seeks to eradicate the ego and dedicates his or her life to the service of others, seeing all in the Self and the Self in all. After experiencing the final state, the karma-yogi lives in the world as a free soul, sharing ineffable peace and happiness with all.

Now, let us turn our attention again to *nirvikalpa samadhi,* the ultimate realization of jnana-yoga, when the aspirant transcends all duality and relativity, and the eternal Brahman shines as Existence-Knowledge-Bliss Absolute. When this goal is reached, knowledge, knower, and the known dissolve into one Pure Consciousness; birth, growth, and death lose their significance in the expanse of infinite Existence; and love, the lover, and the beloved merge in the depth of supreme Bliss. *Nirvikalpa samadhi* is neither communion with the personal God nor the withdrawal of the Self from the bounds of the phenomenal universe. It is union, once and for all, with the absolute Brahman. Having controlled the sense organs and calmed the mind, the jnana-yogi enters the exalted state of *nirvikalpa samadhi* and never cares to return to the world of duality.

The sacred texts firmly state that for the ordinary aspirant there is no return to the phenomenal plane from the state of *nirvikalpa samadhi.* After remaining immersed in that bliss for a few days, the body falls off like a dead leaf. Only those who are born with a special mission of God return to the relative plane of consciousness and live in the world for the good of all beings. Those extraordinary souls are born with a supreme spiritual power by which they transmit holiness and purity to others by a touch, word, look, or thought. Their ego is the purified ego of knowledge, ego of devotion, or ego of a child. They see the universe of name and form filled with the presence of God.

Leaving behind the world of duality perceived by the senses, an aspirant in *samadhi* realizes the Self to be one with the universal Self. This goal of Self-knowledge is the one and only goal of the jnana-yogi. As long as an aspirant is satisfied with anything short of *samadhi,* final knowledge can never be attained. Visions, voices, yogic powers, and mystical experiences are not sure indicators of Self-realization. In all such states of ecstasy and enjoyment, ideas of duality and personality, however exalted, still persist. In the path of bhakti-yoga, for example, the lover and the beloved remain two identities distinct from one another. In the state of *asamprajnata samadhi,* as discussed in the context of raja-yoga, the whole universe is dissolved into two entities: Purusha (Self) and Prakriti (nature).

In jnana-yoga's *nirvikalpa samadhi,* everything dissolves into the oneness of Brahman—the immutable, immortal, one without a second. There is no duality. The raja-yogi cannot resolve the contradiction of multiplicity in Prakriti and oneness in the Purusha. The Purusha withdraws itself from the bonds of Prakriti, while the latter still remains real and distinct. The bhakti-yogi accepts all the diversities of the world as the sport of God. For the jnana-yogi, the universe of multiplicity is not different from Brahman; the jnana-yogi sees the diversities of the universe as the manifold manifestations of one and the same Reality. Brahman is everywhere and in everything; apparent diversities are only diversities in name and form.

The jnana-yogi believes that there is an inherent contradiction in the other three yogas where the Self worships something different from itself and where Reality is an object different from the subject. According to jnana-yoga, an aspirant following the other paths will inevitably feel distanced from Reality—a distance to be overcome by austerity and hardship. For example, the karma-yogi thinks of the effects of past actions as real and feels that he or she is bound to suffer because of them. The karma-yogi then attempts to neutralize the effects of one action by performing a counter-action. The follower of bhakti-yoga believes that he or she is different from God and so practices spiritual disciplines in the form of love in order to commune with God. A follower of raja-yoga thinks that the Purusha (Self) is in bondage and that the bondage is real. The raja-yogi tries to control the mind and achieve liberation of the Purusha. Even the jnana-yogi in the early stages of practice thinks that the Self is in ignorance and tries to remove that ignorance through eradication of the ego. But the jnana-yogi soon realizes that any attempt to eradicate the ego with the help of the ego only gives it a fresh lease on life.

According to jnana-yoga, the ego may take various forms—even harmless forms like the "ego of knowledge"—but is never destroyed. Any attempt to eradicate the ego through spiritual disciplines is futile. One is only deceived by one's own ego. In order to control the ego, the bhakti-yogi aims to purify it with the love of God and so retains the "ego of a child" of God. The karma-yogi tries to exhaust the ego through selfless activity and retains the "ego of a servant" of God. The raja-yogi tries to eradicate it through the power of concentration and breath control. To the jnana-yogi, the whole structure of the ego is false. Through discrimination, the jnana-yogi seeks to destroy the very foundation of the ego so that the whole structure will fall on itself.

The jnana-yogi's renunciation of the ego is considered complete and final. So long as we look upon God as different from our own Self, the surrender of our ego will be partial or reserved. Self-knowledge is not an effort to replace one kind of ego with another. To know one's own ever-pure Self is to know God. Meditation is constantly abiding in the Self, focusing the whole mind on nothing but the reality of the Self.

According to jnana-yoga, Self-knowledge has seven levels differing in their intensity and stability:

1. Desire for enlightenment

2. Inquiry

3. Questioning

4. Self-realization

5. Nonattachment

6. Non-perception of objects

7. Transcendence

The last four indicate the four levels of direct knowledge of Brahman. The aspirant who has reached the stage of nonattachment is greater than one who is at the stage of Self-realization. Higher than the stage of nonattachment is the stage of non-perception of objects; but one who has reached the stage of transcendence has attained the highest Self-knowledge.

In the state of *nirvikalpa samadhi,* the jnana-yogi attains direct perception of Reality. Such an experience transcends all belief, philosophy, ritual, and action. *Nirvikalpa samadhi* is the knowledge of oneness; it is being and becoming. Liberation lies only in realizing one's true nature and in being whole.

Liberation in the path of jnana-yoga has two aspects: *jnana,* or the realization of the oneness of existence within oneself, and *vijnana,* or seeing that unity in the diversities of the universe. *Vijnana* indicates both union and communion with Brahman. Only the yogi who has first experienced union with Brahman in the depths of *samadhi* can commune with Brahman when returning to the world of phenomena. The scriptures describe such a yogi as blessed—one who is alone but not lonely. The *vijnani* looks inward and sees the body, mind, and ego—with all their distractions and diverse thoughts—dissolve into the vastness of the ever-pure Self; the *vijnani* then looks outward and sees the same indivisible Absolute assume different names and forms, playing the roles of manifold beings and things. The *vijnani* stands as a witness to this inscrutable play of the Absolute.

The jnana-yogi is the only one who has discovered the true unity of existence. The basis of all love, peace, and knowledge is this unity. Knowledge of the Self is incomplete if it is not shared with others. Knowledge is not Self-knowledge if it results in indifference and insensitivity toward the world. The more we wake up to the knowledge of our true Self, the more we discover unity and harmony in the midst of apparent diversity. Only with this true vision of unity will all our anonymous anxieties and fears come to an end. Self-knowledge does not separate us from the rest of the world or place us above others; it brings us closer to all. Illumined souls are extraordinary not because they believe themselves to be superior to others but because of their extraordinary realization that they and all others are one. This realization makes illumined souls truly humble, and in humility, they find the greatest peace and joy.

The final goal of jnana-yoga is the discovery of the one Self common to all creatures. Physical science affirms the interdependence of cosmic force and matter. Monotheists speak of a Creator outside creation. Pantheists object to anything extracosmic and believe that God dwells in everything. But all these philosophies end in dualism. The philosophy of jnana-yoga, on the other hand, unites all into one entity. It describes the phenomenal universe as a wavering image of Brahman which is all in all. The rays of the sun glisten on the water; they appear real yet have no reality apart from the sun. They cannot shine unless the sun shines. Everything in this world shines by the radiance of the Self.

Spiritual practices prescribed for this Self-realization consist of hearing about the Self, reflecting on its reality, and direct apprehension of it in the depths of our meditation. But none of these is possible unless we are wholehearted in our spiritual pursuit. The gross impulses within us are too obstinate and obsessive. Our powers of reasoning are often carried away by our emotions, and we easily rationalize any desires we want to fulfill. Our perceptions are distorted by our attachments. Our thoughts are charged with emotional prejudices, and we cannot control them. Our desires are strong and our tendencies deep-seated.

Therefore, the jnana-yogi must develop a sharp and discriminating intellect. The jnana-yogi does not and should not subscribe to any hypothesis or belief about God unless it is tested by the rigors of reason.

Genuine spiritual truth must be verified by the scriptures, amenable to reason, and attainable by direct experience. But reason at times proves to be only an irrational bias in the guise of reason; and untested belief in scriptures can make us dogmatic. All descriptions of Reality contained in the sacred texts are, according to the jnana-yogi, mere suggestions. They describe not what Brahman is to itself but how Brahman appears to us. "To protect the aspirant from error and delusion the seers of Vedanta lay down three criteria of Truth. These are scriptural authority *(Sruti)*, reasoning *(yukti)*, and personal experience *(anubhava)*. Any one of these, singly, may enable a man to realize partial truth, but when all three point to the same conclusion, the aspirant may be assured that he has realized the whole Truth.... In order to free reasoning from the pitfalls of rationalization, rigorous mental disciplines are prescribed so that the aspirant may be grounded in detachment not only from the external world but also from his own pet ideas and exclusive loyalties."[1]

"The ultimate experience of Truth may be an act of faith, but its validity is judged through reason. One may not be able to arrive at Truth exclusively through reason, but one's experience and statement of Truth cannot be valid if they contradict reason...."[2] Reasoning often degenerates into dry intellectualism unless the seeker is established in detachment and inspired by renunciation. Faith insists on acceptance; reason asks for scrutiny. Reason, when not inspired by faith, often ends in empty speculation; on the other hand, emotionalism, if not checked by the scrutiny of reason, lapses into cheap sentimentalism.[3]

21

The Practice of Jnana-Yoga

*The result of dispassion is knowledge, that of
knowledge is withdrawal from sense-pleasures,
which leads to the experience of the Bliss of the Self,
whence follows Peace.*

—SHANKARACHARYA

Jnana-yoga prescribes a rigorous process known as the fourfold discipline in preparation for attaining the ultimate goal of Self-knowledge. The way of jnana-yoga is direct and uphill, and the aspirant is required to be strong, undaunted, and steady. The difficult and hazardous journey must not be made by fits and starts, and the aspirant of jnana-yoga must have a strong moral foundation and spiritual inspiration. The fourfold discipline is marked by the following:

1. Ability to discriminate between the real and the unreal.

2. Burning renunciation that does not hesitate to sacrifice anything that stands in the way of Self-knowledge.

3. Mastery over six spiritual virtues: faith, control of the mind, control of the sense organs, cessation of desires, forbearance, and concentration on the Self.

4. Intense longing for liberation.

Mastery of this discipline is the foundation of jnana-yoga. The aspiring jnana-yogi must pay attention to these means of attaining Self-knowledge and make an active, conscious self-effort rather than continuously dreaming of the goal. Shankaracharya says:

> As a treasure hidden underground requires (for its extraction) competent instruction, excavation, the removal of stones and other such things lying above it and (finally) grasping, but never comes out by being (merely) called out by name, so the transparent Truth of the Self, which is hidden by Maya and its effects, is to be attained through the instructions of a knower of Brahman, followed by reflection, meditation and so forth, but not through perverted arguments.[1]

The process of preparation is a process of self-purification. The aspirant must know that sensuality is a lapse from spirituality and must try to regain lost spiritual balance. The real Self within us is ever free and immortal. But as a result of its deep identification with the body and mind, it has been forced, as it were, to obey their gross urges and to experience the pain and pleasure inevitably associated with them. Such deep-seated identification cannot be explained away by philosophy or reasoning. It is necessary for the aspirant to empty the mind of all attachments and desires and unlearn many things before learning about the reality of the Self and realizing its fullness.

ABILITY TO DISCRIMINATE BETWEEN THE REAL AND THE UNREAL

The first practice of the fourfold discipline is discrimination. Brahman alone is real and all else is illusory. Discrimination is the acknowledgment of this fact. Our view of the world is based more on dreams, fantasies, and half-truths than on reality. Discrimination of the real from the unreal is taking a firm stand against naive and unreflective living. As Sri Ramakrishna explains:

Discrimination means to know the distinction between the
Real and the unreal. God alone is the real and permanent
Substance; all else is illusory and impermanent. The magician
alone is real; his magic is illusory. This is discrimination.[2]

Discrimination is not the suppression of desires but the realization of the futility of worldly desires. The saint-poet Bhartrihari
vividly depicts the knowledge that results from such discrimination by reminding us that every enjoyment in this world is marred
by fear: the wealthy are afraid of thieves, the healthy of disease,
the beautiful of old age, the learned of rivals, the virtuous of evil,
the honored of degradation, and the powerful of their enemies.
From discrimination and renunciation of all desires alone can
one realize freedom from fear.[3]

Discrimination begins with a sense of awakening in a person
who has experienced cracks in his or her foundation of values and
virtues. The seeker comes to the conclusion, "No one in this world
is my own." The world appears to be a foreign land. The seeker
begins to ask, "Where is my real home? Who is my real father?
Who is my real mother? Who is my true friend?"

The process of discrimination involves diving deep into our
being. The human individual, according to jnana-yoga, is a lay-
ered being. That which is real—the Self—remains covered by five
layers of matter: the physical body, the vital force, the mind, the
intellect, and bliss. These five sheaths obscure the light of our true
immortal soul or Self, the indwelling Pure Consciousness ever
shining in every heart. The degree of obscurity varies depending
upon each sheath's density. The sheath of the body, which is the
outermost, is the densest, while the sheath of bliss, the innermost, is the thinnest.

Aspirants on the path of jnana-yoga, following the method
of negation, realize that the material sheaths are not the Self
and penetrate them in search of the Self. The body, they realize,
is made of gross elements, is dependent upon food, was nonexistent before birth, and is subject to the sixfold change of birth,

subsistence, growth, maturity, decline, and death. Such a body cannot be the Self. The body is like a palace in which the Self dwells as the king; when the palace becomes dilapidated, the king does not hesitate to destroy it and build a new one. By following such a process of negation, aspirants reach the next sheath and calmly observe how the vital force maintains the bodily functions of inhalation, nourishment, digestion, elimination, and reproduction. The presence of this sheath keeps human beings alive but does not explain their moral judgments and spiritual aspirations.

Aspirants thus dive deeper and discover the sheath of the mind, which makes human beings thinking, logical, and emotional beings. But carefully observing the activities of the mind, aspirants come to see that the mind also has a beginning and an end, is subject to change, and has no definite identity. The mind is a bundle of countless thoughts, impulses, memories, and desires. The Self, aspirants reflect, must be different from the mind. Thereupon they reach the sheath of the intellect, which lies behind the mind. The intellect is the faculty of judgment and understanding. Identified with the intellect, human beings experience the joys and sorrows of the world in both the waking state and dream state and they experience the absence of the world in dreamless sleep. The intellect, aspirants observe, is less mutable and subtler than all the preceding sheaths. But it is not the true Self.

Aspirants on this quest thus go beyond the sheath of the intellect and discover the sheath of bliss, through which they experience various degrees of joy. Being identified with this sheath, they temporarily transcend the experiences of the waking and dream states and feel detached from the body and mind. But, to their surprise, they find that this sheath too is subject to change. The feeling of withdrawal and self-transcendence that persons experience in dreamless sleep soon leaves them in the face of the harsh realities of life. The sheath of bliss greatly reflects the Self but is not the Self. At last, aspirants reach the immutable and indivisible Self whose nature is that of Existence-Knowledge-Bliss

Absolute. In the Self there is neither thinker nor thought, neither subject nor object. At this stage, all reasoning and analysis come to an end and aspirants enter the state of *samadhi*.

The five sheaths are like five variously designed lamp shades placed one on top of the other, in the center of which shines the light of the effulgent Self. The differences in the textures, designs, and densities of the sheaths make for the differences in the manifestation of the Self in individuals, causing them to appear saintly or sinful. What we know to be our inner disposition is really the particular pattern of our sheaths and not the light of the Self, which shines with the same brightness in every heart.

Discrimination also indicates calm analysis of the three states of our being: the waking state, the dream state, and the state of dreamless sleep. Ordinary persons look upon the waking state as the only real state of existence. The prospects and problems of this state keep us occupied most of the time. In contrast with our daily existence, we look upon the states of dream and dreamless sleep as meaningless and unreal. We do not concern ourselves with our dream problems, nor are we enthusiastic about our dream prospects. But to the jnana-yogi, the dream state is thought of as the dreamer's waking state. Dream experiences, however grotesque and disconnected they may appear in comparison with the experiences of the waking state, are normal and real for the dreamer. In a dream, objects and beings appear real and living, and dreams may seem to endure for long periods of time. The third state is the state of dreamless sleep, in which a person is neither dreaming nor awake. Beyond these three states, there is a fourth state the Upanishads call Turiya, which is the constant witness of the changing phenomena of the first three states.[4] As waves and bubbles subside and become one with the serene water of the ocean, so all names, forms, and experiences of the three states merge into Turiya.

The essence of the practice of discrimination is to let the body, mind, and intellect remain as they are. It is only necessary for the aspirant to remain detached from them. The more one is able to stand aside, the more freedom and peace one enjoys. By detaching oneself from the body, mind, and intellect and their addictions, possessions, perversions, and pretensions, one contemplates the indwelling Self and becomes aware of its serenity and stability. Self-knowledge begins with one's knowledge of the body, mind, and intellect and culminates in the realization of their unity residing in one's true Self.

The practice of discrimination is not speculative regarding the reality of the Self. An aspirant of right discrimination is not a dreamer but a pragmatist. The yogi is determined to delve into the depths of life and not aimlessly float on the surface. Discrimination is a process of introspection by which we seek our true identity that remains hidden behind the façade of the individual body and mind. It is a call to turn our vision inward and directly contact the Self, the foundation of our being. Without this direct contact, religion is no better than dogma. Jesus affirms this and says, "Neither shall they say, Lo here! or, lo there! for, behold, the kingdom of God is within you" (Luke 17:21). Discrimination leads us to the kingdom of God buried within our own Self. "For whosoever will save his life shall lose it; but whosoever will lose his life for my sake, the same shall save it" (Luke 9:24). We refuse to give up our empty dreams and yet want to aspire after life everlasting. We want to have the best of both worlds. We talk of liberation but are content with bondage. We have grown fond of the delusions and attachments that keep our souls imprisoned. Such is the nature of delusion. It never ends until we put an end to it.

BURNING RENUNCIATION

Discrimination, when rightly and sincerely practiced, naturally leads an aspirant to the renunciation of all transitory enjoyments here and hereafter. The Upanishads emphatically declare:

The Hereafter never reveals itself to a person devoid of discrimination, heedless, and perplexed by the delusion of
wealth. "This world alone exists," he thinks, "and there is no
other." Again and again he comes under my sway [i.e., the
sway of death.][5]

An aspirant practicing renunciation is required to give up all desire for the limelight of the world. The jnana-yogi's renunciation
must be uncompromising. He or she must not even entertain curiosity about worldly enjoyment. It is said that a person no longer
interested in eating fish has no reason to be near the fish market.
Renunciation is to be practiced both mentally and physically. An
aspirant with even a trace of curiosity for sense enjoyments is
susceptible to fall. Shankaracharya describes: "Sense-objects are
more virulent in their evil effects than the poison of the cobra.
Poison kills one who takes it, but those others kill one who even
looks at them through the eyes."[6]

Renunciation is not escape from the world. Bondage and freedom are of the mind alone. Renunciation, therefore, is the relinquishment of all desire for sense enjoyments. Sri Ramakrishna
points out:

There are two kinds of renunciation: intense and feeble. Feeble
renunciation is a slow process; one moves in a slow rhythm.
Intense renunciation is like the sharp edge of a razor. It cuts
the bondage of maya easily and at once.[7]

One who has only a mild spirit of renunciation says, "Well, all
will happen in course of time; let me now simply repeat the
name of God." But a man possessed of a strong spirit of renunciation feels restless for God, as the mother feels for her
own child. A man of strong renunciation seeks nothing but
God. He regards the world as a deep well and feels as if he
were going to be drowned in it. He looks on his relatives as
venomous snakes; he wants to fly away from them. And he

does go away. He never thinks, "Let me first make some arrangement for my family and then I shall think of God." He has great inward resolution.[8]

Sri Ramakrishna's final word on renunciation is "If you want to realize God, then you must cultivate intense dispassion. You must renounce immediately what you feel to be standing in your way. You should not put it off till the future."[9]

The spirit of renunciation is never negative. Only by desiring the unbounded joy of the Self can one renounce the fleeting enjoyments of the senses. Desire itself is not contrary to the pursuit of Self-knowledge; it depends upon the objects we desire. If one's desire is the pleasure of the senses, one is sensual; if beauty for beauty's sake, an artist; if Self-knowledge, a yogi. One who remains preoccupied with thoughts of the Self does not need to run away from the world and worldly things.

Renunciation is the bedrock of all spirituality. It is also the measure of spiritual progress. The depth of the spiritual attainment of an aspirant is determined only by steadfastness in renunciation and discrimination. Only those who are well grounded in the virtues of discrimination and renunciation can forge ahead in the path of yoga, working their way through all obstacles and difficulties. The human mind usually seeks the line of least resistance and tries to make a compromise between God and the world, between renunciation and sense enjoyment. Few aspirants realize that the pursuit of worldly enjoyment and the desire for God cannot go together. It often happens that an aspirant lacking in austerity and renunciation is carried away by the whims of emotions and recedes back into the world of fantasy. An effusion of spiritual emotions not accompanied by a corresponding transformation of character and a sincere longing for God has no real value in the path of yoga.

MASTERY OVER SIX SPIRITUAL VIRTUES

Mastery over the following six spiritual virtues is the third practice of the fourfold discipline.

Faith

The aspirant is required to have faith—faith in him- or herself, faith in the teaching, and faith in the teacher. It is faith and sincerity that give us courage and determination on our spiritual adventure. Courage makes some people risk injury and even death for a cause they believe to be just. Moral courage makes others sacrifice everything for their spiritual goal. A person endowed with true faith will not indulge in self-pity when faced with obstacles. Our spiritual practices become fruitful when we do them with faith and self-effort. Loss of faith weakens our commitment to the goal and makes our spiritual efforts halfhearted. Our *japa* and meditation turn dry and become mere mechanical rituals. Our faith is the sole source of our strength. Aspirants who do not have faith in themselves cannot have faith in others, cannot even have faith in God. The spiritual practices of such persons do not produce positive results because they do not believe in what they do. They look for miracles, shortcuts, or mystic attainments to solve their problems overnight.

True faith is not an emotion or belief. It is not blind surrender to the supernatural or the unknown. One believes only so long as one does not know. Faith is an implicit trust in our spiritual destiny. It results from purity of heart, which depends on self-control. Faith sustains us when we become depressed, disillusioned, or when we have to face daunting obstacles in the path of yoga. Depression is a result of self-love. Being intoxicated with self-love, some seek self-gratification in everything and make self-interest their sole concern. Anything that does not serve their self-interest has no meaning for them. Self-love only has selfish desires; as a result, spiritual disciplines and austerities are practiced to gain or possess something. Such a quest of self-love, pursued in the name of spirituality, inevitably ends in despair and disappointment. True faith alone can protect one from the delusion of self-love and selfish desires.

Control of the Mind and the Sense Organs

An aspirant in the path of jnana-yoga requires tremendous courage and tenacity to face the restless mind. The mind can be our best friend but more often is our worst enemy. Shankaracharya warns us: "In the forest-tract of sense-pleasures there prowls a huge tiger called the mind. Let good people who have a longing for liberation never go there."[10] Being impelled by emotions, we often commit acts we later regret, and such regret only proves that our emotions do not represent our true nature.

The mind is a storehouse of the impressions of innumerable past thoughts, feelings, and sense perceptions submerged in the unconscious. Our impulses, likes, and dislikes are influenced by our past thoughts and associations, whether we know it or not. Our conscious, repeated thoughts gradually turn into unconscious habits and desires. Sri Ramakrishna compares the mind to milk and the world to water. As milk mixed with water becomes diluted, so the mind by coming into contact with the world becomes weak. But as the same milk churned with right effort into butter easily floats on the water, so the purified mind easily remains in the world without being affected by it.[11] It is, however, not easy to control the mind because control of the mind depends upon control of the sense organs that are obstinately restless.

While control of the mind consists of not allowing it to wander either outward or inward, control of the sense organs means holding all the organs of perception and action in their respective centers. Of all the unruly sense organs, two are considered to be the most powerful: the sense of sex and the palate. An aspirant in any path of yoga must not entertain the slightest desire for sexual enjoyment or indulgence of the palate. These desires inevitably lead the aspirant's mind downward and wipe out all progress the aspirant has made on the path.

Control of the mind and sense organs seems to be an impossible task. Yet, for a seeker in the path of jnana-yoga, such control is the only means to Self-realization. Shankaracharya warns spiritual seekers to be serious in the path:

> Neither by Yoga, nor by Samkhya, nor by work, nor by learning, but by the realization of one's identity with Brahman is liberation possible, and by no other means.[12]

> A disease does not leave off if one simply utters the name of the medicine, without taking it; (similarly) without direct realization one cannot be liberated by the mere utterance of the word Brahman.[13]

What, then, is the way to control the mind and the sense organs? Is it ever possible for a struggling seeker? In answer, the Bhagavad Gita points out the twofold path of patience and effort:

> Renouncing entirely all the desires born of the will, drawing back the senses from every direction by strength of mind, let a man little by little attain tranquillity with the help of the buddhi [intellect] armed with fortitude. Once the mind is established in the Self, he should think of nothing else.[14]

Practice of self-control becomes fruitful only when it is guided by the spirit of true dispassion toward all sense objects. Shankaracharya says:

> The shark of hankering catches by the throat those seekers after liberation who have got only an apparent dispassion (vairagya) and are trying to cross the ocean of Samsara (relative existence), and violently snatching them away, drowns them half-way.[15]

For a seeker devoid of dispassion and self-control, jnana-yoga ceases to be a path to Self-knowledge and turns into idle imagination.

Cessation of Desires

Control of the mind and the senses is not complete until there is absolute cessation of all desires. The slightest desire, however subtle, can distract the aspirant's mind from the path of yoga. The majority of our desires are unconscious. Unconscious desires remain imperceptible to the conscious mind but greatly influence our thoughts and behavior. One who sincerely aspires after Self-realization must uproot all desires and concentrate on the Self alone:

> Fixing the mind on some particular object like a lump of dough is called concentration.
>
> When the mind is withdrawn from all other objects except one and fixed on the latter, the succession of similar concepts of that one object is called meditation.[16]

Concentration and meditation are not possible until all desires of the mind are weeded out, along with their roots, and all hopes and expectations of worldly pleasures are renounced. When one particular mental state passes into another, the first is not altogether lost; it is preserved in the deeper layers of the mind as a subtle impression that tries to manifest itself whenever a favorable occasion arises. Such subtle impressions are like the deep roots of a plant. Even when a plant is destroyed above the soil, the roots remain and bring forth a new plant in the appropriate season. The subtle impressions manifest in the form of new desires whenever the environment proves suitable for their growth.

The aspirant in the path of jnana-yoga is called upon not only to control the desires of the mind but also to destroy the very roots of those desires lurking in the depths of the mind in the form of subtle impressions. The yogi should not allow gross habits to form into subtle ones but should strike at their very roots. Habits, once formed, are very difficult to root out. The mind that has rid itself of all desires is in perfect equilibrium and is prepared to concentrate on the object of its meditation.

The mind attains the state of cessation of desires in several stages: first, the seeker recognizes worldly objects of enjoyment to be undesirable, and the mind recoils from them; second, the senses are conquered, and the mind becomes balanced, avoiding extreme anxiety and depression; third, the mind becomes indifferent to the rise and fall of its passions and desires; fourth, the seeker realizes the futility of attraction toward external objects and feels no attachment even in their presence. Ultimately, the seeker reaches the highest state of mind. The seeker becomes a yogi, free not only from attachment to worldly enjoyments but from the desire for all pleasures, earthly or heavenly.

Forbearance

We can often control the mind in a peaceful environment, but the mind quickly loses its balance when in direct contact with objects of desire. The aspirant is therefore called upon to practice absolute endurance without resistance, remorse, or retaliation. To quote the words of Swami Vivekananda:

> We may not resist an evil but at the same time we may feel very miserable. A man may say very harsh things to me, and I may not outwardly hate him for it, may not answer him back, and may restrain myself from apparently getting angry; but anger and hatred may be in my mind, and I may feel very badly towards that man. That is not non-resistance. I should be without any feeling of hatred or anger, without any thought of resistance; my mind must be as calm as if nothing had happened. Only when I have got to that state have I attained to non-resistance, and not before. The bearing of all misery,

without any thought of resisting or driving it out, without even any painful feeling in the mind or any remorse—this is titiksha. Suppose I do not resist, and some great evil comes thereby; if I have titiksha, I should not feel any remorse for not having resisted. When the mind has attained to that state, it has become established in titiksha.[17]

Concentration on the Self

Concentration on the Self is not curiosity or an examination of the Self. Shankaracharya says, "Not the mere indulgence of thought (in curiosity) but the constant concentration of the intellect ... on the ever-pure Brahman is what is called *Samadhana,* or self-settledness."[18] The practice of *samadhana* is to concentrate the mind on the Self. If the yearning for Self-realization is sincere, the aspirant will struggle hard for such realization. Every genuine aspirant is bound to feel this intense inner struggle, and only through such struggle comes growth. Every failure one meets with, every mistake one makes is a blessing in disguise. Each apparent setback leads the aspirant onward in the path of Self-knowledge. There are two classes of people who do not struggle: those who have attained Self-realization and those who have not set foot on the spiritual path.

The most important part of one's struggle with the mind is to concentrate the mind upon one, single idea—the Self. The mind must constantly dwell on the Self, paying no attention to the passage of time. There are two aspects of concentrating the mind. First, the aspirant must gather the scattered mind and restrain it from wandering and being restless. Second, the aspirant must practice the conscious witnessing of the mind. The mind becomes divided in meditation, assuming the roles of actor and witness. The aspirant is required to strengthen the witnessing aspect and not spend much energy in restraining the restless mind. He or she may let the mind run on but should watch it. As the witnessing aspect is emphasized, the active mind gradually comes under control until at last the actor ceases to perform for the witness. Steady and daily meditation, even though short, is far more effective than irregular practice, however intense. No one can predict when one's meditation will succeed. Forced meditation is neither possible nor desirable. We should fulfill the conditions of our spiritual life, and the goal will take care of itself. The end is sure to follow if we take care of the means.

INTENSE LONGING FOR LIBERATION

Intense longing for liberation makes the real difference while practicing the spiritual disciplines of discrimination, renunciation, and self-control.

There are eight fetters that bind the soul and make the soul forget its real nature: shame, hatred, fear, pride of caste, pride of lineage, pride of good conduct, grief, and secretiveness.[19] Only through intense longing for liberation can one overcome all bondage and attain liberation. Sri Ramakrishna describes the intensity of the jnana-yogi's longing:

> A disciple asked his teacher, "Sir, please tell me how I can see God." "Come with me," said the guru, "and I shall show you." He took the disciple to a lake, and both of them got into the water. Suddenly the teacher pressed the disciple's head under the water. After a few moments he released him and the disciple raised his head and stood up. The guru asked him, "How did you feel?" The disciple said, "Oh! I thought I should die; I was panting for breath." The teacher said, "When you feel like that for God, then you will know you haven't long to wait for His vision."[20]

Swami Vivekananda says:

> If you want to be spiritual, you must renounce. This is the real test. Give up the world—this nonsense of the senses. There is only one real desire: to know what is true, to be spiritual. No

more of materialism, no more of this egoism. Strong, intense, must be the desire. If a man's hands and feet were so tied that he could not move, and then if a burning piece of charcoal were placed on his body, he would struggle with all his power to throw it off. When I shall have that sort of extreme desire, that restless struggle to throw off this burning world, then the time will have come for me to glimpse the Divine Truth.

Look at me. If I lose my little pocketbook with two or three dollars in it, I go twenty times into the house to find that pocketbook. The anxiety, the worry, and the struggle! If one of you curses me, I remember it twenty years; I cannot forgive and forget it. For the little things of the senses I can struggle like that. Who is there that struggles for God that way? "Children forget everything in their play. The young are mad after the enjoyment of the senses; they do not care for anything else. The old are brooding over their past misdeeds." They are thinking of their past enjoyments—old men who cannot have any enjoyment. Chewing the cud—that is the best they can do. None crave for the Lord in the same intense spirit with which they crave for the things of the senses.[21]

There are some who often talk about their disgust for sense enjoyment and desire for liberation; but as soon as the objects of enjoyment are snatched away from them, they find their lives to be empty, meaningless, and intolerable, only proving that their hunger for liberation was insincere. The yogi must first be sincere. If one sincerely practices the disciplines of discrimination, dispassion, and self-control, one's longing for liberation is certain to intensify.

22
Meditation for Self-Knowledge

His form is not an object of vision; no one beholds Him with the eye. One can know Him when He is revealed by the intellect free from doubt and by constant meditation. Those who know this become immortal.

—KATHA UPANISHAD 2.3.9

Meditation and the practice of the fourfold discipline in jnana-yoga go together. It is dangerous to attempt the one without the other. The practice of meditation without control over the lower urges may cause a violent reaction from the mind, and the suppression of undesirable thoughts without the practice of meditation is impossible. In meditation, the aspirant steadily and patiently concentrates on the object of worship and finally becomes one with it. According to Shankaracharya, the practice of sincere and daily meditation is possible only when the aspirant is lovingly devoted to the object of meditation.[1]

Meditation is always difficult no matter which yoga the aspirant follows and is especially difficult in the path of jnana-yoga, in which the aspirant meditates on the unity of the Atman (individual consciousness) and Brahman (nondual Pure Consciousness). In the other forms of meditation, the aspirant is often advised to fix the mind on a religious symbol or image. The aspirant in the path of jnana-yoga has no such symbol to depend upon. The jnana-yogi should not even concentrate on concepts of the Pure Being, such as empty space, a blue sky, steady fire, or boundless ocean. Meditation on the Absolute is the negation of everything conceivable by the mind by following a process of *"neti, neti,"* or "not this, not this." The aspirant meditates on the Atman, or the indwelling Pure Consciousness, which cannot even be imagined, yet whose presence is always felt within. It is not concentration on a mental image or contemplation on a form but steadily and patiently diving into the deep layers of consciousness by negating all duality.

In karma-yoga, the aspirant gives up attachment to the fruits of action; in raja-yoga, the yogi is instructed to detach the mind from nature—internal and external; in bhakti-yoga, the aspirant is advised to surrender the individual will to the will of God. But in jnana-yoga, the aspirant is required to renounce all duality, knowing it to be illusory and false. The teachers of nondualistic Vedanta, therefore, prescribe the practice of contemplation for the jnana-yogi. Contemplation is likened to a bee buzzing around a flower, about to sit on the flower and sip the honey. Contemplation evokes continuous thought-waves of the object of meditation within the aspirant's mind. It is a halfway house along the way to the realization of the unity of Atman and Brahman. Contemplation includes worship of images and forms, repetition of a mantra, and meditation on a form of the Divine. But true meditation is the highest form of worship. As Sri Ramakrishna says, "There are two kinds of meditation, one on the formless God and the other on God with form. But meditation on the formless God is extremely difficult. In that meditation you must wipe out all that you see or hear. You contemplate only the nature of your Inner Self."[2]

Describing the meaning of concentration, Swami Vivekananda says:

How are we to know that the mind has become concentrated?
The idea of time will vanish. The greater the amount of time
that passes unnoticed, the more deeply concentrated we are.
In everyday life we see that when we are interested in a book
we do not note the time at all, and when we leave the book
we are often surprised to find how many hours have passed.
All time will have a tendency to be unified in the one present.
So the definition is given; when the past and present become
one, the mind is said to be concentrated.[3]

There are three stages in this concentration. In the first stage,
distractions of the mind are checked by one's self-control; in the
second stage, self-control takes full charge of the mind and suppresses the desires; in the third stage, there is neither distraction
nor suppression of desires but only the thought of one single object. The goal of concentration and meditation is to dissolve all
pluralities into one substance. Mind, intellect, and the sense of
ego are dissolved into the Self and the Self into Brahman.

Meditation, according to jnana-yoga, is the natural state of the
mind. Left to itself, the mind gravitates toward meditation. The
necessity for meditation arises due to the distractions of the mind.
That such distractions make us feel restless proves that they are
foreign to us. The goal of jnana-yoga is to attain freedom by dis-
solving everything into Brahman, Existence-Knowledge-Bliss
Absolute. By realizing Brahman within and without, the jnana-
yogi becomes Brahman. The human mind longs to move from
lesser happiness to greater happiness, from lesser awareness to
greater awareness, and from lesser freedom to greater freedom.
Realization of Brahman as the Self of all takes us to the very source
of all happiness, awareness, and freedom. Self-knowledge is an intuitive revelation, and meditation prepares us for this revelation.

The technique of jnana-yoga follows the threefold process of
sravana, or hearing of the Vedic texts; *manana*, or reflecting upon

what has been heard; and *nididhyasana,* or right apprehension of Brahman.

In order to proceed toward Self-knowledge we must first begin with a working hypothesis, and the Vedic statements "That Thou art"[4] and "I am Brahman"[5] fulfill that need. The truth is to be heard. As Sri Ramakrishna says, "Better than reading is hearing, and better than hearing is seeing."[6] This hearing is not ordinary, halfhearted hearing but spiritual hearing with an open mind toward what is heard, which becomes especially effective when we hear about the Self from a knower of Self. We do not perceive the presence of the Self within us because we have repeatedly ignored it. This repeated self-denial makes us think and behave in a self-forgetful way; but persistent hearing about the positive presence of the Self infuses us with faith in our spiritual destiny. Hearing about the Self leaves no impression on the mind unless we have faith in what we hear.

The second step in the process is to reflect on what we have heard. Hearing does not mean credulous acceptance of what has been heard. We often cling to our preconceived ideas, arbitrary opinions, and want to hear only from those who support those ideas and opinions. That predisposition of mind leads us to read literature and listen to lectures that only reinforce rather than challenge our views. This same attitude impels us to seek guidance not from impartial critics but from likeminded persons and flatterers, which keeps us just as miserable and restless as we were before. Religion without reflection, therefore, often leads to dogmatism, fundamentalism, and fanaticism. Without reflection, life is disrupted at every step by our unstable emotions and uncontrolled gross impulses.

We can only have faith in ourselves and devotion to our goal if what we hear is properly understood through continuous reflection and meditation. Sri Ramakrishna says, "A real devotee develops the power of assimilating instruction. An image can not be impressed on bare glass, but only on glass stained with a black solution, as in photography. The black solution is devotion to God."[7]

Along the spiritual path, idle fancy often passes as faith and emotional bias of the mind as objectivity. This trickery of the mind can only be dealt with through reflection, which encourages honest doubt and objective analysis. It is true that reflection alone cannot tell us what truth is, but it can tell us what truth is not. Reflection provides us a steady ground to land on when assailed by doubt and disbelief. Genuine faith is like a flaming fire that consumes deep-seated beliefs and doubts. But we need reflection to kindle the flame of faith within us. Reflection in jnana-yoga is not conventional reasoning and rationalizing. True spiritual reflection concludes "Brahman alone exists, and I must realize that my existence is one with it."

The third step in the technique of jnana-yoga is right apprehension of Brahman. Hearing about truth from an enlightened teacher stirs up the mind with strong suggestions about the Self; reflection on what we have heard protects our newborn faith from countervailing prejudices, negative emotions, untested doctrines, and uncritically accepted notions; but right apprehension transforms our new faith into an all-consuming, immediate, and natural intuition. The mind takes the form of that which we perceive through our senses. The objects of the senses act only as suggestions toward that perception. One, therefore, sees Brahman within only when the entire mind is directed toward it and is possessed by it.

There is a marked difference between right apprehension (nididhyasana) and dualistic meditation (dhyana), which is generally practiced with the aid of physical, mental, or verbal symbols. Nididhyasana depends more upon the nature of the thing to be known than on the knower's mind. Dualistic meditation is practiced on Saguna Brahman, or Brahman with attributes, and rarely on Nirguna Brahman, or Brahman as Pure Consciousness without attributes. It is less difficult to concentrate the mind on something concrete than on formless Pure Consciousness. Therefore, beginners on the path of jnana-yoga are advised to practice meditation on Saguna Brahman with the help of a visual or auditory symbol.

Right apprehension (*nididhyasana*) is more than meditation on the Self as Brahman; it is the right and direct experience of Brahman. By repudiating all pretensions and addictions of the mind, the Self is grasped as Brahman, or undifferentiated Pure Consciousness. While the practice of meditation depends upon scriptural prescriptions and the aspirant's faith in them, right apprehension depends upon the nature of the object to be known and the means adopted for such knowledge. Again, the imagination has a role to play in the practice of meditation. The image or deity, for example, is taken as a symbol of God. But in right apprehension, there is no imagination. Right apprehension directly leads to *samadhi,* or realization of the Absolute. By realizing the Self as Brahman, the aspirant sees Brahman everywhere; everything outside becomes nothing but a reflection of everything inside. The more the yogi realizes "I am Brahman," the more the yogi sees "All this is verily Brahman." By following the course of *nididhyasana,* the jnana-yogi ultimately reaches Brahman, the bedrock of the individual and universal consciousness.

The intense bliss of Self-knowledge overwhelms the jnana-yogi, and he or she remains immersed in that bliss and does not care to return to the world from the realm of the Self. If and when the jnana-yogi comes back to the world of diversity, the spell of the Absolute does not recede and all perceptions of diversity are overpowered by an awareness of an all-pervasive unity. The *Mundaka Upanishad* describes the nature of this realization:

> As flowing rivers disappear in the sea, losing their names and forms, so a wise man, freed from name and form, attains the Purusha, who is greater than the Great.

He who knows the Supreme Brahman verily becomes Brahman.[8]

The human mind, the jnana-yogi contends, has become obsessed with the notion of duality. It separates the spiritual from the secular, transcendent from empirical, mediate from immediate, and energy from matter. The whole cosmos is in reality but one undivided substance, manifesting itself in diverse ways through various forms. There is one life force that runs through all things like a continuous chain of which various forms are various links. The bedrock of Ultimate Reality, therefore, is not the duality but non-duality of Being. The more our discursive intellect tries to objectify the truth, the more it eludes our grasp. Meaningful liberation frees us from all obsessions of duality—birth and death, pain and pleasure, good and bad, holy and unholy, pure and impure, and so forth.

According to jnana-yoga, liberation is to be attained here and now. The *Katha Upanishad* says:

What is here, the same is there; and what is there, the same is here. He goes from death to death who sees any difference here.

By the mind alone is Brahman to be realized; then one does not see in It any multiplicity whatsoever. He goes from death to death who sees multiplicity in It. This, verily, is That.[9]

In contrast, liberation in raja-yoga is the detachment of the mind from the Self; in jnana-yoga, the mind is united with Brahman. Liberation in raja-yoga may be said to be negative, described as the cessation of all miseries. The emphasis of jnana-yoga, on the other hand, is on the positive attainment of absolute bliss.

Nididhyasana is not constructing a new theory of God but deepening our Self-awareness in order to discover the unity of Brahman. It is a one-pointed dive into the Self, with the one goal of realizing the unity of the Absolute. In the process of

Self-realization, the aspirant first repudiates all diversities of the universe as unreal. But with the dawning of Self-knowledge within, the aspirant begins to see that the diversities negated before were not unreal but rather disguises of the Absolute. In the depth of *nididhyasana,* all the names and forms of the Divine dissolve into one—the one Supreme Reality. Any concept of Reality that is parochial and provincial is not to be mistaken for the Absolute. While our beliefs, theories, and systems of thought change, the Absolute is eternal and changeless. Even the testimony of the scriptures proves imperfect when this realization is attained. There is nothing more to be known and nothing more to be gained. As Shankaracharya says, the scriptures are intended for the unillumined. "Scripture cannot directly describe the true nature of the non-dual Atman. It is of no use to the knower of Ultimate Reality."[10]

Self-realization is the inescapable destiny of every human being. The ignorant think that realization of Brahman is impossible to attain. The illumined say that it is impossible for the ignorant to forget Brahman and remain ignorant forever.

23

Two Aspects of Liberation

The yogi endowed with complete enlightenment sees, through the eye of Knowledge, the entire universe in his own Self and regards everything as the Self and nothing else.

—SHANKARACHARYA

There are two stages of liberation in jnana-yoga: the ascent and descent of the mind. These two stages indicate two distinct movements of consciousness—one from without to within and the other from within to without. One is realizing the Self in isolation; the other is seeing the same Self behind the veil of names and forms. One is known as *jnana,* or realizing the spirit through negation, the other as *vijnana,* or the spiritualization of everything. As described by Sri Ramakrishna:

> Jnana is the realization of Self through the process of "Neti, neti." "Not this, not this." One goes into samadhi through this process of elimination and realizes the Atman.
>
> But vijnana means Knowledge with a greater fullness.... After having the vision of God one talks to Him as if He were an intimate relative. That is vijnana.[1]

The movement from *jnana* to *vijnana* is the movement from realizing Brahman to be the individual Self to realizing Brahman to be the totality. The *vijnani* sees that Reality is *nirguna*, without attributes, as well as *saguna*, with attributes, and enjoys both stages of *jnana* and *vijnana*—that is to say, realizing Brahman in *samadhi* and realizing Brahman in the whole universe.

ASCENT OF THE MIND

Jnana-yoga describes in metaphorical language seven planes of consciousness or seven levels of an aspirant's inner unfoldment. These seven planes are similar to the six centers of consciousness described by raja-yoga.

The first plane, which lies at the base of the spine, is the center of all body consciousness. Dwelling on this plane, a person's mind remains focused only on the pursuit of bodily pleasures. Above the first plane, at the organ of generation, lies the second plane, the focal point of the individual ego, which holds together all instincts and urges and asserts its claim over them. The third plane is located at the level of the navel. On rising to this plane, one witnesses the various sense organs busy in their activities. The mind ascending and descending between these first three planes only thinks of three things in this world: eating, sleeping, and sexual gratification.

Rising above gross consciousness, the mind reaches the fourth plane located at the level of the heart. The fifth plane, located at the throat, is the seat of the pure intellect free from all attachments. The sixth plane lies between the eyebrows and is the abode of the universal ego—the ego that is free from the constraints of individuality. The seventh plane is at the crown of the head. It is the summit of pure existence, the abode of nondual pure being, beyond the experiences of life and its flow of changes. Ascending step by step to these latter four planes, the mind dwells only on thoughts of God and the ever-pure Self.

Following the course of spiritual awakening, aspirants experience these seven levels of consciousness that hitherto had remained unperceived. The ascent is the process of isolating the Self from the influences of body, mind, ego, and pure intellect. In the process of ascent, as aspirants reach the second plane, they begin to look toward the body from the perspective of a third person. Before, they were totally identified with the body, but now they feel the body to be a separate entity. Remaining detached, aspirants ascend to the third plane and calmly observe the mind and its various desires. From this plane, they watch the outgoing nature of the sense organs that constantly draw in sense data from the outside world, which flood the unconscious. They were previously harassed by their sense organs, but now as detached witnesses to their activities, they feel a sense of freedom and rest.

Such detached observers then reach the fourth plane and discover that all emotions and feelings are characteristics of an egocentric identity, which cares more for itself than for others. As aspirants detect this fact, they dissociate themselves from the ego and reach the fifth plane of pure intellect. Ascending to this plane, they perceive the intellect in its pure form, free from all inhibition and fixation, and recall that this pure intellect was once intimidated and overpowered by the ego. They then decide to go further. They detach themselves from the intellect and reach the sixth plane, and here they clearly and fully witness their own minds—made of thoughts, consciousness, and ego-self—which, through their various ramifications, have built the structures of their individualities. The sixth plane is the last of the layers of embodiment such aspirants have yet to transcend. From the sixth plane, they catch a glimpse of the limitless Self, the undivided Pure Consciousness. The seventh plane is the peak of the ascent. It is the plane of pure being in which all three concepts of perception—knowledge, knower, and the known—become one. As Sri Ramakrishna says:

After passing the six centres the aspirant arrives at the seventh plane. Reaching it, the mind merges in Brahman. The individual soul and the Supreme Soul become one. The aspirant goes into samadhi. His consciousness of the body disappears. He loses the knowledge of the outer world. He does not see the manifold anymore. His reasoning comes to a stop.[2]

DESCENT OF THE MIND

The seventh plane of consciousness is not a stopping ground but a stepping-stone toward a beatific vision that reveals everything as the dynamic transfiguration of one's own Self. The course of this dynamic beatitude is known as the descent of the mind from the bliss and stillness of the Absolute to the harmony and peace of relative existence as perceived through the categories of time, space, and causation.

The fundamental principle of jnana-yoga is that the external world is nothing but the reflection of our own minds. As we change within, we perceive corresponding changes without. The *jnani* who has reached the seventh plane becomes a *vijnani* who sees the universe and all living beings as the diverse manifestations of the Absolute. Everything that was negated as not-Self during the ascent is now looked upon as various aspects of the one Absolute—the one without a second. All difference between faith and reason and all contradiction between the Self and the not-Self vanish once and for all. There is nothing to discard or negate where the Self alone exists. The question of accepting one thing and rejecting another does not arise when everything is the transfiguration of one's own being. Ideas of negation and affirmation exist only in our minds and not in the Absolute. Yet, the jnana-yogi has first to adopt the method of negation and then affirmation. It is not possible to accept all as Self until that Self is discovered by discarding the superimposition of not-Self.

While the ascent is a movement upward from the bounds of body, senses, mind, intellect, and ego to the summit of our existence, the descent is a conscious and voluntary coming down from the stillness of absolute being to the planes of manifold becoming. If the ascent leads to the knowledge of the Self in its isolated form, the descent is a recognition of the same Self everywhere and in everything.

The descent of the mind is a process of gradual spiritualization of the inner life as well as of the outer world. As the mind emerges from the stillness of the seventh plane and comes down to the sixth, the aspirant assumes an ego, which is impartial, universal, and free from the biases of race, class, caste, culture, and tradition. The aspirant feels that the individual ego is connected to all things and beings of the universe in an equal manner. With this universal ego, the aspirant descends to the fifth plane, the plane of the intellect. The discursive intellect—which until now justified its self-aggrandizement—becomes inspired with a new vision of universal interdependence and unity. The sense of spiritual identification with all things and beings of the universe illumines the horizon of the mind and frees the aspirant from fear. Fear arises from a sense of duality. The conviction of spiritual unity with the cosmos breaks down all barriers of attachment as the mind descends to the plane of the heart, the fountainhead of all feelings. Egocentric feelings now become cosmocentric. The flow of the mind, until now obstructed by possessiveness, becomes spontaneous and unobstructed. The aspirant becomes infused with a feeling of universal sympathy and affinity.

The light of illumination, which had so far spiritualized the realms of ego, intellect, and heart, now enters the level of the senses and shines through all the doors of perception. Whatever the jnana-yogi sees, hears, touches, tastes, or smells becomes reminiscent of the Self. Whatever the yogi does—physically, mentally, intellectually, or spiritually—becomes a form of *yajna,* or offering in the fire of Self-knowledge. Sri Ramakrishna describes such a yogi as one who lives, as it were, in a house made of glass where light shines both inside and outside.[3]

The process of jnana-yoga first silences the ego, and then reveals an all-pervading Self common to all. This common Self of all creatures is the basis of all love and goodness. While the ascent of the mind leads the jnana-yogi to the realization of the cosmic Self—the center of perfect tranquility—the descent indicates a gradual return to the everyday world without losing that center. In a sense, the descent fulfills the purpose of ascent. The aim of jnana-yoga is not to achieve a sheltered haven of *kaivalya,* as in raja-yoga, but to liberate the soul and also the body and the mind. The jnana-yogi remains firmly established in the knowledge of oneness even while living in the midst of the diversities of this world. Like the needle of a compass that always points toward the true north, the mind of the jnana-yogi always points toward the true Absolute.

The realization of the Self as one and many at the same time, which the jnana-yogi attains by following the course of ascent and descent, is absolute liberation in this very life. The yogi who has achieved this liberation is no longer deluded by ignorance. The liberated can have no fear of falling. Psychic visions may come and go. Yogic powers may be attained or lost. Ecstasies and emotions may have their ebb and flow. But the liberation that comes in the wake of Self-knowledge is everlasting. Once one has tasted the bliss of this liberation, one no longer desires any desire and forever remains in a state of divine inebriation. Shankaracharya vividly describes the behavior of such as liberated sage and says:

> Sometimes a fool, sometimes a sage, sometimes possessed
> of regal splendor; sometimes wandering, sometimes behav-
> ing like a motionless python, sometimes wearing a benignant
> expression; sometimes honoured, sometimes insulted, some-

times unknown—thus lives the man of realization, ever happy
with Supreme Bliss.[4]

Such a liberated soul is an enigma to the ordinary world plagued
by vanity, lust, greed, competition, and aggression. The liberated
jnana-yogi's value structure, way of life, and actions are seen to
be quite different from others. For the vast majority, to be normal is to be agitated, excited, and stressed—self-interest and sense
gratification are the laws of this world. While others float day and
night upon a stream of aimless thoughts and endless desires, the
jnana-yogi wields absolute mastery over all distracting thoughts
and emotions. The liberated soul lives and moves in the world
firmly fixed on the oneness of the Self. In everyday life, the liberated soul remains silent while others indulge in idle gossip or
futile arguments. The liberated soul never imposes his or her will
on others and never teaches those who do not want to be taught.
The liberated soul always looks upon the imperfections of others
with sympathetic understanding and patience, knowing that the
evolution of human nature cannot be hastened. The liberated
soul teaches others through the example of his or her own life.
The liberated soul is never secretive but always honest, truthful,
and at peace in the Self.

Although the liberated yogi and the ignorant person see the
same world, their angles of vision are radically different. One enjoys the world while the other is deluded by it. The ignorant person is like a pot that sinks in water because it attracts water into
it; the liberated person is like a boat floating on water without allowing the water to enter it. The liberated soul ever remains in a
state of meditation. There is no such thing as worldly activity for
one who is liberated, since the definitions of worldly activity and
meditation depend on the motive and not on the act itself. The
liberated soul, like a bird in the sky or a fish in water, leaves no
footprints behind. The liberated soul mingles with the world but
remains unidentified. The world looks upon the liberated soul as
the most impractical person and may never learn anything from

his or her life. Yet the liberated soul learns a great deal from the world and is amused to see how ignorance passes for knowledge, appearance for reality, and bondage for freedom. Shankaracharya aptly depicts the enigmatic character of the knower of Self:

> Though without riches, yet ever content; though helpless, yet very powerful; though not enjoying the sense-objects, yet eternally satisfied; though without an exemplar, yet looking upon all with an eye of equality.
>
> Though doing, yet inactive; though experiencing fruits of past actions, yet untouched by them; though possessed of a body, yet without identification with it; though limited, yet omnipresent is he.[5]

The liberated soul's life and actions demonstrate for us the reality of the Self, the divinity of the individual, and the unity of the cosmos. Having realized the Self in all, and all in the Self, the liberated soul looks upon the pleasure and pain of others as his or her own pain and pleasure. Though active, the liberated soul is not the doer of action. Whether at rest or active, whether the results of past actions bear fruit or not, the liberated soul is always at peace. Just as a drunken person is unaware of having on clothes, the liberated soul is unaware of the body. The world is like a theater, the Absolute a screen, and the changing phenomena moving pictures. The liberated soul enjoys seeing the movie, being aware of the screen. The Absolute is like a mirror and the multiplicities of the universe like passing reflections. The liberated soul sees the mirror and the reflections at the same time. Free from all attachments, from fear and worry, the liberated soul never broods over the past, never worries about the future, and lives only in the present.

The final conclusion of jnana-yoga is that we are self-exiles. We are pockets of isolated existence threatened by death and shadowed by fear and anxiety. We are unable to truly and unselfishly love anyone or anything in this world and are therefore deprived of love from others. We do not trust others because we do not trust ourselves. There is no permanent rest for us until we realize the Self. There is no permanent peace until we return to the deserted shrine of the heart, the abode of the Self. Attaining this wisdom makes a person a *jivanmukta,* or one liberated in this very life. The *jivanmukta* resolves the contradictions of life by spiritualizing all things and looking upon everything as the reflection of the great Self.

Life demands creative self-expression, the core of which is self-expansion. Ideas of exclusiveness, self-interest, and fanaticism on an individual or social level thwart this urge for self-expansion and give rise to various forms of isolation. These complexes—heightened by emotion, nurtured in the name of cultural refinement, religious fervor, economic gain, and political interest—breed separateness and degenerate into hatred, love of power, and a sense of prestige. Such developments are the symptoms of isolated existence. In every such isolated individual there is a deep anguish born of inner restlessness and desperation.

The way of the jnana-yogi is completely different. The yogi knows that hatred cannot be conquered by hatred and that there is no peace in isolation. Since our individual personality is part of the sum total of all personalities, our peace, happiness, and security depend on the peace, happiness, and security of all others. By complying with the laws of morality and ethics, we ensure the peace, happiness, and security of others and thus do good to ourselves. The Bible teaches us, "Thou shalt love thy neighbor as thyself" (Matt. 19:19). To one who asks, "Why should I love my neighbor?" the jnana-yogi answers, "Love thy neighbor as thyself because you and your neighbor are not different but one."

Jnana-yoga is ultimately a process of ego-analysis that lays bare the very root of our ego and helps us to discover our common Self. Self-knowledge is not just the knowledge of our own existence but of our common existence. Any idea that separates us from others is superstition. The basic assumption of all the systems of yoga is that humans are divine, and this divinity is indivisible. The *jivanmukta* calls upon us to analyze ourselves before analyzing everyone else. This analysis gives us the key to all the problems of life. Life without self-analysis is a psychological chaos that makes destiny uncertain, the goal of life indeterminable, and the purpose of life self-defeating. The ever-present Self cannot be ignored. One who runs away from it confronts it at every turn.

24
Obstacles in Jnana-Yoga

This, the firm control of the senses, is what is called
yoga. One must then be vigilant; for yoga can be both
beneficial and injurious.
—KATHA UPANISHAD 2.3.11

The path of jnana-yoga is for rationally and philosophically
minded spiritual seekers. Such seekers confront obstacles
that make it difficult for them to stay on the path. These obstacles are argumentation, egotism, loss of faith, mistaking intellectual understanding of the Self for Self-knowledge, selfishness,
and four distinctive obstacles in jnana-yoga meditation.

ARGUMENTATION

In the practice of discrimination, the seeker is likely to indulge in
many arguments that are inconclusive and futile and may thus
begin to take pleasure in arguing for argument's sake. There is
nothing like vain argumentation to inflame the mind and make it
unfit for the practice of concentration and meditation. For this reason, a seeker is advised not to express his or her philosophical
views unless asked and to refrain from the habit of contradicting
others. One should scrupulously avoid all gossip and also those

who indulge in it. The yogi must maintain an inner composure and tranquility at any cost to stay on the path of yoga. One who refuses to learn from one's past mistakes and the mistakes of others never makes progress in the path of jnana-yoga.

EGOTISM

Egotism is the most formidable enemy of the jnana-yogi. The ego pursues us like a shadow, assuming different forms and disguises. Though jnana-yoga directly leads to the perception of Reality and is regarded as the highest of yogas, a seeker in this path may easily become egotistic and overconfident. Blinded by egotism, the aspiring yogi may slight the worldly as incorrigibly ignorant and regard other forms of worship as imperfect, incomplete, and inferior. An egotistic person becomes intolerant of others, assumes the role of a reformer or teacher, and practices austerity and discrimination from a sense of self-righteousness, which is the worst form of self-deception. True Self-knowledge is incompatible with any kind of vanity or egotism. Self-knowledge is an all-consuming fire that burns to ashes all the seeker's prejudices and rationalizations. For a seeker of Self-knowledge, there is nothing more harmful than egotism and the premature desire to teach others.

LOSS OF FAITH

The philosophy of jnana-yoga greatly emphasizes reason. It says that we cannot have faith unless we have learned to question the unfounded authority of our prejudices and perversions that appear to be religious. But, as Swami Vivekananda says:

> The Devil can and indeed does quote the scriptures for his own purpose; and thus the way of knowledge appears to offer justification for what the bad man does, as much as it offers inducements for what the good man does. This is the great danger in Jnana-Yoga.[1]

Faith, according to jnana-yoga, is not mere opinion. It is an inner conviction born out of one's own experience and never from the experience of another. True faith never contradicts reason. Sincere faith and reason cooperate with each other in revealing the truth. Faith without reason promotes dogmatism, and reason without faith is mere intellectual gymnastics.

The goal of jnana-yoga reasoning is not to disprove the reality of the universe but to prove the reality of Brahman. Such reasoning is positive, open minded, and goal oriented. It proceeds from the particular to the general until it points toward the one, nondual Pure Consciousness. But reasoning becomes distorted when it fails to focus on the goal. When reason is not supported by the steadfast practice of meditation and not inspired by an intense longing for liberation, it becomes self-defeating. It can reduce the aspiring yogi to a bundle of opinions that makes him or her unable to commit to anything worthwhile to follow in practice. Having lost faith in the goal, the aspiring yogi lives in a universe devoid of divine presence and staggers under the weight of his or her own infirmity and limitation. In the words of Sri Ramakrishna:

> The jnanis follow the path of discrimination. Sometimes it happens that, discriminating between the Real and the unreal, a man loses his faith in the existence of God. But a devotee who sincerely yearns for God does not give up his meditation even though he is invaded by atheistic ideas. A man whose father and grandfather have been farmers continues his farming even though he doesn't get any crop in a year of drought.[2]

With this loss of faith, seekers can gradually give up their practice of meditation and discrimination. They feel weary and the path of jnana-yoga very soon becomes dry, dull, and deluding.

INTELLECTUAL UNDERSTANDING

A seeker can mistake an intellectual understanding of the Self for Self-knowledge. Intellectual understanding, however, does not stand up under trying circumstances and cannot take the seeker very far in yoga. A seeker must not remain satisfied with an intellectual understanding of the Self. Until one has tasted the bliss of Atman, one should continue onward and forward in the path of yoga.

SELFISHNESS

Seekers in the path of jnana-yoga often become selfish and insensitive, despising all expressions of human emotion as unspiritual and inimical to knowledge of the Self. In order to shield themselves from the temptations of the world, they indiscriminately brand everything as distracting and unholy. Reasoning makes them heartless, callous, and indifferent to the sufferings of others. In quest of God as the indweller, they overlook God manifested in all things and beings and develop strong hatred toward everything human. Their so-called piety and devotion to the pursuit of Self-knowledge actually spring from repression and frustration.

As a remedy for this obstacle, seekers may borrow practices from karma-yoga. If one is unwilling to sacrifice the selfish ego for the sake of the Self or for the service of others, one is not ready for the steep path of jnana-yoga.

OBSTACLES IN MEDITATION

There are four other obstacles in jnana-yoga a seeker should be careful to avoid. These are particular to jnana-yoga meditation: inertia, lack of control over the mind, mistaking lower stages of *samadhi* for higher stages, and a distaste for meditation itself.

Inertia, or *laya*, is the state of mind overcome by drowsiness, dullness, lethargy, and sleep. While practicing meditation, the seeker often falls into the state of *laya*, the mind being concentrated neither on Brahman nor on the world. Most seekers of meditation lapse into this state of *laya* and are held down by it because of their carelessness in the practice of the fourfold discipline. To overcome *laya*, the struggling seeker should study the scriptures, engage in unselfish activity, and seek holy company.

Sometimes the mind of the meditator vacillates from one object to another. This is known as *vikshepa*. Various manifestations of *vikshepa* are idle imaginations, aimless wanderings of the mind, a lack of control over sense desires, jealousy, anger, lust, and depression. Sometimes long-forgotten memories of sense enjoyments hidden in the unconscious mind suddenly appear before the mind of a struggling seeker, taking the mind by surprise and throwing it off balance. The mind that is accustomed to enjoy wandering in the midst of gross external objects finds it extremely difficult to dwell on a single object within. To overcome *vikshepa*, one must pacify the mind by cultivating positive, spiritual thoughts. Anger should be overcome by patience, lust by repetition of a mantra, and greed by renunciation. The seeker is advised to patiently bring the mind back to its object of meditation each time it wanders away.

Seekers moving along the path of jnana-yoga can also mistake lower stages of *samadhi* for higher stages, which prevents them from reaching the ultimate goal. This is known as *rasaswada*, which literally means "experiencing the joy of self-conquest." Seekers who finally defeat their deadliest enemies—passions and attachments—after a long life-and-death struggle often feel proud of their conquest and forget their ultimate goal. But if seekers prolong their enjoyment of a particular stage, they may altogether forget the goal and fail to understand the difference between the lesser degrees of joy and the absolute bliss of *nirvikalpa samadhi*. They may have experienced an end of suffering, intoxication of the Divine, and freedom of the soul, but these are trivial compared to the supreme bliss of the Self.

To overcome this obstacle, seekers are advised not to dwell too long on any experience of joy. However alluring is the joy of any stage along the path, they must not stop until the goal is reached. Commenting on jnana-yoga, Swami Vivekananda observes:

> Meditating on this reality [i.e., the unity of the Atman and Brahman] always and reminding the soul of its real nature are the only ways in this Yoga. It is the highest, but most difficult. Many persons get an intellectual grasp of it, but very few attain realisation.[3]

Finally, it can happen that the meditator begins to find meditation itself distasteful. This is known as *kashaya*. The seeker feels averse to meditation due to the mind's hidden attachments to sense enjoyments. The seeker may find all spiritual progress abruptly coming to a halt. Under such circumstances, the struggling seeker is advised to persevere, be patient, and never give up. The benefits of yoga are sure to come in due time.

PART FIVE

Conclusion

25
Harmony of the Yogas

The ultimate goal of mankind, the aim and end of all religions, is but one—reunion with God, or, what amounts to the same, with the divinity which is every man's true nature. But while the aim is one, the method of attaining may vary with the different temperaments of men. Both the goal and the methods employed for reaching it are called Yoga.

—SWAMI VIVEKANANDA

The goal of the four yogas is essentially the same. In karma-yoga, the goal is freedom, which takes the form of God-vision or Self-knowledge. In bhakti-yoga, the goal is communion with God in the form of the Chosen Ideal of the seeker. In raja-yoga, it is realization of the Self as Pure Consciousness, immortal, and ever free. In jnana-yoga, it is Self-knowledge that reveals the all-pervading, ever-blissful Self of the universe to be also the inmost Self of all beings.

The obstacles, too, are the same for all four yogas, namely, ignorance and all its ramifications. In karma-yoga, it is the ignorant ego that brings in its wake attachment, aversion, and desire for the results of action. In bhakti-yoga, the same ignorance creates self-love, which is at the root of all separateness of the individual soul from God, the universal soul. In raja-yoga, distractions and restlessness of the mind result from the same ignorance. In jnana-yoga, the same ignorance brings about spiritual blindness that blocks the perception of our true Self, the center of our being.

The exclusive practice of any of the four yogas is difficult. There are many obstacles that beset each path unless the seeker is extraordinary in his or her fitness and longing for the goal. Such an extraordinary seeker is rare. Hence the necessity for a harmonious practice of the four yogas.

Although each of the four yogas has been presented as an independent path to the Divine, the four are interconnected. When any one of the four yogas leads the way, the other three remain in the background. For example, in bhakti-yoga, when devotion leads the way, the other three yogas—of action, meditation, and knowledge—remain in the background to support the leader.

Practice of a harmonious combination of the four yogas is important because of the pitfalls and dangers on the way.

Karma-yoga calls for working with nonattachment to the results of action. But it is nearly impossible for an average seeker to practice nonattachment perfectly. Attaining this state of perfection requires a strong motivation for the goal, and to maintain this motivation, the seeker must practice the concentration and meditation of raja-yoga with the discrimination and dispassion of jnana-yoga. Without these foundational practices, the follower of karma-yoga often becomes addicted to activity and fails to pay attention to the motivation for action. As a result, karma-yoga becomes only karma and ceases to be yoga. Furthermore, only rare souls can work with nonattachment without succumbing to the praise or blame of others. The desire for fame and recognition distracts even the most extraordinary karma-yogis. Doing good must be preceded by being good. To see the presence of the Self in all and serve all calls for first seeing the presence of the Self within ourselves.

Bhakti-yoga is the path of love and devotion for God. There is the danger in this path that during practice the bhakti-yogi may attain only a foretaste of the Divine but take it to be everything and stop proceeding on the path. Sentiments and emotions often masquerade as devotion. True devotion in bhakti-yoga is always backed up by the discrimination and renunciation of a jnana-yogi. A seeker cannot attain true love of God without having the universal outlook of the path of knowledge and without practicing concentration and nonattachment. It is not unusual for a seeker in the path of bhakti-yoga to neglect the cultivation of knowledge, reason, and discrimination and become fanatic and dogmatic about his or her own sect, creed, and particular form of God. Self-surrender in this path can be an escape and divine grace can be misunderstood. So Sri Ramakrishna says:

> A man must work. Only then can he see God.... one cannot develop love of God or obtain the vision of Him without work. Work means meditation, worship and the like. The chanting of God's name and glories is work too. You may also include charity, sacrifice, and so on.... It is not that God can be realized by this work and not by that. The vision of God depends on His grace. Still a man must work a little with longing for God in his heart. If he has longing he will receive the grace of God.[1]

Followers of raja-yoga are often distracted by the lure of yogic powers and psychic attainments and neglect strengthening their moral foundation. Seekers on this path sometimes become anxious to forcibly awaken their spiritual consciousness through *pranayama, asana,* and austerities. But to raise the spiritual consciousness without having a strong motivation for attaining a spiritual goal is extremely dangerous. The only practice in this path is concentration and meditation, guided by strong willpower and total commitment to the goal. The raja-yogi can become preoccupied only with the practices of concentration and meditation and neglect the foundational practices of purity, chastity, and austerity. As a result, the seeker fails to make any progress. The raja-yogi should not forget the supporting practices of discrimination and renunciation of jnana-yoga, purification of bhakti-yoga, and nonattachment of karma-yoga to succeed on his or her path.

Jnana-yoga is the direct path of knowledge and calls for rejecting the world of the senses as illusory and for mercilessly practicing detachment and dispassion. Unless the jnana-yogi is careful, he or she can become egocentric, cold, dry, and insensitive. In the name of dispassion and discrimination, the jnana-yogi may brand all human emotions—including devotion to God—as human weaknesses and aberrations of the mind. The follower of this path may forget that knowledge has its counterpart in devotion. Overemphasizing the Vedic statement "I am Brahman," he or she forgets its counterpart, "That Thou art." Knowledge that fails to express itself as devotion for God is sterile and meaningless. Self-knowledge, when not expressed as self-dedication for the good of all, is no knowledge at all.

Swami Vivekananda compared the harmony of the yogas to the flight of a bird:

> Three things are necessary for a bird to fly: the two wings, and the tail as a rudder for steering. Jnana is the one wing, bhakti the other, and raja-yoga is the tail that maintains the balance. For those who cannot pursue all these three forms of worship together in harmony, and take up, therefore, bhakti alone as their way, it is necessary always to remember that forms and ceremonials, though absolutely necessary for the progressing soul, have no other value than to lead us to that state in which we feel the most intense love of God.[2]

Sri Ramakrishna emphasized the common goal of the four yogas: Self-knowledge or God-realization. As long as this goal is kept in sight, it is not important which path a seeker chooses to follow. Each yoga reveals a particular aspect of one and the same God. In the words of Sri Ramakrishna, "Whichever you follow, it is God that you will ultimately reach. The jnani looks on God in one way and the bhakta looks on Him in another way. The God of the jnani is full of brilliance, and the God of the bhakta is full of sweetness."[3]

The purpose of the spiritual quest is to attain the knowledge of Brahman, the Ultimate Reality, and a seeker may decide whether he or she wants to control the mind, purify the mind, persuade the mind, or remove the false ego of the mind in order to attain knowledge of Brahman. Sri Ramakrishna says, "The upshot of the whole thing is that, no matter what path you follow, yoga is impossible unless the mind becomes quiet. The mind of a yogi is under his control; he is not under the control of his mind."[4] By the harmonious practice of all the four yogas, the seeker avoids the pitfalls and roadblocks on the path of yoga and attains the goal of the spiritual quest.

Notes

Introduction

1. Swami Nikhilananda, *Vivekananda: The Yogas and Other Works* (New York: Ramakrishna-Vivekananda Center, 1996), 499.

2. Ibid., 454.

3. Ibid., 582.

4. Quoted in Swami Nikhilananda, trans., *Self-Knowledge* (New York: Ramakrishna-Vivekananda Center, 1989), 217.

5. Swami Nikhilananda, trans., *The Gospel of Sri Ramakrishna* (New York: Ramakrishna-Vivekananda Center, 2000), 113.

6. Swami Nikhilananda, *Vivekananda: The Yogas and Other Works*, 493–94.

7. *Complete Works of Swami Vivekananda*, vol. 3 (Calcutta: Advaita Ashrama, 1973), 321.

Chapter 1: The Message of Karma-Yoga

1. Swami Nikhilananda, *Vivekananda: The Yogas and Other Works*, 498–99.

2. See Swami Vireswarananda, trans., *Srimad Bhagavad Gita* 3.30 (Chennai: Sri Ramakrishna Math, n.d.), 160.

3. See Swami Nikhilananda, trans., *The Bhagavad Gita* 18.41, (New York: Ramakrishna-Vivekananda Center, 1992), 358–60.

4. See ibid., 9.27–28, pp. 230–31.

5. See Swami Madhavananda, trans., *Vivekachudamani of Sri Sankaracarya*, v. 24, (Calcutta: Advaita Ashrama, 1970), 9.

6. Swami Nikhilananda, *Vivekananda: The Yogas and Other Works*, 805–6.

7. See Swami Nikhilananda, *Bhagavad Gita* 10.8, p. 239.

8. See Swami Nikhilananda, *Gospel of Sri Ramakrishna*, 436.

9. Swami Nikhilananda, *Bhagavad Gita* 12.5–11, pp. 273–77.

CHAPTER 2: THE PHILOSOPHY AND PSYCHOLOGY OF KARMA-YOGA

1. Swami Nikhilananda, *Vivekananda: The Yogas and Other Works*, 497.

2. See Swami Nikhilananda, *Bhagavad Gita* 5.18–19, 6.29, pp. 155, 170.

3. See ibid., 12.13–14, 2.48–50, pp. 279, 88–90.

4. See Swami Nikhilananda, *Vivekananda: The Yogas and Other Works*, 453.

5. See Swami Nikhilananda, *Bhagavad Gita* 2.55–72, pp. 93–101.

6. See ibid., 7.14, pp. 187–89.

7. See ibid., 11.32, p. 261.

8. See ibid., 13.12, pp. 288–89.

CHAPTER 3: KARMA-YOGA AND TRUE RENUNCIATION

1. Swami Nikhilananda, *Vivekananda: The Yogas and Other Works*, 463.

2. *Complete Works of Swami Vivekananda*, vol. 6 (Calcutta: Advaita Ashrama, 1972), 84.

3. Swami Nikhilananda, *Bhagavad Gita* 4.18, p. 132.

4. Swami Nikhilananda, *Vivekananda: The Yogas and Other Works*, 820.

5. Swami Nikhilananda, *Bhagavad Gita* 3.11–12, p. 108.

6. Ibid., 140.

CHAPTER 4: THE PRACTICE OF KARMA-YOGA

1. Swami Nikhilananda, *Bhagavad Gita* 3.26, p. 114.

2. Ibid., 3.4, p. 104.

3. Ibid., 3.6, p. 105.

4. Swami Nikhilananda, *Gospel of Sri Ramakrishna*, 139, 194, 672.

5. Swami Nikhilananda, *Vivekananda: The Yogas and Other Works*, 480–81.

6. Swami Nikhilananda, *Bhagavad Gita* 3.35, p. 119.

7. See ibid., 17.11–13, pp. 331–35.

8. Ibid., 18.13–14, p. 349.

9. Swami Nikhilananda, *Vivekananda: The Yogas and Other Works*, 806.

10. *Sayings of Sri Ramakrishna* (Chennai: Sri Ramakrishna Math, 2003), 289.

11. See Swami Nikhilananda, *Bhagavad Gita* 18.26, p. 354.

12. See ibid., 3.27, p. 155.

CHAPTER 5: KARMA-YOGA FOR SELF-KNOWLEDGE

1. Swami Nikhilananda, *Bhagavad Gita* 6.3–4, p. 162.

2. Swami Nikhilananda, *Vivekananda: The Yogas and Other Works*, 458.

3. Swami Nikhilananda, *Bhagavad Gita* 8.7, p. 199.

4. Ibid., 6.14, p. 166.

5. Ibid., 18.57, p. 366.

6. See Swami Nikhilananda, *Vivekananda: The Yogas and Other Works*, 650.

7. Quoted in Swami Nikhilananda, *Bhagavad Gita*, 241.

8. Ibid., 4.24, p. 136.

9. Swami Nikhilananda, *Gospel of Sri Ramakrishna*, 478.

10. See Swami Nikhilananda, *Bhagavad Gita* 2.55–72, pp. 93–101.

11. Ibid., 5.24, p. 158.

CHAPTER 6: OBSTACLES IN KARMA-YOGA

1. See Swami Nikhilananda, *Bhagavad Gita* 2.62–63, pp. 96–97.

2. See Swami Nikhilananda, *Gospel of Sri Ramakrishna*, 81.

3. Swami Nikhilananda, *Vivekananda: The Yogas and Other Works*, 479.

CHAPTER 7: THE MESSAGE OF BHAKTI-YOGA

1. Swami Nikhilananda, *Vivekananda: The Yogas and Other Works*, 432.

2. Ibid., 432–33.

3. Ibid., 433.

4. Swami Nikhilananda, *Bhagavad Gita* 9.31, p. 232.

CHAPTER 8: THE PHILOSOPHY AND PSYCHOLOGY OF BHAKTI-YOGA

1. *Chhandogya Upanishad* 3.14.1, in *The Upanishads*, vol. 4, trans. Swami Nikhilananda (New York: Ramakrishna-Vivekananda Center, 1994), 206.

2. *Mundaka Upanishad* 1.1.7, in *The Upanishads*, vol. 1, trans. Swami Nikhilananda (New York: Ramakrishna-Vivekananda Center, 1990), 264.

3. *Taittiriya Upanishad* 3.6.1, in *Upanishads*, vol. 4, 73.

4. Swami Nikhilananda, trans., *The Gospel of Sri Ramakrishna*, abridged ed. (New York: Ramakrishna-Vivekananda Center, 1996), 233.

5. Swami Nikhilananda, *Gospel of Sri Ramakrishna*, 478.

6. Ibid., 277.

7. Swami Madhavananda, trans., *Uddhava Gita or The Last Message of Sri Krishna* 9.20–22 (Calcutta: Advaita Ashrama, 1971), 132.

8. Swami Prabhavananda, trans., *Narada's Way of Divine Love*, vv. 31, 32 (Hollywood: Vedanta Press, 1971), 75.

9. Swami Nikhilananda, *Gospel of Sri Ramakrishna*, 83.

10. Swami Nikhilananda, *Vivekananda: The Yogas and Other Works*, 417.

11. Swami Madhavananda, *Uddhava Gita* 4.22, p. 66.

12. Swami Nikhilananda, *Gospel of Sri Ramakrishna*, 844.

13. Ibid., 542.

14. Ibid., 703.

15. Swami Nikhilananda, *Gospel of Sri Ramakrishna*, abridged ed., 245–46.

CHAPTER 9: PREPARATORY PRACTICES IN BHAKTI-YOGA

1. Swami Nikhilananda, *Gospel of Sri Ramakrishna*, 95.

2. Ibid., 255.

3. Ibid., 659.

4. Ibid., 465.

5. *Complete Works of Swami Vivekananda*, vol. 4 (Calcutta: Advaita Ashrama, 1966), 5.

6. *Complete Works of Swami Vivekananda*, vol. 4, 11.

7. Swami Nikhilananda, *Vivekananda: The Yogas and Other Works*, 426.

CHAPTER 10: CHARACTERISTICS OF THE TEACHER AND THE ASPIRANT

1. Swami Nikhilananda, *Gospel of Sri Ramakrishna*, 168.

2. Swami Nikhilananda, *Vivekananda: The Yogas and Other Works*, 415.

3. Ibid., 418–19.

4. Swami Nikhilananda, *Gospel of Sri Ramakrishna*, 648–49.

5. Swami Tapasyananda, trans., *Srimad Bhagavatam: The Holy Book of God* 11.2.55 (Madras: Sri Ramakrishna Math, 1982), 14.

6. Swami Nikhilananda, *Bhagavad Gita* 12.13–19, pp. 279–81.

7. Ibid., 9.30–31, p. 232.

8. Swami Madhavananda, *Uddhava Gita* 9.18, p. 131.

CHAPTER 11: SPIRITUAL DISCIPLINES IN BHAKTI-YOGA

1. Swami Nikhilananda, *Gospel of Sri Ramakrishna*, 680.

2. Vishnu Puri, *Bhakti Ratnavali or A Necklace of Devotional Gems*, trans. Swami Tapasyananda (Madras: Sri Ramakrishna Math, 1979), 151.

3. Swami Nikhilananda, *Gospel of Sri Ramakrishna*, abridged ed., 213.

4. See Swami Hitananda, *Worship of Sri Ramakrishna* (Madras: Sri Ramakrishna Math, 1982), 30.

5. Quoted in Swami Nikhilananda, *Hinduism: Its Meaning for the Liberation of the Spirit* (New York: Ramakrishna-Vivekananda Center of New York, 1992), 170.

6. Swami Madhavananda, *Uddhava Gita* 6.33, p. 94.

7. Swami Nikhilananda, *Gospel of Sri Ramakrishna*, 588.

8. Quoted in Swami Tyagisananda, trans., *Narada Bhakti Sutras* (Madras: Sri Ramakrishna Math, 1972), 188.

9. See *Chhandogya Upanishad* 1.1.10, in *Upanishads*, vol. 4, 116.

10. *Complete Works of Swami Vivekananda*, vol. 5 (Calcutta: Advaita Ashrama, 1970), 324.

11. See Swami Nikhilananda, *Gospel of Sri Ramakrishna*, 105.

12. Quoted in Swami Tyagisananda, *Narada Bhakti Sutras*, 51.

13. Ibid., 51.

14. Ibid., 52.

15. Quoted in Swami Nikhilananda, *Vivekananda: The Yogas and Other Works*, 406.

16. Swami Nikhilananda, *Gospel of Sri Ramakrishna*, 114.

17. Ibid., 255.

18. Swami Prabhavananda, *Narada's Way of Divine Love*, v. 6, p. 33.

19. Swami Nikhilananda, *Gospel of Sri Ramakrishna*, 611.

20. Ibid., 369.

21. Swami Saradananda, *Sri Ramakrishna, The Great Master*, trans. Swami Jagadananda (Madras: Sri Ramakrishna Math, 1970), 455–56.

22. Swami Nikhilananda, *Gospel of Sri Ramakrishna*, 115.

23. Quoted in Aswini Kumar Datta, *Bhaktiyoga* (Bombay: Bharatiya Vidya Bhavan, 1971), 190.

24. Ibid.

25. See ibid., 190–91.

26. Ibid., 191–92.

27. Swami Nikhilananda, *Gospel of Sri Ramakrishna*, 449.

28. Ibid., 77.

CHAPTER 12: OBSTACLES IN BHAKTI-YOGA

1. Swami Nikhilananda, *Bhagavad Gita* 2.62–63, p. 96.

2. Quoted in Aswini Kumar Datta, *Bhaktiyoga*, 39.

3. Ibid., 56.

4. Swami Nikhilananda, *Holy Mother: Being the Life of Sri Sarada Devi, Wife of Sri Ramakrishna, and Helpmate in His Mission* (New York: Ramakrishna-Vivekananda Center of New York, 1962), 319.

5. *Complete Works of Swami Vivekananda*, vol. 5, 386.

6. Swami Nikhilananda, *Gospel of Sri Ramakrishna*, 729.

7. *Complete Works of Swami Vivekananda*, vol. 7 (Calcutta: Advaita Ashrama, 1972), 254–55.

8. Swami Nikhilananda, *Vivekananda: The Yogas and Other Works*, 415.

CHAPTER 13: THE MESSAGE OF RAJA-YOGA

1. Swami Nikhilananda, *Vivekananda: The Yogas and Other Works*, 582.

2. Ibid., 545.

3. Ibid., 547.

4. Quoted in Georg Feuerstein, *Sacred Paths* (Burdett, N.Y.: Larson Publications, 1991), 113.

5. Swami Nikhilananda, *Vivekananda: The Yogas and Other Works*, 618.

CHAPTER 14: THE PHILOSOPHY AND PSYCHOLOGY OF RAJA-YOGA

1. Swami Nikhilananda, *Gospel of Sri Ramakrishna*, 653.

2. Swami Nikhilananda, *Vivekananda: The Yogas and Other Works*, 632–33.

3. Ibid., 629–30.

4. Ibid., 633.

5. Ibid., 214.

CHAPTER 15: PREPARATORY PRACTICES IN RAJA-YOGA

1. Swami Nikhilananda, *Vivekananda: The Yogas and Other Works*, 610–11.

2. Swami Nikhilananda, *Bhagavad Gita* 17.14–16, p. 338.

3. See *Katha Upanishad* 1.2.11-5, in *Upanishads*, vol. 1, 136–38.

CHAPTER 16: THE EIGHT-LIMBED PRACTICE

1. Swami Nikhilananda, *Gospel of Sri Ramakrishna*, 312.

2. See Swami Nikhilananda, *Vivekananda: The Yogas and Other Works*, 859, 870, 872.

3. Ibid., 606.

4. Ibid., 664.

5. *Complete Works of Swami Vivekananda*, vol. 1 (Calcutta: Advaita Ashrama, 1972), 520, 518.

6. Swami Madhavananda, *Vivekachudamani*, v. 13, p. 5.

7. Swami Hariharananda Aranya, *Yoga Philosophy of Patanjali* (Albany: State University of New York Press, 1983), 245.

8. Swami Nikhilananda, *Vivekananda: The Yogas and Other Works*, 609.

9. Ibid., 666.

10. Ibid., 608.

11. See ibid., 667.

12. Ibid., 631–32.

13. Ibid., 617.

14. Ibid., 604.

15. Ibid., 609–10.

16. Ibid., 587.

17. Ibid., 659–60.

CHAPTER 17: OBSTACLES IN RAJA-YOGA

1. Swami Nikhilananda, *Vivekananda: The Yogas and Other Works*, 637.

2. Ibid., 637–38.

3. Ibid., 611.

4. Ibid., 584.

5. See ibid., 606.

6. Ibid., 661.

7. Ibid., 587.

8. Ibid., 610.

CHAPTER 18: THE MESSAGE OF JNANA-YOGA

1. *Brihadaranyaka Upanishad* 1.4.8, in *The Upanishads,* vol. 3, trans. Swami Nikhilananda (New York: Ramakrishna-Vivekananda Center, 1990), 121.

2. See Swami Nikhilananda, *Hinduism,* 116.

3. *Katha Upanishad* 1.2.12, in *Upanishads,* vol. 1, 136.

CHAPTER 19: THE PHILOSOPHY AND PSYCHOLOGY OF JNANA-YOGA

1. Swami Nikhilananda, *Gospel of Sri Ramakrishna,* 216.

CHAPTER 20: THE GOAL OF JNANA-YOGA: SELF-KNOWLEDGE

1. Swami Nikhilananda, *Self-Knowledge,* 17.

2. Ibid., 15.

3. See ibid.

CHAPTER 21: THE PRACTICE OF JNANA-YOGA

1. Swami Madhavananda, *Vivekachudamani,* v. 65, p. 23.

2. Swami Nikhilananda, *Gospel of Sri Ramakrishna,* 179.

3. See Swami Madhavananda, trans., *The Vairagya-Satakam or The Hundred Verses on Renunciation,* v. 31 (Calcutta: Advaita Ashrama, 1971), 19.

4. See *Brihadaranyaka Upanishad* 5.14.3, in *Upanishads,* vol. 3, 340.

5. *Katha Upanishad* 1.2.6, in *Upanishads,* vol. 1, 132.

6. Swami Madhavananda, *Vivekachudamani,* v. 77, p. 28.

7. Swami Nikhilananda, *Gospel of Sri Ramakrishna,* 410.

8. Ibid., 165–66.

9. Ibid., 750.

10. Swami Madhavananda, *Vivekachudamani,* v. 176, p. 68.

11. See Swami Nikhilananda, *Gospel of Sri Ramakrishna*, 82.

12. Swami Madhavananda, *Vivekachudamani*, v. 56, p. 20.

13. Ibid., v. 62, p. 22.

14. Swami Nikhilananda, *Bhagavad Gita* 6.24–25, p. 168.

15. Swami Madhavananda, *Vivekachudamani*, v. 79, p. 29.

16. Quoted in First Disciples of Shri Ramakrishna, *Spiritual Talks* (Calcutta: Advaita Ashrama, 1968), 212.

17. Swami Nikhilananda, *Vivekananda: The Yogas and Other Works*, 744–45.

18. Swami Madhavananda, *Vivekachudamani*, v. 26, p. 9.

19. Swami Nikhilananda, *Gospel of Sri Ramakrishna*, 243–44.

20. Ibid., 674.

21. Swami Nikhilananda, *Vivekananda: The Yogas and Other Works*, 799–800.

CHAPTER 22: MEDITATION FOR SELF-KNOWLEDGE

1. See Swami Madhavananda, *Vivekachudamani*, v. 31, p. 11.

2. Swami Nikhilananda, *Gospel of Sri Ramakrishna*, 403–4.

3. Swami Nikhilananda, *Vivekananda: The Yogas and Other Works*, 669.

4. *Chhandogya Upanishad* 6.8.7, in *Upanishads*, vol. 4, 309.

5. *Brihadaranyaka Upanishad* 1.4.10, in *Upanishads*, vol. 3, 122–23.

6. Swami Nikhilananda, *Gospel of Sri Ramakrishna*, 476.

7. Ibid., 244.

8. *Mundaka Upanishad* 3.2.8–9, in *Upanishads*, vol. 1, 309.

9. *Katha Upanishad* 2.1.10–11, in *Upanishads*, vol. 1, 165–66.

10. Swami Nikhilananda, trans., *The Upanishads*, vol. 2 (New York: Ramakrishna-Vivekananda Center, 2004), 273.

CHAPTER 23: TWO ASPECTS OF LIBERATION

1. Swami Nikhilananda, *Gospel of Sri Ramakrishna*, 417.

2. Ibid., 245.

3. See ibid., 242.

4. Swami Madhavananda, *Vivekachudamani*, v. 542, p. 202.

5. Ibid., vv. 543–44, pp. 202–3.

CHAPTER 24: OBSTACLES IN JNANA-YOGA

   1. Swami Nikhilananda, *Vivekananda: The Yogas and Other Works*, 437.

   2. Swami Nikhilananda, *Gospel of Sri Ramakrishna*, 238.

   3. Ibid., 155.

CHAPTER 25: HARMONY OF THE YOGAS

   1. Swami Nikhilananda, *Gospel of Sri Ramakrishna*, 645–46.

   2. Swami Nikhilananda, *Vivekananda: The Yogas and Other Works*, 406.

   3. Swami Nikhilananda, *Gospel of Sri Ramakrishna*, 768.

   4. Ibid., 248.

Glossary

Advaita Nonduality; a school of Vedanta philosophy, declaring the oneness of God, soul, and universe.

agami **(karma)** The action that will be performed by an individual in the future. Karma, or the result of past actions, is divided into three categories: *prarabdha, agami,* and *sanchita. Prarabdha* is that which has already begun to fructify; *agami* is that which is ready to fructify; and *sanchita* is that which is stored up or held in reserve. It is illustrated by the familiar example from archery. *Prarabdha* is like an arrow that has left the bow; it must strike the target. *Agami* is like an arrow that is attached to the bow string; it is ready to be released but can be withheld. And *sanchita* is like an arrow in the quiver; it is held in reserve.

Ananda Bliss.

Arjuna A hero of the epic *Mahabharata* and a friend and disciple of Sri Krishna. Sri Krishna delivered the teachings of the Bhagavad Gita to Arjuna.

artha Attainment of worldly prosperity; one of the four values of life.

Atman Self or soul; denotes also the Supreme Soul, which, according to the Advaita Vedanta, is one with the individual soul.

avidyamaya   Maya, or illusion causing duality, has two aspects, namely, *avidyamaya* and *vidyamaya*. *Avidyamaya*, or the "maya of ignorance," consisting of anger, passion, and so on, entangles one in worldliness. *Vidyamaya*, or the "maya of knowledge," consisting of kindness, purity, unselfishness, and so on, leads one to liberation. Both belong to the relative world. See **maya.**

Bhagavad Gita   An important Hindu scripture, part of the *Mahabharata* epic, containing the teachings of Sri Krishna.

Bhagavatam   A sacred book of the Hindus describing the life of Sri Krishna.

bhakta   A follower of the path of *bhakti*, or divine love; a worshiper of the personal God.

bhakti   Devotion; love of God.

bhakti-yoga   The path of devotion followed by dualistic worshipers.

Bharata   Literally, a descendent of the ancient King Bharata. In the Bhagavad Gita, Bharata refers to Arjuna, a descendent of King Bharata. See **Arjuna.**

bhava   Existence; feeling; emotion; ecstasy; *samadhi;* also denotes any one of the five attitudes that a dualistic worshiper assumes toward God. The first of these attitudes is that of peace; assuming the other four attitudes, the devotee regards God as the Master, Child, Friend, or Beloved.

bhava samadhi   Ecstasy in which the devotee retains his or her ego and enjoys communion with the personal God.

brahmachari   A celibate student undergoing mental and moral training under a preceptor in the old Hindu style; a novice in a Hindu monastery preparing for the life of a monk.

brahmacharya   The state of a *brahmachari;* the life of an unmarried student.

Brahman   The Absolute; the Supreme Reality.

buddhi   The intelligence or discrimination faculty; the seat of wisdom.

Chaitanya, Sri　A prophet born in 1485, who lived at Navadip, Bengal, and emphasized the path of divine love for the realization of God.

chetana samadhi　Communion with God in which the devotee retains "I-consciousness" and is aware of his or her relationship with God.

Chit　Consciousness.

chitta　The "mind-stuff"; one of four functions of the mind (along with *buddhi, ahamkara,* and *manas*); that part of the inner organ which is the storehouse of memory.

Dhananjaya　A name given to Arjuna in honor of his having subdued the kings of India and acquired their wealth. See **Arjuna.**

Gayatri　(1) The Gayatri mantra, a sacred verse of the Vedas, repeated by brahmins as part of their devotions. (2) The *gayatri* meter, an important meter in Vedic verses, containing twenty-four syllables.

Ghosh, Girish Chandra　One of the greatest Bengali dramatists and an ardent disciple of Sri Ramakrishna.

guna　One of the basic modifications of nature. According to the Samkhya philosophy, Prakriti (nature), in contrast with Purusha (Spirit), consists of three *gunas* (qualities or strands), known as *sattva, rajas,* and *tamas.*

Hari　God; a name of Vishnu.

Holy Mother　See **Sarada Devi, Sri.**

Ishtadevata　The form or an aspect of the deity one specially selects for devotional purposes; Chosen Ideal.

jada samadhi　Communion with God in which the aspirant appears lifeless, like an inert object.

japa　Silent repetition of a divine name or mystic syllable, keeping count either with a rosary or fingers. This kind of repetition occupies an important place in the Hindu system of spiritual practice.

jiva　The embodied soul; a living being; an ordinary person.

jivanmukta   One who has attained liberation from maya while living in the body.

jivanmukti   Liberation from maya while living in the body.

jnana   Knowledge of God arrived at through reasoning and discrimination; also denotes the process of reasoning by which the ultimate Truth is attained. The word is generally used to denote knowledge by which one is aware of one's identity with Brahman.

jnana-yoga   Spiritual discipline mainly based upon philosophical discrimination between the real and the unreal and upon renunciation of the unreal.

jnani   One who follows the path of knowledge, consisting of discrimination to realize God; generally used to denote a nondualist.

Kali   An epithet of the Divine Mother, the Primal Energy.

kama   Enjoyment of legitimate pleasures; one of the four values of life.

karma   (1) Action in general; duty. (2) The law of cause and effect.

karma-yoga   Spiritual discipline based upon the unselfish performance of duty without attachment to the fruits of action.

kosha   Literally, sheath or covering; one of five layerings or bodies that cover the soul, which is unaffected by any of them. They are the gross sheath or physical body *(annamayakosha)*, the vital sheath *(pranamayakosha)*, the mental sheath *(manomayakosha)*, the sheath of intelligence or intellect *(vijnanamayakosha)*, and the sheath of bliss *(anandamayakosha)*.

Krishna, Sri   A divine incarnation, described in the *Mahabharata* and *Bhagavatam*.

kundalini   The spiritual energy lying coiled up, or dormant, at the base of the spine in all individuals; when awakened through spiritual practice, it rises through the spinal column, passes through various centers, or *chakras*, and at last reaches the brain, whereupon the yogi experiences *samadhi*.

lila Divine sport or play; creation is often explained by the Vaishnavas as the spontaneous *lila* of God.

Mahabharata A celebrated Hindu epic.

mahabhava The most intense ecstatic love of God. See **bhava.**

Mahamaya The Great Illusionist; a name of Kali, the Divine Mother.

mantra A sacred word or mystic syllable in Sanskrit, used in *japa.*

maya Ignorance obscuring the vision of God; the Cosmic Illusion on account of which the One appears as many, the Absolute as the relative; it is also used to denote attachment.

moksha Liberation or final emancipation; one of the four values of life.

Narada A great sage and lover of God in Hindu mythology.

"Neti, neti" Literally, "not this, not this"; the negative process of discrimination, advocated by the followers of nondualistic Vedanta.

Nirguna Brahman Brahman without qualities or attributes.

Nirvana Final absorption in Brahman, or the all-pervading Reality, by the annihilation of the individual ego.

nirvikalpa samadhi The highest state of *samadhi,* in which the aspirant realizes total oneness with Brahman.

nishtha Single-minded devotion or love.

Nyaya Indian Logic; one of the six systems of orthodox Hindu philosophy.

ojas The highest form of energy in the human body. That part of human energy expressed through sexual action and sexual thought, when checked and controlled, easily becomes changed into *ojas* and is stored in the brain.

Om The most sacred word of the Vedas; a symbol of God and of Brahman.

Pandava Literally, son of Pandu; refers to Arjuna, the third son of Pandu. See **Arjuna.**

Partha Literally, son of Pritha; an epithet of Arjuna. See **Arjuna.**

Patanjali The author of the Yoga system, one of the six systems of orthodox Hindu philosophy.

Prakriti Primordial nature, which, in association with Purusha, creates the universe; it is one of the categories of the Samkhya philosophy.

prana (1) The vital energy or life force. (2) The breath. (3) One of five functions of the vital force: *prana, apana, vyana, udana,* and *samana.* (4) A name of the Cosmic Soul as endowed with activity.

pranayama Control of breath; one of the disciplines of yoga.

prarabdha karma The action that has begun to fructify, the fruit of which is being reaped in this life. See *agami.*

prema Ecstatic love; divine love of the most intense kind.

Purusha A term of the Samkhya philosophy, denoting the eternal Conscious Principle; the universe evolves from the union of Prakriti and Purusha. The word also denotes the soul and the Absolute.

Radha The great woman contemporary and devotee of Sri Krishna.

rajas The principle of activity or restlessness. See *guna.*

rajasika Pertaining to, or possessed of, *rajas.*

raja-yoga A system of Yoga ascribed to Patanjali, dealing with concentration and its methods, control of the mind, *samadhi,* and similar matters.

Rama, Sri The hero of the *Ramayana,* regarded by Hindus as a divine incarnation.

Ramakrishna, Sri (1836–1886) A great saint of Bengal, regarded as a divine incarnation, whose life inspired the modern renaissance of Vedanta.

Ramanuja (1017–1137) A great philosopher-saint of India, the foremost interpreter of the school of qualified nondualistic Vedanta.

Ramprasad A Bengali mystic and writer of songs about the Divine Mother.

sadhana   Spiritual discipline.

sadhu   Holy person; a term generally used with reference to a monk.

Saguna Brahman   Brahman with attributes and qualities; the Absolute conceived as the creator, preserver, or destroyer of the universe; the personal God, according to Vedanta.

samadhi   Total absorption in the object of meditation or in the Godhead; ecstasy.

Samkhya   One of the six systems of orthodox Hindu philosophy.

samskara   A tendency, habit, predisposition, or mental impression created by thoughts and actions.

sanchita karma   The vast storehouse of accumulated actions done in the past, the fruits of which have not yet been reaped. See *agami.*

sandhya   Devotions or ritualistic worship.

sannyasa   Literally, "complete renunciation"; monastic life or renunciation practiced by monks in the form of giving up all desire for progeny, wealth, and happiness in heaven after death.

sannyasi(n)   A monk who renounces the world in order to realize God.

Sarada Devi, Sri   (1853–1920) Wife and spiritual companion of Sri Ramakrishna; also known as the Holy Mother.

Sat   Reality; Being; Existence.

Sat-Chit-Ananda (Satchidananda)   Literally, Existence-Knowledge-Bliss; a name of Brahman, the Ultimate Reality.

sattva   The principle of balance or wisdom. See *guna.*

sattvika   Pertaining to, or possessed of, *sattva.*

savikalpa samadhi   In Vedanta, the first of two stages of *samadhi,* in which the seeker remains conscious of his or her realization of the unity of the inmost Self with the Supreme Self.

Shankaracharya   (788–820) One of the greatest philosophers of India; an exponent of Advaita Vedanta.

Shanti(h)   Peace.

Sri   (also Shri) Literally, "blessed" or "holy"; a prefix used with names or the titles of certain scriptures. It also serves as an honorific title before the name of a deity or holy person.

Srimad Bhagavatam   One of the Puranas; a well-known scripture dealing with the life of Sri Krishna. Also known as the *Bhagavata Purana*.

tamas   The principle of inertia or dullness. See *guna*.

tamasika   Pertaining to, or possessed of, *tamas*.

Tantra   A system of religious philosophy in which the Divine Mother, or Power, is the Ultimate Reality; also the scriptures dealing with this philosophy.

tapas   Austerity.

Turiya   Literally the "fourth"; the state of the transcendental Self, beyond the three states of waking, dream, and dreamless sleep.

Uddhava   The name of a devotee and follower of Sri Krishna.

Uddhava Gita   A text that forms part of the *Srimad Bhagavatam*. It is the parting instructions of Sri Krishna to his beloved devotee and follower Uddhava.

Upanishads   Scriptures that contain the inner or mystic teachings of the Vedas, dealing with the ultimate Truth and its realization.

Vedanta   One of the six systems of orthodox Hindu philosophy.

Vedas   The revealed scriptures of the Hindus, consisting of the *Rig Veda, Sama Veda, Yajur Veda,* and *Atharva Veda.*

videha   Detached from the body; without body consciousness.

vijnana   Special knowledge of the Absolute, by which one affirms the universe and sees it as the manifestation of Brahman.

vijnani   One endowed with *vijnana*.

Vivekachudamani   A treatise on Vedanta by Shankaracharya.

Vivekananda, Swami   (1863–1902) The foremost of Sri Ramakrishna's *sannyasin* disciples, also known by the premonastic names of Narendranath, Narendra, or Naren.

vritti   A "thought-wave" in the mind; restricting these mental desires and distractions is the aim of yoga, according to Patanjali.

yajna   Sacrifice; denotes ritual, worship, oblations to God, or any action performed with a spiritual motive.

Yoga   (1) Union of the individual soul with the Universal Soul. (2) The method by which to realize union through control of mind and concentration. (3) One of the six systems of orthodox Hindu philosophy. The Yoga system of Patanjali.

yogi   One who practices yoga.

Credits

Grateful acknowledgment is given for permission to use material from the following sources:

From *Uddhava Gita or The Last Message of Sri Krishna* translated by Swami Madhavananda, 1971; *Complete Works of Swami Vivekananda*, vol. 5, 1970; *Vivekachudamani of Sri Sankaracarya* translated by Swami Madhavananda, 1970, used by permission of the publisher, Advaita Ashrama, Calcutta, West Bengal, India.

From *The Upanishads*, vols. 1–4 translated by Swami Nikhilananda, © 1949, 1952, 1956, and 1959; *The Bhagavad Gita* translated by Swami Nikhilananda, © 1944; *Vivekananda: The Yogas and Other Works* edited by Swami Nikhilananda, © 1953; *The Gospel of Sri Ramakrishna* translated by Swami Nikhilananda, © 1942; *The Gospel of Sri Ramakrishna*, abridged ed. translated by Swami Nikhilananda, © 1958, used by permission of the publisher, Ramakrishna-Vivekananda Center of New York.

Index

About the Author

Swami Adiswarananda, a senior monk of the Ramakrishna Order of India, is the Minister and Spiritual Leader of the Ramakrishna-Vivekananda Center of New York. Born in 1925 in West Bengal, India, Swami received his undergraduate and master's degrees from the University of Calcutta. He joined the monastic order of Sri Ramakrishna in 1954 and was ordained a monk in 1963. Before being sent by the Ramakrishna Order to its New York center in 1968, he taught religious subjects in one of the premier colleges of the Order and was later editor of *Prabuddha Bharata: Awakened India*, the English-language monthly journal on religion and philosophy published by the Order. Swami is a frequent lecturer at colleges, universities, and other religious, educational, and cultural institutions, and his writings appear regularly in many scholarly journals on religion and philosophy. He is the author of *The Spiritual Quest and the Way of Yoga: The Goal, the Journey and the Milestones; The Vedanta Way to Peace and Happiness;* and *Meditation and Its Practices: A Definitive Guide to Techniques and Traditions of Meditation in Yoga and Vedanta.* He is also the editor of *Sri Ramakrishna, the Face of Silence* and *Sri Sarada Devi, The Holy Mother: Her Teachings and Conversations* (all SkyLight Paths).

Global Spiritual Perspectives

Spiritual Perspectives on America's Role as Superpower
by the Editors at SkyLight Paths

Are we the world's good neighbor or a global bully? From a spiritual perspective, what are America's responsibilities as the only remaining superpower? Contributors:

Dr. Beatrice Bruteau • Rev. Dr. Joan Brown Campbell • Tony Campolo • Rev. Forrest Church • Lama Surya Das • Matthew Fox • Kabir Helminski • Thich Nhat Hanh • Eboo Patel • Abbot M. Basil Pennington, ocso • Dennis Prager • Rosemary Radford Ruether • Wayne Teasdale • Rev. William McD. Tully • Rabbi Arthur Waskow • John Wilson

5½ x 8½, 256 pp, Quality PB, ISBN 1-893361-81-0 **$16.95**

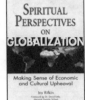

Spiritual Perspectives on Globalization, 2nd Edition
Making Sense of Economic and Cultural Upheaval
by Ira Rifkin; Foreword by Dr. David Little, Harvard Divinity School

What is globalization? Surveys the religious landscape, explaining in clear and non-judgmental language the beliefs that motivate spiritual leaders, activists, theologians, academics, and others involved on all sides of the issue. Includes a new Afterword and Discussion Guide designed for group use.

5½ x 8½, 256 pp, Quality PB, ISBN 1-59473-045-8 **$16.99**

Hinduism / Vedanta

Meditation & Its Practices: A Definitive Guide to Techniques and Traditions of Meditation in Yoga and Vedanta
by Swami Adiswarananda

The complete sourcebook for exploring Hinduism's two most time-honored traditions of meditation.

6 x 9, 504 pp, HC, ISBN 1-893361-83-7 **$34.95**

The Spiritual Quest and the Way of Yoga: The Goal, the Journey and the Milestones *by Swami Adiswarananda*

The Yoga way to attain the goal of life and overcome obstacles on the spiritual path.

6 x 9, 288 pp, HC, ISBN 1-59473-113-6 **$29.99**

Sri Ramakrishna, the Face of Silence
by Swami Nikhilananda and Dhan Gopal Mukerji
Edited with an Introduction by Swami Adiswarananda; Foreword by Dhan Gopal Mukerji II

Classic biographies present the life of Sri Ramakrishna and explain systems of Indian thought intimately connected with his life.

6 x 9, 352 pp, HC, ISBN 1-59473-115-2 **$29.99**

Sri Sarada Devi, The Holy Mother: Her Teachings and Conversations
Translated and with Notes by Swami Nikhilananda
Edited and with an Introduction by Swami Adiswarananda

Brings to life the Holy Mother's teachings on human affliction, self-control, and peace.

6 x 9, 288 pp, HC, ISBN 1-59473-070-9 **$29.99**

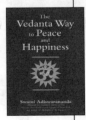

The Vedanta Way to Peace and Happiness
by Swami Adiswarananda

Introduces the timeless teachings of Vedanta—divinity of the individual soul, unity of all existence, and oneness with the Divine.

6 x 9, 240 pp, HC, ISBN 1-59473-034-2 **$29.99**

Children's Spirituality—Board Books

How Did the Animals Help God? (A Board Book)
by Nancy Sohn Swartz, Full-color illus. by Melanie Hall
Abridged from Nancy Sohn Swartz's *In Our Image*, God asks all of nature to offer gifts to humankind—with a promise that they will care for creation in return.
5 x 5, 24 pp, Board Book, Full-color illus., ISBN 1-59473-044-X **$7.99** *For ages 0–4*

Where Is God? (A Board Book)
by Lawrence and Karen Kushner; Full-color illus. by Dawn W. Majewski
A gentle way for young children to explore how God is with us every day, in every way. Abridged from *Because Nothing Looks Like God* by Lawrence and Karen Kushner.   5 x 5, 24 pp, Board, Full-color illus., ISBN 1-893361-17-9 **$7.99** *For ages 0–4*

What Does God Look Like? (A Board Book)
by Lawrence and Karen Kushner; Full-color illus. by Dawn W. Majewski
A simple way for young children to explore the ways that we "see" God. Abridged from *Because Nothing Looks Like God* by Lawrence and Karen Kushner.
5 x 5, 24 pp, Board, Full-color illus., ISBN 1-893361-23-3 **$7.95** *For ages 0–4*

How Does God Make Things Happen? (A Board Book)
by Lawrence and Karen Kushner; Full-color illus. by Dawn W. Majewski
A charming invitation for young children to explore how God makes things happen in our world. Abridged from *Because Nothing Looks Like God* by Lawrence and Karen Kushner.   5 x 5, 24 pp, Board, Full-color illus., ISBN 1-893361-24-1 **$7.95** *For ages 0–4*

What Is God's Name? (A Board Book)
by Sandy Eisenberg Sasso; Full-color illus. by Phoebe Stone
Everyone and everything in the world has a name. What is God's name? Abridged from the award-winning *In God's Name* by Sandy Eisenberg Sasso.
5 x 5, 24 pp, Board, Full-color illus., ISBN 1-893361-10-1 **$7.99** *For ages 0–4*

What You Will See Inside ...

This important new series of books is designed to show children ages 6–10 the Who, What, When, Where, Why and How of traditional houses of worship, liturgical celebrations, and rituals of different world faiths, empowering them to respect and understand their own religious traditions—and those of their friends and neighbors.

What You Will See Inside a Catholic Church
by Reverend Michael Keane; Foreword by Robert J. Keeley, Ed.D.
Full-color photographs by Aaron Pepis
Visually explains the common use of the altar, processional cross, baptismal font, votive candles, and more.   8½ x 10½, 32 pp, HC, ISBN 1-893361-54-3 **$17.95**
Also available in Spanish: **Lo que se puede ver dentro de una iglesia católica**
8½ x 10½, 32 pp, Full-color photos, HC, ISBN 1-893361-66-7 **$16.95**

What You Will See Inside a Hindu Temple
by Dr. Mahendra Jani and Dr. Vandana Jani; Photographs by Neirah Bhargava and Vijay Dave
Colorful, full-page photographs set the scene for concise but informative descriptions of the ways and whys of Hindu worship, faith, and religious life.
8½ x 10½, 32 pp, Full-color photos, HC, ISBN 1-59473-116-0 **$17.99**

What You Will See Inside a Mosque
by Aisha Karen Khan; Photographs by Aaron Pepis
Featuring full-page pictures and concise descriptions, demystifies the celebrations and ceremonies of Islam throughout the year.
8½ x 10½, 32 pp, Full-color photos, HC, ISBN 1-893361-60-8 **$16.95**

What You Will See Inside a Synagogue
by Rabbi Lawrence A. Hoffman and Dr. Ron Wolfson; Full-color photos by Bill Aron
A colorful, fun-to-read introduction that explains the ways and whys of Jewish worship and religious life.
8½ x 10½, 32 pp, Full-color photos, HC, ISBN 1-59473-012-1 **$17.99**

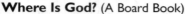

Children's Spiritual Biography

Ten Amazing People
And How They Changed the World
by Maura D. Shaw; Foreword by Dr. Robert Coles
Full-color illus. by Stephen Marchesi

For ages 7 & up

Black Elk • Dorothy Day • Malcolm X • Mahatma Gandhi • Martin Luther King, Jr. • Mother Teresa • Janusz Korczak • Desmond Tutu • Thich Nhat Hanh • Albert Schweitzer

This vivid, inspirational, and authoritative book will open new possibilities for children by telling the stories of how ten of the past century's greatest leaders changed the world in important ways.

8½ x 11, 48 pp, HC, Full-color illus., ISBN 1-893361-47-0 **$17.95** *For ages 7 & up*

Spiritual Biographies for Young People—For ages 7 and up

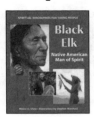
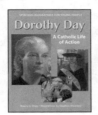
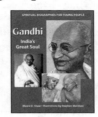
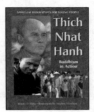

Black Elk: Native American Man of Spirit
by Maura D. Shaw; Full-color illus. by Stephen Marchesi
Through historically accurate illustrations and photos, inspiring age-appropriate activities, and Black Elk's own words, this colorful biography introduces children to a remarkable person who ensured that the traditions and beliefs of his people would not be forgotten.
6¾ x 8¾, 32 pp, HC, Full-color illus., ISBN 1-59473-043-1 **$12.99**

Dorothy Day: A Catholic Life of Action
by Maura D. Shaw; Full-color illus. by Stephen Marchesi
Introduces children to one of the most inspiring women of the twentieth century, a down-to-earth spiritual leader who saw the presence of God in every person she met. Includes practical activities, a timeline, and a list of important words to know.
6¾ x 8¾, 32 pp, HC, Full-color illus., ISBN 1-59473-011-3 **$12.99**

Gandhi: India's Great Soul
by Maura D. Shaw; Full-color illus. by Stephen Marchesi
There are a number of biographies of Gandhi written for young readers, but this is the only one that balances a simple text with illustrations, photographs, and activities that encourage children and adults to talk about how to make changes happen without violence. Introduces children to important concepts of freedom, equality, and justice among people of all backgrounds and religions.
6¾ x 8¾, 32 pp, HC, Full-color illus., ISBN 1-893361-91-8 **$12.95**

Thich Nhat Hanh: Buddhism in Action
by Maura D. Shaw; Full-color illus. by Stephen Marchesi
Warm illustrations, photos, age-appropriate activities, and Thich Nhat Hanh's own poems introduce a great man to children in a way they can understand and enjoy. Includes a list of important Buddhist words to know.
6¾ x 8¾, 32 pp, HC, Full-color illus., ISBN 1-893361-87-X **$12.95**

Children's Spirituality

Because Nothing Looks Like God
by Lawrence and Karen Kushner; Full-color illus. by Dawn W. Majewski
Real-life examples of happiness and sadness—from goodnight stories, to the hope and fear felt the first time at bat, to the closing moments of life—introduce children to the possibilities of spiritual life.

11 x 8½, 32 pp, HC, Full-color illus., ISBN 1-58023-092-X **$16.95**

For ages 4 & up (a Jewish Lights book)

Also available:

Teacher's Guide, 8½ x 11, 22 pp, PB, ISBN 1-58023-140-3 **$6.95** *For ages 5–8*

Becoming Me: A Story of Creation
by Martin Boroson; Full-color illus. by Christopher Gilvan-Cartwright
Told in the personal "voice" of the Creator, here is a story about creation and relationship that is about each one of us.

8 x 10, 32 pp, Full-color illus., HC, ISBN 1-893361-11-X **$16.95** *For ages 4 & up*

But God Remembered: Stories of Women from Creation to the Promised Land   *by Sandy Eisenberg Sasso; Full-color illus. by Bethanne Andersen*

A fascinating collection of four different stories of women only briefly mentioned in biblical tradition and religious texts; all teach important values through their actions and faith.   9 x 12, 32 pp, HC, Full-color illus., ISBN 1-879045-43-5 **$16.95**
For ages 8 & up (a Jewish Lights book)

Cain & Abel: Finding the Fruits of Peace
by Sandy Eisenberg Sasso; Full-color illus. by Joani Keller Rothenberg
A sensitive recasting of the ancient tale shows we have the power to deal with anger in positive ways. Provides questions for kids and adults to explore together. "Editor's Choice"—American Library Association's *Booklist*

9 x 12, 32 pp, HC, Full-color illus., ISBN 1-58023-123-3 **$16.95** *For ages 5 & up (a Jewish Lights book)*

Does God Hear My Prayer?
by August Gold; Full-color photo illus. by Diane Hardy Waller
This colorful book introduces preschoolers as well as young readers to prayer and how prayer can help them express their own fears, wants, sadness, surprise, and joy.   10 x 8½, 32 pp, Quality PB, Full-color photo illus., ISBN 1-59473-102-0 **$8.99**

The 11th Commandment: Wisdom from Our Children
by The Children of America
"If there were an Eleventh Commandment, what would it be?" Children of many religious denominations across America answer this question—in their own drawings and words. "A rare book of spiritual celebration for all people, of all ages, for all time." —*Bookviews*

8 x 10, 48 pp, HC, Full-color illus., ISBN 1-879045-46-X **$16.95** *For ages 4 & up (a Jewish Lights book)*

For Heaven's Sake
by Sandy Eisenberg Sasso; Full-color illus. by Kathryn Kunz Finney
Everyone talked about heaven: "Thank heavens." "Heaven forbid." "For heaven's sake, Isaiah." But no one would say what heaven was or how to find it. So Isaiah decides to find out, by seeking answers from many different people.

9 x 12, 32 pp, HC, Full-color illus., ISBN 1-58023-054-7 **$16.95** *For ages 4 & up (a Jewish Lights book)*

God in Between
by Sandy Eisenberg Sasso; Full-color illus. by Sally Sweetland
If you wanted to find God, where would you look? A magical, mythical tale that teaches that God can be found where we are: within all of us and the relationships between us.   9 x 12, 32 pp, HC, Full-color illus., ISBN 1-879045-86-9 **$16.95**
For ages 4 & up (a Jewish Lights book)

Spiritual Poetry—The Mystic Poets

Experience these mystic poets as you never have before. Each beautiful, compact book includes: A brief introduction to the poet's time and place; a summary of the major themes of the poet's mysticism and religious tradition; essential selections from the poet's most important works; and an appreciative preface by a contemporary spiritual writer.

Hafiz: The Mystic Poets
Preface by Ibrahim Gamard
Hafiz is known throughout the world as Persia's greatest poet, with sales of his poems in Iran today only surpassed by those of the Qur'an itself. His probing and joyful verse speaks to people from all backgrounds who long to taste and feel divine love and experience harmony with all living things.
5 x 7¼, 144 pp, HC, ISBN 1-59473-009-1 **$16.99**

Hopkins: The Mystic Poets
Preface by Rev. Thomas Ryan, CSP
Gerard Manley Hopkins, Christian mystical poet, is beloved for his use of fresh language and startling metaphors to describe the world around him. Although his verse is lovely, beneath the surface lies a searching soul, wrestling with and yearning for God.
5 x 7¼, 112 pp, HC, ISBN 1-59473-010-5 **$16.99**

Tagore: The Mystic Poets
Preface by Swami Adiswarananda
Rabindranath Tagore is often considered the "Shakespeare" of modern India. A great mystic, Tagore was the teacher of W. B. Yeats and Robert Frost, the close friend of Albert Einstein and Mahatma Gandhi, and the winner of the Nobel Prize for Literature. This beautiful sampling of Tagore's two most important works, *The Gardener* and *Gitanjali*, offers a glimpse into his spiritual vision that has inspired people around the world.
5 x 7¼, 144 pp, HC, ISBN 1-59473-008-3 **$16.99**

Whitman: The Mystic Poets
Preface by Gary David Comstock
Walt Whitman was the most innovative and influential poet of the nineteenth century. This beautiful sampling of Whitman's most important poetry from *Leaves of Grass*, and selections from his prose writings, offers a glimpse into the spiritual side of his most radical themes— love for country, love for others, and love of Self.
5 x 7¼, 192 pp, HC, ISBN 1-59473-041-5 **$16.99**

Kabbalah from Jewish Lights Publishing

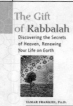

Ehyeh: A Kabbalah for Tomorrow by Dr. Arthur Green
6 x 9, 224 pp, Quality PB, ISBN 1-58023-213-2 **$16.99**; HC, ISBN 1-58023-125-X **$21.95**

The Enneagram and Kabbalah: Reading Your Soul by Rabbi Howard A. Addison
6 x 9, 176 pp, Quality PB, ISBN 1-58023-001-6 **$15.95**

Finding Joy: A Practical Spiritual Guide to Happiness by Dannel I. Schwartz with Mark Hass
6 x 9, 192 pp, Quality PB, ISBN 1-58023-009-1 **$14.95**; HC, ISBN 1-879045-53-2 **$19.95**

The Gift of Kabbalah: Discovering the Secrets of Heaven, Renewing Your Life on Earth
by Tamar Frankiel, Ph.D.
6 x 9, 256 pp, Quality PB, ISBN 1-58023-141-1 **$16.95**; HC, ISBN 1-58023-108-X **$21.95**

Zohar: Annotated & Explained
Translation and annotation by Dr. Daniel C. Matt. Foreword by Andrew Harvey
5½ x 8½, 160 pp, Quality PB, ISBN 1-893361-51-9 **$15.99**

Meditation / Prayer

Prayers to an Evolutionary God
by William Cleary; Afterword by Diarmuid O'Murchu
How is it possible to pray when God is dislocated from heaven, dispersed all around us, and more of a creative force than an all-knowing father? Inspired by the spiritual and scientific teachings of Diarmuid O'Murchu and Teilhard de Chardin, Cleary reveals that religion and science can be combined to create an expanding view of the universe—an evolutionary faith.
6 x 9, 208 pp, HC, ISBN 1-59473-006-7 **$21.99**

The Song of Songs: A Spiritual Commentary
by M. Basil Pennington, OCSO; Illustrations by Phillip Ratner
Join M. Basil Pennington as he ruminates on the Bible's most challenging mystical text. You will follow a path into the Songs that weaves through his inspired words and the evocative drawings of Jewish artist Phillip Ratner—a path that reveals your own humanity and leads to the deepest delight of your soul.
6 x 9, 160 pp, HC, 14 b/w illus., ISBN 1-59473-004-0 **$19.99**

Women of Color Pray: Voices of Strength, Faith, Healing, Hope, and Courage   Edited and with Introductions by Christal M. Jackson
Through these prayers, poetry, lyrics, meditations and affirmations, you will share in the strong and undeniable connection women of color share with God. It will challenge you to explore new ways of prayerful expression.
5 x 7¼, 208 pp, Quality PB, ISBN 1-59473-077-6 **$15.99**

The Art of Public Prayer, 2nd Edition: Not for Clergy Only
by Lawrence A. Hoffman 6 x 9, 288 pp, Quality PB, ISBN 1-893361-06-3 **$18.95**

Finding Grace at the Center: The Beginning of Centering Prayer
by M. Basil Pennington, ocso, Thomas Keating, ocso, and Thomas E. Clarke, SJ
5 x 7¼, 112 pp, HC, ISBN 1-893361-69-1 **$14.95**

A Heart of Stillness: A Complete Guide to Learning the Art of Meditation
by David A. Cooper 5½ x 8½, 272 pp, Quality PB, ISBN 1-893361-03-9 **$16.95**

Meditation without Gurus: A Guide to the Heart of Practice
by Clark Strand 5½ x 8½, 192 pp, Quality PB, ISBN 1-893361-93-4 **$16.95**

Praying with Our Hands: Twenty-One Practices of Embodied Prayer from the World's Spiritual Traditions by Jon M. Sweeney; Photographs by Jennifer J. Wilson; Foreword by Mother Tessa Bielecki; Afterword by Taitetsu Unno, PhD
8 x 8, 96 pp, 22 duotone photographs, Quality PB, ISBN 1-893361-16-0 **$16.95**

Silence, Simplicity & Solitude: A Complete Guide to Spiritual Retreat at Home
by David A. Cooper 5½ x 8½, 336 pp, Quality PB, ISBN 1-893361-04-7 **$16.95**

Three Gates to Meditation Practice: A Personal Journey into Sufism, Buddhism, and Judaism by David A. Cooper 5½ x 8½, 240 pp, Quality PB, ISBN 1-893361-22-5 **$16.95**

Women Pray: Voices through the Ages, from Many Faiths, Cultures, and Traditions
Edited and with introductions by Monica Furlong
5 x 7¼, 256 pp, Quality PB, ISBN 1-59473-071-7 **$15.99**;
Deluxe HC with ribbon marker, ISBN 1-893361-25-X **$19.95**

Midrash Fiction

Daughters of the Desert: Tales of Remarkable Women from Christian, Jewish, and Muslim Traditions   *by Claire Rudolf Murphy, Meghan Nuttall Sayres, Mary Cronk Farrell, Sarah Conover, and Betsy Wharton*

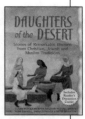

Breathes new life into the old tales of our female ancestors in faith. Uses traditional scriptural passages as starting points, then with vivid detail fills in historical context and place. Chapters reveal the voices of Sarah, Hagar, Huldah, Esther, Salome, Mary Magdalene, Lydia, Khadija, Fatima, and many more. Historical fiction ideal for readers of all ages. Quality paperback includes reader's discussion guide.

5½ x 8½, 208 pp, Quality PB, ISBN 1-59473-106-3 **$14.99**; HC, 192 pp, ISBN 1-893361-72-1 **$19.95**

The Triumph of Eve & Other Subversive Bible Tales
by Matt Biers-Ariel

Many people were taught and remember only a one-dimensional Bible. These engaging retellings are the antidote to this—they're witty, often hilarious, always profound, and invite you to grapple with questions and issues that are often hidden in the original text.

5½ x 8½, 192 pp, HC, ISBN 1-59473-040-7 **$19.99**

Also available:
The Triumph of Eve & Other Subversive Bible Tales Teacher's Guide
  8½ x 11, 44 pp, PB, ISBN 1-59473-152-7 **$8.99**

Religious Etiquette / Reference

How to Be a Perfect Stranger, 3rd Edition: The Essential Religious Etiquette Handbook   *Edited by Stuart M. Matlins and Arthur J. Magida*
The indispensable guidebook to help the well-meaning guest when visiting other people's religious ceremonies. A straightforward guide to the rituals and celebrations of the major religions and denominations in the United States and Canada from the perspective of an interested guest of any other faith, based on information obtained from authorities of each religion. Belongs in every living room, library, and office. Covers:
African American Methodist Churches • Assemblies of God • Bahá'í • Baptist • Buddhist • Christian Church (Disciples of Christ) • Christian Science (Church of Christ, Scientist) • Churches of Christ • Episcopalian and Anglican • Hindu • Islam • Jehovah's Witnesses • Jewish • Lutheran • Mennonite/Amish • Methodist • Mormon (Church of Jesus Christ of Latter-day Saints) • Native American/First Nations • Orthodox Churches • Pentecostal Church of God • Presbyterian • Quaker (Religious Society of Friends) • Reformed Church in America/Canada • Roman Catholic • Seventh-day Adventist • Sikh • Unitarian Universalist • United Church of Canada • United Church of Christ
6 x 9, 432 pp, Quality PB, ISBN 1-893361-67-5 **$19.95**

The Perfect Stranger's Guide to Funerals and Grieving Practices: A Guide to Etiquette in Other People's Religious Ceremonies   *Edited by Stuart M. Matlins*
6 x 9, 240 pp, Quality PB, ISBN 1-893361-20-9 **$16.95**
The Perfect Stranger's Guide to Wedding Ceremonies: A Guide to Etiquette in Other People's Religious Ceremonies   *Edited by Stuart M. Matlins*
6 x 9, 208 pp, Quality PB, ISBN 1-893361-19-5 **$16.95**

Sacred Texts—SkyLight Illuminations Series
Andrew Harvey, series editor

Offers today's spiritual seeker an enjoyable entry into the great classic texts of the world's spiritual traditions. Each classic is presented in an accessible translation, with facing pages of guided commentary from experts, giving you the keys you need to understand the history, context and meaning of the text. This series enables readers of all backgrounds to experience and understand classic spiritual texts directly, and to make them a part of their lives. Andrew Harvey writes the foreword to each volume, an insightful, personal introduction to each classic.

Bhagavad Gita: Annotated & Explained
Translation by Shri Purohit Swami; Annotation by Kendra Crossen Burroughs
"The very best Gita for first-time readers." —Ken Wilber. Millions of people turn daily to India's most beloved holy book, whose universal appeal has made it popular with non-Hindus and Hindus alike. This edition introduces you to the characters, explains references and philosophical terms, shares the interpretations of famous spiritual leaders and scholars, and more.
5½ x 8½, 192 pp, Quality PB, ISBN 1-893361-28-4 **$16.95**

Dhammapada: Annotated & Explained
Translation by Max Müller and revised by Jack Maguire; Annotation by Jack Maguire
The Dhammapada—believed to have been spoken by the Buddha himself over 2,500 years ago—contain most of Buddhism's central teachings. This timeless text concisely and inspirationally portrays the route a person travels as he or she advances toward enlightenment and describes the fundamental role of mental conditioning in making us who we are.
5½ x 8½, 160 pp, b/w photographs, Quality PB, ISBN 1-893361-42-X **$14.95**

The Divine Feminine in Biblical Wisdom Literature
Selections Annotated & Explained
Translation and annotation by Rabbi Rami Shapiro; Foreword by Rev. Dr. Cynthia Bourgeault
Uses the Hebrew books of Psalms, Proverbs, Song of Songs, Ecclesiastes and Job, and the Wisdom literature books of Sirach and the Wisdom of Solomon to clarify who Wisdom is, what She teaches, and how Her words can help us live justly, wisely, and with compassion.
5½ x 8½, 240 pp, Quality PB, ISBN 1-59473-109-8 **$16.99**

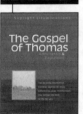

The Gospel of Thomas: Annotated & Explained
Translation and annotation by Stevan Davies
Discovered in 1945, this collection of aphoristic sayings sheds new light on the origins of Christianity and the intriguing figure of Jesus, portraying the Kingdom of God as a present fact about the world, rather than a future promise or future threat.
5½ x 8½, 192 pp, Quality PB, ISBN 1-893361-45-4 **$16.95**

Hasidic Tales: Annotated & Explained
Translation and annotation by Rabbi Rami Shapiro
Introduces the legendary tales of the impassioned Hasidic rabbis, which demonstrate the spiritual power of unabashed joy, offer lessons for leading a holy life, and remind us that the Divine can be found in the everyday.
5½ x 8½, 240 pp, Quality PB, ISBN 1-893361-86-1 **$16.95**

The Hebrew Prophets: Selections Annotated & Explained
Translation and annotation by Rabbi Rami Shapiro; Foreword by Zalman M. Schachter-Shalomi
Focuses on the central themes covered by all the Hebrew prophets: moving from ignorance to wisdom, injustice to justice, cruelty to compassion, and despair to joy, and challenges us to engage in justice, kindness and humility in every aspect of our lives.
5½ x 8½, 224 pp, Quality PB, ISBN 1-59473-037-7 **$16.99**

Sacred Texts—SkyLight Illuminations Series

Andrew Harvey, series editor

The Hidden Gospel of Matthew: Annotated & Explained
Translation and annotation by Ron Miller

Takes you deep into the text cherished around the world to discover the words and events that have the strongest connection to the historical Jesus. Reveals the underlying story of Matthew, a story that transcends the traditional theme of an atoning death and focuses instead on Jesus's radical call for personal transformation and social change.

5½ x 8½, 272 pp, Quality PB, ISBN 1-59473-038-5 **$16.99**

The Secret Book of John
The Gnostic Gospel—Annotated & Explained
Translation and annotation by Stevan Davies

Introduces the most significant and influential text of the ancient Gnostic religion. This central myth of Gnosticism tells the story of how God fell from perfect Oneness to imprisonment in the material world, and how by knowing our divine nature and our divine origins—that we are one with God—we reverse God's descent and find our salvation.

5½ x 8½, 208 pp, Quality PB, ISBN 1-59473-082-2 **$16.99**

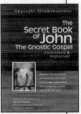

Rumi and Islam: Selections from His Stories, Poems, and Discourses—
Annotated & Explained
Translation and annotation by Ibrahim Gamard

Offers a new way of thinking about Rumi's poetry. Focuses on Rumi's place within the Sufi tradition of Islam, providing insight into the mystical side of the religion—one that has love of God at its core and sublime wisdom teachings as its pathways.

5½ x 8½, 240 pp, Quality PB, ISBN 1-59473-002-4 **$15.99**

Selections from the Gospel of Sri Ramakrishna
Annotated & Explained
Translation by Swami Nikhilananda; Annotation by Kendra Crossen Burroughs

The words of India's greatest example of God-consciousness and mystical ecstasy in recent history. Introduces the fascinating world of the Indian mystic and the universal appeal of his message that has inspired millions of devotees for more than a century.

5½ x 8½, 240 pp, b/w photographs, Quality PB, ISBN 1-893361-46-2 **$16.95**

Spiritual Writings on Mary: Annotated & Explained
Annotation by Mary Ford-Grabowsky

Selections from influential writers, thinkers, and theologians—ancient and modern, from Western and Eastern backgrounds—examine the role of Mary, the mother of Jesus, as a source of inspiration in history and in life today.

5½ x 8½, 288 pp, Quality PB, ISBN 1-59473-001-6 **$16.99**

The Way of a Pilgrim: Annotated & Explained
Translation and annotation by Gleb Pokrovsky

This classic of Russian spirituality is the delightful account of one man who sets out to learn the prayer of the heart—also known as the "Jesus prayer"—and how the practice transforms his life.

5½ x 8½, 160 pp, Illus., Quality PB, ISBN 1-893361-31-4 **$14.95**

Zohar: Annotated & Explained
Translation and annotation by Daniel C. Matt

The best-selling author of *The Essential Kabbalah* brings together in one place the most important teachings of the Zohar, the canonical text of Jewish mystical tradition. Guides you step by step through the midrash, mystical fantasy, and Hebrew scripture that make up the Zohar, explaining the inner meanings in facing-page commentary.

5½ x 8½, 176 pp, Quality PB, ISBN 1-893361-51-9 **$15.99**

Spiritual Biography—SkyLight Lives

SkyLight Lives reintroduces the lives and works of key spiritual figures of our time—people who by their teaching or example have challenged our assumptions about spirituality and have caused us to look at it in new ways.

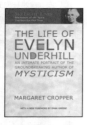 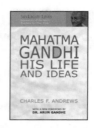 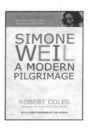 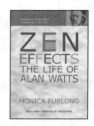

The Life of Evelyn Underhill
An Intimate Portrait of the Groundbreaking Author of *Mysticism*
by Margaret Cropper; Foreword by Dana Greene

Evelyn Underhill was a passionate writer and teacher who wrote elegantly on mysticism, worship, and devotional life. This is the story of how she made her way toward spiritual maturity, from her early days of agnosticism to the years when her influence was felt throughout the world.
6 x 9, 288 pp, 5 b/w photos, Quality PB, ISBN 1-893361-70-5 **$18.95**

Mahatma Gandhi: His Life and Ideas
by Charles F. Andrews; Foreword by Dr. Arun Gandhi

Examines from a contemporary Christian activist's point of view the religious ideas and political dynamics that influenced the birth of the peaceful resistance movement, the primary tool that Gandhi and the people of his homeland would use to gain India its freedom from British rule.
6 x 9, 336 pp, 5 b/w photos, Quality PB, ISBN 1-893361-89-6 **$18.95**

Simone Weil: A Modern Pilgrimage
by Robert Coles

The extraordinary life of the spiritual philosopher who's been called both saint and madwoman. Robert Coles' intriguing study of Weil is an insightful portrait of the beloved and controversial thinker whose life and writings influenced many (from T. S. Eliot to Adrienne Rich to Albert Camus), and continue to inspire seekers everywhere.
6 x 9, 208 pp, Quality PB, ISBN 1-893361-34-9 **$16.95**

Zen Effects: The Life of Alan Watts
by Monica Furlong

Through his widely popular books and lectures, Alan Watts (1915–1973) did more to introduce Eastern philosophy and religion to Western minds than any figure before or since. Here is the first and only full-length biography of one of the most charismatic spiritual leaders of the twentieth century.
6 x 9, 264 pp, Quality PB, ISBN 1-893361-32-2 **$16.95**

More Spiritual Biography

Bede Griffiths: An Introduction to His Interspiritual Thought
by Wayne Teasdale 6 x 9, 288 pp, Quality PB, ISBN 1-893361-77-2 **$18.95**

Inspired Lives: Exploring the Role of Faith and Spirituality in the Lives of Extraordinary People
by Joanna Laufer and Kenneth S. Lewis 6 x 9, 256 pp, Quality PB, ISBN 1-893361-33-0 **$16.95**

Spiritual Innovators: Seventy-Five Extraordinary People Who Changed the World in
the Past Century *Edited by Ira Rifkin and the Editors at SkyLight Paths; Foreword by Robert Coles*
6 x 9, 304 pp, b/w photographs, Quality PB, ISBN 1-893361-50-0 **$16.95**; HC, ISBN 1-893361-43-8 **$24.95**

White Fire: A Portrait of Women Spiritual Leaders in America
by Rabbi Malka Drucker; Photographs by Gay Block
7 x 10, 320 pp, 30+ b/w photos, HC, ISBN 1-893361-64-0 **$24.95**

Spirituality

Autumn: A Spiritual Biography of the Season
Edited by Gary Schmidt and Susan M. Felch; Illustrations by Mary Azarian

Rejoice in autumn as a time of preparation and reflection. Includes Wendell Berry, David James Duncan, Robert Frost, A. Bartlett Giamatti, Kimiko Hahn, P. D. James, Julian of Norwich, Garret Keizer, Tracy Kidder, Anne Lamott, May Sarton.
6 x 9, 320 pp, 5 b/w illus., Quality PB, ISBN 1-59473-118-7 **$18.99**; HC, ISBN 1-59473-005-9 **$22.99**

Awakening the Spirit, Inspiring the Soul
30 Stories of Interspiritual Discovery in the Community of Faiths
Edited by Brother Wayne Teasdale and Martha Howard, MD; Foreword by Joan Borysenko, PhD

Thirty original spiritual mini-biographies that showcase the varied ways that people come to faith—and what that means—in today's multi-religious world.
6 x 9, 224 pp, HC, ISBN 1-59473-039-3 **$21.99**

Summer: A Spiritual Biography of the Season
Edited by Gary Schmidt and Susan M. Felch; Illustrations by Mary Azarian

"A sumptuous banquet.... These selections lift up an exquisite wholeness found within an everyday sophistication."— ★ *Publishers Weekly* starred review
Includes Anne Lamott, Luci Shaw, Ray Bradbury, Richard Selzer, Thomas Lynch, Walt Whitman, Carl Sandburg, Sherman Alexie, Madeleine L'Engle, Jamaica Kincaid.
6 x 9, 304 pp, 5 b/w illus., Hardcover, ISBN 1-59473-083-0 **$21.99**

Winter: A Spiritual Biography of the Season
Edited by Gary Schmidt and Susan M. Felch; Illustrations by Barry Moser

"This outstanding anthology features top-flight nature and spirituality writers on the fierce, inexorable season of winter.... Remarkably lively and warm, despite the icy subject." — ★ *Publishers Weekly* starred review.
Includes Will Campbell, Rachel Carson, Annie Dillard, Donald Hall, Ron Hansen, Jane Kenyon, Jamaica Kincaid, Barry Lopez, Kathleen Norris, John Updike, E. B. White.
6 x 9, 288 pp, 6 b/w illus., Deluxe PB w/flaps, ISBN 1-893361-92-6 **$18.95**;
HC, ISBN 1-893361-53-5 **$21.95**

The Alphabet of Paradise: An A–Z of Spirituality for Everyday Life
by Howard Cooper 5 x 7¾, 224 pp, Quality PB, ISBN 1-893361-80-2 **$16.95**

Creating a Spiritual Retirement: A Guide to the Unseen Possibilities in Our Lives
by Molly Srode 6 x 9, 208 pp, b/w photos, Quality PB, ISBN 1-59473-050-42 **$14.99**;
HC, ISBN 1-893361-75-6 **$19.95**

The Geography of Faith: Underground Conversations on Religious, Political and Social Change *by Daniel Berrigan and Robert Coles; Updated introduction and afterword by the authors* 6 x 9, 224 pp, Quality PB, ISBN 1-893361-40-3 **$16.95**

God Lives in Glass: Reflections of God for Adults through the Eyes of Children
by Robert J. Landy, PhD; Foreword by Sandy Eisenberg Sasso
7 x 6, 64 pp, HC, Full-color illus., ISBN 1-893361-30-6 **$12.95**

God Within: Our Spiritual Future—As Told by Today's New Adults *Edited by Jon M. Sweeney and the Editors at SkyLight Paths* 6 x 9, 176 pp, Quality PB, ISBN 1-893361-15-2 **$14.95**

Jewish Spirituality: A Brief Introduction for Christians *by Lawrence Kushner*
5½ x 8½, 112 pp, Quality PB, ISBN 1-58023-150-0 **$12.95** *(a Jewish Lights book)*

A Jewish Understanding of the New Testament
by Rabbi Samuel Sandmel; New preface by Rabbi David Sandmel
5½ x 8½, 384 pp, Quality PB, ISBN 1-59473-048-2 **$19.99**

Journeys of Simplicity: Traveling Light with Thomas Merton, Bashō, Edward Abbey, Annie Dillard & Others *by Philip Harnden* 5 x 7¼, 128 pp, HC, ISBN 1-893361-76-4 **$16.95**

Keeping Spiritual Balance As We Grow Older: More than 65 Creative Ways to Use Purpose, Prayer, and the Power of Spirit to Build a Meaningful Retirement
by Molly and Bernie Srode 8 x 8, 224 pp, Quality PB, ISBN 1-59473-042-3 **$16.99**

The Monks of Mount Athos: A Western Monk's Extraordinary Spiritual Journey on Eastern Holy Ground *by M. Basil Pennington, ocso; Foreword by Archimandrite Dionysios*
6 x 9, 256 pp, 10+ b/w line drawings, Quality PB, ISBN 1-893361-78-0 **$18.95**

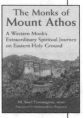

One God Clapping: The Spiritual Path of a Zen Rabbi *by Alan Lew with Sherril Jaffe*
5½ x 8½, 336 pp, Quality PB, ISBN 1-58023-115-2 **$16.95** *(a Jewish Lights book)*

Spirituality

Prayer for People Who Think Too Much
A Guide to Everyday, Anywhere Prayer from the World's Faith Traditions   *by Mitch Finley*
5½ x 8½, 224 pp, Quality PB, ISBN 1-893361-21-7 **$16.99**; HC, ISBN 1-893361-00-4 **$21.95**

The Shaman's Quest: Journeys in an Ancient Spiritual Practice
by Nevill Drury; with a Basic Introduction to Shamanism by Tom Cowan
5½ x 8½, 208 pp, Quality PB, ISBN 1-893361-68-3 **$16.95**

Show Me Your Way: The Complete Guide to Exploring Interfaith Spiritual Direction
by Howard A. Addison   5½ x 8½, 240 pp, Quality PB, ISBN 1-893361-41-1 **$16.95**;
HC, ISBN 1-893361-12-8 **$21.95**

Spirituality 101: The Indispensable Guide to Keeping—or Finding—Your Spiritual Life
on Campus   *by Harriet L. Schwartz, with contributions from college students at nearly thirty campuses across the United States*   6 x 9, 272 pp, Quality PB, ISBN 1-59473-000-8 **$16.99**

Spiritually Incorrect: Finding God in All the Wrong Places
by Dan Wakefield; Illus. by Marian DelVecchio
5½ x 8½, 192 pp, b/w illus., Quality PB, ISBN 1-59473-137-3 **$15.99**; HC, ISBN 1-893361-88-8 **$21.95**

Spiritual Manifestos: Visions for Renewed Religious Life in America from Young
Spiritual Leaders of Many Faiths   *Edited by Niles Elliot Goldstein; Preface by Martin E. Marty*
6 x 9, 256 pp, HC, ISBN 1-893361-09-8 **$21.95**

A Walk with Four Spiritual Guides: Krishna, Buddha, Jesus, and Ramakrishna
by Andrew Harvey   5½ x 8½, 192 pp, 10 b/w photos & illus., Quality PB, ISBN 1-59473-138-1 **$15.99**;
HC, ISBN 1-893361-73-X **$21.95**

What Matters: Spiritual Nourishment for Head and Heart
by Frederick Franck   5 x 7¼, 144 pp, 50+ b/w illus., HC, ISBN 1-59473-013-X **$16.99**

Who Is My God?, 2nd Edition
An Innovative Guide to Finding Your Spiritual Identity
Created by the Editors at SkyLight Paths   6 x 9, 160 pp, Quality PB, ISBN 1-59473-014-8 **$15.99**

Spirituality—A Week Inside

Come and Sit: A Week Inside Meditation Centers
by Marcia Z. Nelson; Foreword by Wayne Teasdale
The insider's guide to meditation in a variety of different spiritual traditions. Traveling through Buddhist, Hindu, Christian, Jewish, and Sufi traditions, this essential guide takes you to different meditation centers to meet the teachers and students and learn about the practices, demystifying the meditation experience.
6 x 9, 224 pp, b/w photographs, Quality PB, ISBN 1-893361-35-7 **$16.95**

Lighting the Lamp of Wisdom: A Week Inside a Yoga Ashram
by John Ittner; Foreword by Dr. David Frawley
This insider's guide to Hindu spiritual life takes you into a typical week of retreat inside a yoga ashram to demystify the experience and show you what to expect from your own visit. Includes a discussion of worship services, meditation and yoga classes, chanting and music, work practice, and more.   6 x 9, 192 pp, b/w photographs,
Quality PB, ISBN 1-893361-52-7 **$15.95**; HC, ISBN 1-893361-37-3 **$24.95**

Making a Heart for God: A Week Inside a Catholic Monastery
by Dianne Aprile; Foreword by Brother Patrick Hart, ocso
This essential guide to experiencing life in a Catholic monastery takes you to the Abbey of Gethsemani—the Trappist monastery in Kentucky that was home to author Thomas Merton—to explore the details. "More balanced and informative than the popular *The Cloister Walk* by Kathleen Norris." — *Choice: Current Reviews for Academic Libraries*   6 x 9, 224 pp, b/w photographs,
Quality PB, ISBN 1-893361-49-7 **$16.95**; HC, ISBN 1-893361-14-4 **$21.95**

Waking Up: A Week Inside a Zen Monastery
by Jack Maguire; Foreword by John Daido Loori, Roshi
An essential guide to what it's like to spend a week inside a Zen Buddhist monastery.
6 x 9, 224 pp, b/w photographs, Quality PB, ISBN 1-893361-55-1 **$16.95**;
HC, ISBN 1-893361-13-6 **$21.95**

Spiritual Practice

Divining the Body
Reclaim the Holiness of Your Physical Self   *by Jan Phillips*
A practical and inspiring guidebook for connecting the body and soul in spiritual practice. Leads you into a milieu of reverence, mystery and delight, helping you discover a redeemed sense of self.
8 x 8, 256 pp, Quality PB, ISBN 1-59473-080-6 **$16.99**

Finding Time for the Timeless
Spirituality in the Workweek   *by John McQuiston II*
Simple, refreshing stories that provide you with examples of how you can refocus and enrich your daily life using prayer or meditation, ritual and other forms of spiritual practice.   5½ x 6½, 208 pp, HC, ISBN 1-59473-035-0 **$17.99**

The Gospel of Thomas: A Guidebook for Spiritual Practice
by Ron Miller; Translations by Stevan Davies
An innovative guide to bring a new spiritual classic into daily life. Offers a way to translate the wisdom of the Gospel of Thomas into daily practice, manifesting in your life the same consciousness revealed in Jesus of Nazareth. Written for readers of all religious backgrounds, this guidebook will help you to apply Jesus's wisdom to your own life and to the world around you.
6 x 9, 160 pp, Quality PB, ISBN 1-59473-047-4 **$14.99**

The Knitting Way: A Guide to Spiritual Self-Discovery
by Linda Skolnik and Janice MacDaniels
Through sharing stories, hands-on explorations and daily cultivation, Skolnik and MacDaniels help you see beyond the surface of a simple craft in order to discover ways in which nuances of knitting can apply to the larger scheme of life and spirituality. Includes original knitting patterns.
7 x 9, 240 pp, Quality PB, ISBN 1-59473-079-2 **$16.99**

Earth, Water, Fire, and Air: Essential Ways of Connecting to Spirit
by Cait Johnson   6 x 9, 224 pp, HC, ISBN 1-893361-65-9 **$19.95**

Forty Days to Begin a Spiritual Life
Today's Most Inspiring Teachers Help You on Your Way
Edited by Maura Shaw and the Editors at SkyLight Paths; Foreword by Dan Wakefield
7 x 9, 144 pp, Quality PB, ISBN 1-893361-48-9 **$16.95**

Labyrinths from the Outside In
Walking to Spiritual Insight—A Beginner's Guide
by Donna Schaper and Carole Ann Camp
6 x 9, 208 pp, b/w illus. and photographs, Quality PB, ISBN 1-893361-18-7 **$16.95**

Practicing the Sacred Art of Listening: A Guide to Enrich Your Relationships
and Kindle Your Spiritual Life—The Listening Center Workshop
by Kay Lindahl   8 x 8, 176 pp, Quality PB, ISBN 1-893361-85-3 **$16.95**

The Sacred Art of Bowing: Preparing to Practice
by Andi Young   5½ x 8½, 128 pp, b/w illus., Quality PB, ISBN 1-893361-82-9 **$14.95**

The Sacred Art of Chant: Preparing to Practice
by Ana Hernandez   5½ x 8½, 192 pp, Quality PB, ISBN 1-59473-036-9 **$15.99**

The Sacred Art of Fasting: Preparing to Practice
by Thomas Ryan, CSP   5½ x 8½, 192 pp, Quality PB, ISBN 1-59473-078-4 **$15.99**

The Sacred Art of Listening: Forty Reflections for Cultivating a Spiritual Practice
by Kay Lindahl; Illustrations by Amy Schnapper
8 x 8, 160 pp, Illus., Quality PB, ISBN 1-893361-44-6 **$16.99**

Sacred Speech: A Practical Guide for Keeping Spirit in Your Speech
by Rev. Donna Schaper   6 x 9, 176 pp, Quality PB, ISBN 1-59473-068-7 **$15.99**;
HC, ISBN 1-893361-74-8 **$21.95**

About SKYLIGHT PATHS Publishing

SkyLight Paths Publishing is creating a place where people of different spiritual traditions come together for challenge and inspiration, a place where we can help each other understand the mystery that lies at the heart of our existence.

Through spirituality, our religious beliefs are increasingly becoming a part of our lives—rather than *apart* from our lives. While many of us may be more interested than ever in spiritual growth, we may be less firmly planted in traditional religion. Yet, we do want to deepen our relationship to the sacred, to learn from our own as well as from other faith traditions, and to practice in new ways.

SkyLight Paths sees both believers and seekers as a community that increasingly transcends traditional boundaries of religion and denomination—people wanting to learn from each other, *walking together, finding the way.*

For your information and convenience, at the back of this book we have provided a list of other SkyLight Paths books you might find interesting and useful. They cover the following subjects:

Buddhism / Zen	Gnosticism	Mysticism
Catholicism	Hinduism /	Poetry
Children's Books	Vedanta	Prayer
Christianity	Inspiration	Religious Etiquette
Comparative	Islam / Sufism	Retirement
Religion	Judaism / Kabbalah /	Spiritual Biography
Current Events	Enneagram	Spiritual Direction
Earth-Based	Meditation	Spirituality
Spirituality	Midrash Fiction	Women's Interest
Global Spiritual	Monasticism	Worship
Perspectives		

Or phone, fax, mail or e-mail to: SKYLIGHT PATHS Publishing
Sunset Farm Offices, Route 4 • P.O. Box 237 • Woodstock, Vermont 05091
Tel: (802) 457-4000 • Fax: (802) 457-4004 • www.skylightpaths.com
Credit card orders: (800) 962-4544 (8:30AM–5:30PM ET Monday–Friday)
Generous discounts on quantity orders. SATISFACTION GUARANTEED. Prices subject to change.

**For more information about each book,
visit our website at www.skylightpaths.com**